A DISCOURSE ON DISENCHANTMENT

SUNY Series in Political Theory: Contemporary Issues
Philip Green, editor

A DISCOURSE ON DISENCHANTMENT

Reflections on Politics and Technology

Gilbert G. Germain

STATE UNIVERSITY OF NEW YORK PRESS

Published by
State University of New York Press, Albany

©1993 State University of New York

For information, address the State University of New York Press,
State University Plaza, Albany, NY 12246

Production by Christine Lynch
Marketing by Lynne Lekakis

Library of Congress Cataloging-in-Publication Data

Germain, Gilbert G., 1954-
   A discourse on disenchantment : reflections on politics and
technology / Gilbert G. Germain.
      p.   cm. — (SUNY series in political theory. Contemporary
issues)
   Includes bibliographical references (p.   ) and index.
   ISBN 0-7914-1319-5 (CH : acid-free). — ISBN 0-7914-1320-9 (PB :
acid-free)
   1. Political science—Philosophy. 2. Technology—Political
aspects. 3. Philosophy of nature. 4. Pessimism. 5. Human ecology.
I. Title. II Title: Disenchantment. III. Series.
   JA80.G47 1993
320'.01—dc20   92-284
                                                          CIP

10 9 8 7 6 5 4 3 2 1

For my parents

Contents

Preface

Most people, it seems, take perverse delight in acknowledging those events which, while having contributed to the realization of some end, were themselves largely fortuitous. I assume this response arises from the tension between the perceived facticity of that which has been realized—its presence as a completed and therefore apparently necessary 'thing'—and the awareness that it did not have to be what it is. Delight is aroused because realizations of this sort appeal to what seems to be our innate love of the unconditioned and unexpected. But the pleasure is perverse because this same attraction often undermines the sense of reassurance that accompanies a belief in the necessity of unfolding events.

I think every author, when looking back on the origin and execution of his or her work, experiences something of the same. It is for this reason that I gain as much satisfaction from reflecting on the process through which this book came to be as I do from the completed text itself. For I know this text as 'object' is the product of an amalgam of forces not always within my capacity to foresee or control.

A good example of one such force pertains to the very theme of this volume—disenchantment. It originally was brought to my attention by a professor at Carleton University in Ottawa, Canada, whom I was visiting while on leave from my doctoral studies at the University of Notre Dame. I had been pursuing an interest in Hegel at that time, or perhaps I should say Kojève's Hegel, and felt vaguely uncomfortable with certain aspects of the undertaking. The "end of history" thesis *per se* was not one of them. It seemed to me then that Kojève's depiction of the universal and homogeneous state—the generic term for the post-historical liberal state—captured perfectly the essence of contemporary political life.

My difficulty with the thesis was its overly descriptive character, its satisfaction in merely taking stock of the world as it is. But of course Kojève's whole point was to argue, following Hegel, that because the existing liberal democratic state satisfies the most basic of all human desires—the desire for universal and reciprocal recognition of individuals as individuals—it is incapable of becoming other than what it is.[1] By definition, then, all there is left to do is reflect on the immutably given. So by accepting the premises of Kojève's thesis, as I had done, but not submitting wholly to its conclusions, I was evidently either failing to grasp the totality of the argument or stubbornly refusing to embrace those aspects of it that were too painful to embrace. My quandary, in short, was attributable either to ignorance or cowardice.

This book was written in indirect response to the tyranny of truth that pervades the Kojèvean portrayal of the new world. I have tried to exorcize the ghost of Kojève's Hegel by presenting an account of a world that, like his, appears to be locked into some kind of procedural grid, yet which allows for substantive critique.

Despite their obvious differences, both Kojève and Max Weber, the originator of the disenchantment thesis, agree on at least one point: the preoccupation with form (or means) within contemporary society indicates that questions relating to the ends of human existence are no longer as problematic for people as they once were. For Kojève, such questions have been decisively settled by the ubiquitous liberal democratic state, which satisfies the fundamental human desire for universal recognition by enshrining laws that protect the individual rights of its citizenry. To the extent that this political development responds to a definitive need of the species, it is a good for Kojève.

Weber, by contrast, looks upon the routinization of life much more circumspectly. He does not, for example, ascribe modernity's growing neglect of the ends of existence to the fact that they already have been satisfied, as does Kojève. Rather, he claims that questions concerning ends are being displaced by a fascination with the realm of means, with the powers of control which modern science and technology have handed to us. Thus below the shining surface of the technological order lies for Weber the multiform and protean realm of ends, enfeebled, to be sure, but not beyond revitalization.

It should be noted at this point that I do not think Weber's proposed solution to the problematics of disenchantment is ultimately viable. So my sympathy lies not with the particulars of his argument but with its implied sense of hope, with its guiding belief that modernity's "iron cage" need not become an iron vault. I share his belief, and it animates this study.

A note or two on the purpose and scope of the ensuing investigation. A theme as far-reaching as disenchantment can be approached from various angles. I obviously have had to make a choice as to which perspective is most appropriate for my intentions in writing this book. It was my aim to have the work appeal to two different kinds of audiences simultaneously. On the one hand, it was written to pique the interest of those who are concerned with theoretical issues centering on the relationship between politics and technology, but who are not deeply familiar with the theme of disenchantment. For these individuals I have laid out the various arguments in a relatively straightforward and descriptive manner. On the other hand, I wanted the text to appeal to readers who are more familiar with the debate, but who nonetheless might be interested in a new slant on the theme. The evaluative component of the book should be of primary interest to these.

Given these intentions it became apparent the book would have to be organized in such a way as to satisfy the complementary demands of this dual constituency. It seemed to me that Jürgen Habermas's recent reflections on Weber's disenchantment thesis in *The Theory of Communicative Action* could provide the means to do so. Hence, for instance, those deemed here to be major contributors to the discourse on disenchantment are largely the same individuals Habermas considers in his critique of Weber's theory of rationalization. An independent account of their arguments constitutes the introductory component of this text. These contributors are then revisited when I review Habermas's critique of their respective positions. The result is both a deepening of our understanding of the debate and an appreciation of Habermas's own stand in relation to Weber's thoughts on disenchantment. Using Habermas's analysis to delimit the general contours of the discussion has the added benefit of setting the stage for a critique of the disenchantment thesis, both in its original Weberian formulation and its reinterpretation in the hands of Habermas.

By adopting this approach I necessarily have passed over certain individuals who might seem to be logical candidates for inclusion. Chief among them is Martin Heidegger.[2] Doubtless there are those who may argue that the exclusion of someone of Heidegger's stature from a discourse on politics and technology is inexcusable on any grounds. Be that as it may, I have reasons for the course I have chosen. First, the subtlety and complexity of Heidegger's reflections on technology are such that including him within the debate would have required a rather lengthy analysis (perhaps in the form of a separate chapter), and this addition I believe would have detracted from the esthetic unity of the text. But beyond this defense there is the stronger claim that Heidegger need not be explicitly included in the analysis because his presence already pervades it in a thinly veiled form. Specifically, my appropriation of Merleau-Ponty's "philosophy of the flesh" as an antidote to disenchantment bears a great deal of resemblance to Heidegger's admonition to "let Being be." Both of these thinkers worked within a post-Cartesian paradigm and both struggled to formulate a way of conceiving a decentered 'subject.' However, as will become apparent, there are reasons for preferring Merleau-Ponty's approach over Heidegger's, given the nature of the particular problem that confronts us here.

I would like to make one final observation with regard to the form of the discourse. Because I generally have not incorporated into the discussion secondary commentary on its key figures, those who come to this analysis expecting to find out what the contemporary academic world is saying about Weber's understanding of *Zweckrationalität*, for instance, will be disappointed. As stated, it has not been my intention in writing this book to provide the reader with a comprehensive analysis of its subject. My more immediate aim was simply to highlight the relevance of the disenchantment thesis to contemporary debates on the status of the modern condition. Given this and the fact that I wanted to ensure the book's accessibility to as wide an audience as possible, it was necessary to find ways to limit the scope of an investigation that could easily have become unmanageable. Staying close to primary sources was one way to accomplish this.

Among the various academics I have known and worked with over the years, two especially stand out, and therefore deserve special mention. The first is Tom Darby, who, over a decade ago, showed me what it means to live a life of inquiry. For this I will be forever grateful. The second is Fred Dallmayr, without whose guidance this undertaking certainly would have never seen the light of day. Like so many others, I come away from the experience of having worked with him with deep respect and admiration for his insight, his breadth of vision, and his generosity of spirit. I also would like to acknowledge the contributions of Edward Goerner and Alfons Beitzinger, both of whom embody the best of a tradition that upholds the inseparability of intellect and character. I wish as well to extend my gratitude to the following: to Fabio Dasilva, to the anonymous reviewers of my manuscript, to the editors of the State University of New York Press, and to my wife, Sheri McBride.

INTRODUCTION

Humans are natural beings to the extent that they are born of nature and retain a certain primordial bond with that from which they have risen. But to speak in these terms, to say in effect that humans are both rooted in nature and beyond it, demands explanation. Of course, one can assert that humans are beyond nature insofar as they are reflexive beings, that is, beings whose relation to the world is mediated through their own conceptual thought. However, a much more difficult task remains in attempting to determine precisely the manner in which humans, as reflective beings, retain a primordial link with the natural world. It will be argued here that as a tree's roots provide the foundation upon which it is able to break ranks with the confines of its immediate nutritive environment, it is from a pre-reflective union with the world that our mediating capacities have evolved and continue to be sustained. The primary task of this study, then, is to suggest a way in which this elemental connection can be articulated. This work receives its impetus by showing the consequences of neglecting our reflexive relations with the natural world and with other human beings.

The ensuing investigation unfolds as a discourse on the theme of disenchantment. It is, in actuality, a discourse on discourses—a synthetic discourse—in that it orders previously articulated analyses so as to form a coherent overview of an ongoing dialogue. This extended dialogue reveals a discernible development with respect to changes in the interpretation of the relationship between ourselves and nature. We see that (Western) peoples over time have defined themselves and their rational capacities as increasingly devoid of any connection to a natural or worldly substrate. This "outward journey," as it may be called, then is complemented by a kind of return. Yet it is not a simple return, either in the directness of the route traveled or in the site of its final destination. As with Odysseus' return to his native Ithaca, the journey home is not without its hardships—its obstacles and impasses—which to overcome will affect irreversibly the traveler's understanding of his refound homeland.

The discourse begins in earnest with Descartes, who was the leading figure in the epistemological revolution that precipitated the birth of modern philosophy, and one of the chief architects of disenchantment. His contribution to the discourse, we shall see, hinges on the claim that the *cogito* (the thinking ego) is the ultimate reference point for knowledge of the extended or material world. Kantian epistemol-

1

ogy further entrenched the disjunction between ego and 'other' by providing a masterful account of the manner in which our experience of the world issues from a cognitive process which pre-exists that experience. Yet despite its remove from the phenomenal world, the Kantian ego was able to account for its relationship to that world and thus forge a bond of sorts between the two.

The same, however, cannot be said of the *cogito* for Max Weber. The thinking or reasoning ego for Weber is incapable of making definitive claims of a Kantian sort because doing so would require of it something it does not possess—a transcendental status. Following Nietzsche, Weber argues that the ego is conditioned by the contingencies that attend a spatially and temporally situated being. It therefore does not occupy a vantage point outside the flux of worldly existence. But this is not to say that for Weber the situated ego is worldly in the sense that it is intimately connected with the material substrate of the natural order. Rather, it simply means that the *cogito* confronts the world from a historically and culturally conditioned position.

Because the thinking ego is radically subjectivized in this manner, it is incapable of giving a rational account of itself as a determinate 'thing.' Both this and the fact the thinking ego *(cogito)* is cut off from the world means that reason for Weber has lost its traditional capacity to reveal the intelligible structure of the whole. Since questions pertaining to comprehensive issues of this sort cannot be answered by rational means, they are said to fall within the domain of personal "interests" or "values." People's values, then, serve to orient them within a rationally ambiguous universe. Values lend it meaning and stability. Beyond this, values for Weber also serve to frame the act of reasoning itself. Thus reason in modernity is said to be relegated to the task of calculating the means required to further subjectively valued ends or interests. It is, in short, an instrument of an extra-rational force.

Georg Lukács and the early Frankfurt School theorists such as Theodor Adorno and Max Horkheimer essentially agree with Weber's depiction of the instrumental or purposive character of modern rationality. They agree as well on the negative impact that value-neutral reasoning has had on issues related to the human–nature relationship and the status of meaning. However, they part company with Weber (and with each other) insofar as they interpret purposive rationality using different sets of assumptions. Lukács, for example, offers a Marxist reading of the genealogy of modern rationality. *Reification* is the term he employs to describe the process in which the objectified relations of production within bourgeois society condition the nature of interhuman relations. The result is that the world, both human and non-human, tends to assume the character of a reified "commodity."

Horkheimer and Adorno, on the other hand, claim that purposive rationality is linked directly to the drive to dominate nature. Reason, they assert, becomes an "instrument"—a mere tool of manipulation— when it is abstracted from the context of its use. By systematically ignoring the being of the 'other' (i.e., nature), it tends to absorb all substantively particular content in its predetermined concepts and principles. Nature consequently is objectified, reduced to a controllable 'thing.' But in the process, they argue, nature avenges herself by seeing to it that "the subjective spirit which cancels the animation of nature [does so] only by imitating its rigidity and by despiritualizing itself in turn."[1] In short, by disenchanting nature, reason ends up reducing its own capabilities to a mere reckoning with consequences. Thus it is argued that some kind of reconciliation with nature is needed in order to undercut the "tyranny" of modern rationality.

It is within the mode of analysis known as "systems theory" or "cybernetics" that we are most removed from the human–nature nexus. Even though Weber is portrayed in this study as the consummate spokesman for an era in which the breach between humans and nature had been rendered all but complete, there remains in his thought a peculiar ambiguity with respect to its finality. Because he held that science was a value-related enterprise and hence conditioned by the interests of its practitioners, there is no reason to assume, in principle at least, that these interests must remain for all time within the ambit of the prevailing ethos of domination.

In contrast, systems theorists such as Jacques Ellul argue that no such free play of valuations exists: A society informed by instrumental rationality, he says, is in fact an autonomous, self-steering "system" which accepts no extrinsic limitations on its functioning. The production of values is internally generated and they therefore necessarily serve the needs of the system alone.

We have now reached the outer threshold of our investigative journey. Subsequent arguments have as their theme the renewal of an equilibrium between the realms of means (technology) and ends (meaning, value). The possibility of such a restoration, of course, presumes that it is within the power of the subject (or subjects) to effect such a rapproachment, a view which systems analysts dispute. Nonetheless, of those who assume a possible reconciliation, two individuals will be the focus of discussion. I first will address Hans Blumenberg, who argues that the most adventitious way of redressing this imbalance is to embrace those ends that technology itself is best suited to fulfill, such as the extension of our control over nature and the resultant expansion of our freedom from necessity.

Jürgen Habermas, unlike Blumenberg, acknowledges the difficulties associated with the proliferation of technical rationality in modernity. He therefore cannot subscribe to a wholesale endorsement of the modern. Still, he argues, it can be saved if those forces which presently are crippling contemporary society are utilized in a way that satisfies truly human needs as opposed to merely the imperatives of technology itself. This calls for a "paradigm shift," a relocation of the controlling force in society from the realm of instrumental action (the "system") to that of communicative action (the "lifeworld"). It is within this latter domain—what might broadly be termed the political sphere—that questions concerning the "ends" of the societal order are to be addressed and finally settled. The agreed-upon ends then can serve to steer the system in a direction unimpeded by latter's internal dictates and toward the fulfillment of the desired goals.

There are a number of difficulties with Habermas's proposal, but, from the perspective I adopt in this study, its most glaring shortcoming lies in the suggestion that our instrumental control of nature can and should be neatly isolated from our communicative relations with fellow human beings. I will argue that Habermas's reliance on communicative action as a means of actualizing modernity's full potential only exacerbates the problem of domination by rationalizing the need for an even greater expansion of our powers of control, extending it to include subsystems themselves.

Because the path Habermas follows leads ultimately to a dead end, the return journey must be redirected, only this time with the advantage of having his insights act as a marker delimiting the range of possible alternatives open to us. What Habermas has taught us, if only through the consequences of its neglect, is the need to be attentive to the ontological interrelation of humans and the non-human natural world. Hence I will argue that all viable alternatives to disenchantment must have as their objective the articulation of this interconnection.

A re-examination of Adorno's positive critique of instrumental rationality, I maintain, aids greatly in the consolidation of this new line of inquiry. Thus we return to his account of art and the esthetic experience for insight into a way of conceiving a non-antagonistic relationship between the human and non-human natural realms. Of central importance to his argument is the claim that artists, rather than recreating or representing the world as 'object' in their art, give concrete expression to its essential quality (its aura or mood) as they experience it. They function, in short, as a medium through which nature comes to express itself. The artists' de-centered relationship with the world is viewed here as indicating a way out of disenchantment. The failure of Adorno's esthetic theory, however, is that it does not adequately explain the manner in which artists come to speak for nature. For this reason that I turn in the final section to Merleau-Ponty and his "philosophy of the flesh," for it provides us with precisely such an explanation and shows the extent to which the problem of human–nature relations is a general condition of human existence.

The study closes with a look at the political ramifications of Merleau-Ponty's ontology. An analysis of "embodied politics" will provide the forum for a discussion of human interaction within a post-disenchanted framework.

In terms of its organizational structure, this discourse consists of five chapters and a few brief concluding remarks. The first chapter provides a concise account of the pertinent developments within modern philosophical thought which prefigure Weber's disenchantment thesis. The main points of focus include Descartes's conception of a "practical philosophy," the epistemological revolution precipitated by Kant, various manifestations of neo-Kantianism in nineteenth-century Germany, and the Romantic rebellion as articulated by Nietzsche against the Enlightenment.

The primary objective of the second chapter is to present a full description of the disenchantment thesis, both in its initial Weberian configuration and in subsequent reinterpretations. Prior to this, however, I will recount the extent to which Weber appropriates certain themes from both Enlightenment and Romantic traditions in the formulation of his own understanding of rationality. Then our attention will shift to those theorists who have developed further Weber's critical insight into the disenchantment of the world. Arguments advanced by Lukács, Horkheimer, Adorno, Ellul, and Niklas Luhmann will be reviewed.

The third chapter presents an exegesis of two arguments which have as their objective the defense of modernity. My analysis of both Blumenberg and Habermas will be limited to those concerns that relate directly to the problem of disenchantment.

The fourth chapter is both evaluative and expository. It opens with a critique of Habermas's plan to assuage the corrosive effects of instrumentalism on the body politic. It concludes with an analysis of further refinements in our understanding of the human–nature nexus as expressed in Adorno's esthetic theory and Merleau-Ponty's reflections on art and his general theory of perception.

The final, fifth chapter will address the issue of politics within the context of a renewed understanding of man's ontological embeddedness in the world. Merleau-Ponty's political writings will provide a basis for the discussion.

I want to note, in closing, that there is a certain self-acknowledged risk in adopting the Weberian viewpoint as descriptive of the contemporary state of affairs and in having it serve as a reference point for arguments whose goal is to overcome disenchantment. To speak of disenchantment is to provoke expectations concerning the desirability of a 're-enchanted' world where man and nature co-exist in simple (and in my view, naive) harmony. This risk, however, is worth taking, for at least two reasons. First, the portrayal of the world as disenchanted provides us with a highly persuasive account of the forces operating in an environment governed increasingly by rule-bound processes and procedures. It is, put simply, too powerful an explanatory model of the apparent trajectory of modernity not to be taken seriously. Secondly, Weber's thesis in itself suggests ways to move beyond disenchantment which are not constrained by the parameters of his own discourse. The burden of this investigation, then, is to prove that only by collapsing the illusory tension that pits a 'live' or spirited world against a 'dead' or de-spirited one, can we begin to address and resolve the very real difficulties that confront us.

PART ONE

THE OUTWARD JOURNEY

I

THE SETTING

"I suppose Descartes brought me to the point
where he brought himself—to faith. Fact or
fiction—in the end you can't distinguish between
them—you just have to choose."

Graham Greene, *Monsignor Quixote*

The primary aim of this chapter is to trace the philosophical in-
fluences that contributed directly to Max Weber's formulation of
the disenchantment thesis. But before we begin to outline these
forces it is necessary to situate the investigation within a more comprehensive context. For it is crucial that we first gain some insight
into the general assumptions which underlay such a conception and
lend it its distinctively "modern" air. One way to do this is to
familiarize ourselves with a pre-modern understanding of the thinking subject's relationship to the non-human natural world and have
this earlier conception serve as a standard against which the disenchantment problematic can be articulated and assayed. The investigation begins, then, as have so many other inquiries into the modern
condition, by turning our eyes to the classical world—specifically, to
its assessment of the man–nature nexus.

The Turn Toward Epistemology

Nature, as conceived by the ancients, was neither straightforwardly
'alive' nor mere inert 'stuff.' Having long since abandoned animism,
they had yet to interpret the natural world as simple extended matter.
That is to say, although the gods no longer were perceived to inhabit
nature directly, they nonetheless regarded nature within the context
of an overarching metaphysical world view.

Aristotle is perhaps the best exponent of such an outlook in the classical world. In Book II of his *Physics* he argues that existing entities are characterized by a capacity for change. They exist to the extent that they have the potential to become something other than what they are. For Aristotle there were two primary causes of change within the material world and hence two basic kinds of being. There are, on the one hand, those objects whose principle of motion lies within themselves, and, on the other, those in which the agent of change lies without. The former type are categorized as natural objects and the latter as products of artifice, or artifacts. The primary difference, then, between the two kinds of being is that one (the natural world) is self-generating and hence not of human making, whereas the other owes its existence to the intervention of human agency. Thus the natural world, by virtue of its autogenetic character, possesses a kind of necessity—an order— that the fabricated world does not.

The 'nature' in a natural object is manifested in the process by which the object actualizes what it has the potential to become. All natural processes are linked together in terms of this fundamental movement— the realization of potency. But this understanding of nature reveals as well nature's imperfection according to classical understanding. For nature, by definition, is a becoming in search of being, and as such it presupposes the existence of an entity (Being) whose very essence is pure act, i.e., the divine *nous*, the so-called "Unmoved Mover." The being of nature thus is predicated upon Being as pure act.

For Aristotle, as for Plato, the greatest good for man is that activity which leads to an understanding of that which is highest. It is axiomatic for the Greeks that the highest is that which must be, the necessary order of things. Because nature is such an order, its study (the science of physics) is accorded an exalted rank in the hierarchy of sciences. However, because the natural realm implies the supernatural—the unchanging ground of all mutable being—the highest of the sciences for Aristotle is metaphysics. This differentiation in rank notwithstanding, it is important to note that both types of inquiry fall under the rubric of the "theoretical" sciences insofar as their aim is to contemplate the given, not to effect a change within it.

It was precisely because the ancients took the natural order to be necessary that they gave place to the theoretical science of physics over those sciences that have as their subject matter contingent processes and objects. The science of necessary objects, then, yields necessary knowledge, while that of contingent objects begets provisional knowledge. The productive sciences, in contrast, are conditional in a different sense, for they seek neither necessary nor provisional knowledge of what is but knowledge of the means to realize what might be. In attempting to further clarify this conception, it helps to recall the fact that the products of nature's 'artifice' originate from nature itself. To the extent that nature "makes itself," it cannot be other than what it is. In contrast, the products of human artifice by definition do not make themselves. Rather, their origin lies in the mind of the artificer, or, more precisely, in the artificer's conceptual image of a proposed artifact. Because there is nothing in the 'nature' of a natural object that suggests it has been made into a determinate product, there is no necessity in the process by which the human producing agent determines the form its shape will take. Indeed, there is no 'science' of image fabrication. For Aristotle the science of production pertains only to the determination of the means best suited to realize a preconceived image. Knowledge in such matters, then, is a kind of technical know-how (an art) that perhaps is best captured by the term *craftsmanship*.

If, as Aristotle argued, the objects of human artifice are not what they must be, then the science of production could not possibly be interpreted as the highest form of rational inquiry. It is for this reason that the classical world view devalued the appropriation of nature as a use-object in favor of its treatment as an object for contemplation.

Theoretical science for the ancients was the most useful type of rational inquiry insofar as its practice led to the fullest realization of that which distinguishes man from beast, that is, his capacity to rationally comprehend the ground of his existence. The theoretical life therefore was acknowledged as the most human form of existence. Against this, the life of the artisan was considered less evolved to the extent that the reasoning that informs it is unconcerned with essences and focuses instead on technical matters relating to the manipulation of the material world for productive or creative ends.[1] It is a life guided by a subsidiary mode of reasoning, by reasoning conceived as mere contrivance or reckoning with consequences.[2]

Despite its various reinterpretations, the classical schema that ranked theory (contemplation) over art (production) retained its canonical authority until the onset of the modern era. It is with Descartes that we begin to see a self-conscious and systematic attempt to overturn the theory/art distinction formulated by Aristotle. Descartes does so by arguing that the highest science has as its appropriate end the investigation of nature for the purpose of mastering nature. In Descartes's estimation the most evolved scientific endeavor is no longer, as it was for the ancients, the act of contemplating the order of things, natural or otherwise. He redirects science away from such ontological concerns and toward the realm of the ontic. Nowhere is this better illustrated than in his assertion, in *Discourse on Method*, that "it is possible to reach knowledge that will be of much utility in this life, and that instead of the speculative philosophy now taught in the schools we can find a practical one, by which . . . [we can] render ourselves the masters and possessors of nature."[3]

In this passage Descartes defines "practical philosophy" to indicate precisely the direction in which he wishes the activity of science to shift. Whereas for Aristotle "practical" or "political" science refers to the activity that has as its end the determination of those practices (the virtues) that facilitate *eupraxia*, "practical philosophy" carries no such ethical or political overtones for Descartes. Rather, it discloses his intention to collapse theory (science) and art *(technē)* for the immanent purpose of "conserving health," which Descartes assumes to be the basis "of all the other goods in this life."[4] The highest and most useful science now aims at promoting mere existence and not the good life.

Descartes's understanding of "practical philosophy" is grounded in his radical reinterpretation of what constitutes metaphysics. He begins by defining it as "perfect knowledge of all things that man can know . . . so that we must begin with the investigation of first causes, i.e., principles."[5] However, the Aristotelian tenor of this provisional account of the term is undercut when he adds that mind *(res cogitans)* and body *(res extensa)* are the two first principles (or "simple natures") of knowledge, and that, when taken together, they comprise the sum total of mind's knowledge. Unlike their classical counterparts, Cartesian first principles are wholly immanent. The philosophical repercussions of this revision cannot be overestimated: Now the highest science by definition must have as its proper subject matter the investigation of mind, body, and their interrelation. By reinterpreting metaphysics as epistemology, Descartes in effect argues that philosophy has as its primary focus not the essence but the existence of nature as a material datum.

What remains unexplained at this point is how the turn toward epistemology is related, in Descartes's thought, to the philosophical justification of the practice of modern science. The answer lies in the way Descartes perceives the linkage between mind and body. Simply put, he claims these first principles are known intuitively, knowledge of which, he adds, "arises from the light of reason alone." Moreover, knowledge of first principles is said to be arrived at "without any fear of error."[6] These pivotal assertions expose two major assumptions that underpin much of modern philosophical thought. On the one hand, it reveals the extent to which the ego is posited as autonomous and the source of knowledge of both mind and body. On the other hand, it illustrates Descartes's conviction that knowledge of first principles can be free of error and illusion only if 'mind' is perceived as removed from, or other than, "extended matter."[7] Implied in this latter assertion is the view that the obstacles in the path to clear reasoning are due to a perception of mind as embodied, an understanding of fateful consequence for the disenchantment thesis.

No immediate purpose would be served by recounting the argument that led Descartes to rank mind over body. What is important to note, however, is that given this starting point, the only way he could have avoided the trap of epistemological idealism—the conclusion that because only mind truly exists, all it can know is itself—was to maintain that *res extensa* possesses a discrete reality of its own. But this presents Descartes with a new challenge, namely, to account for the manner in which these distinct substances interrelate, or to explain how mind comes to have knowledge of what is not-mind.

The Cartesian solution is decisive. He asserts that knowledge of extended matter cannot possibly be a product of sensual apprehension, for this presupposes, wrongly in his view, that the organ of apprehension is likewise embodied. Descartes therefore is forced to argue that knowledge of the "other" must arise from an intuitive mental act, from pure intellection.[8] What in fact the mind intuits in this regard is something analogous to "abstract matter" or "generic mass." Specifically, it is that uniform substance which is said to "stand under" the accidents (sensory qualities) of corporeal objects. Since this substance is universal, in the sense that it is the common substrate that grounds particular manifestations of material being, qualitative differences between objects are reduced for Descartes to simple quantitative proportions. It is by regarding corporeal being as knowable only as *res extensa* that he was able to "mathematize" matter, and ultimately to render it accessible to the universalizing power of a controlling mind, to the power of technical rationality.

In review, the particular cognitive paradigm that the Cartesian revolution ushered in rests on two basic presuppositions that will prove to be of crucial significance to our discourse on disenchantment. The first is the claim that the proper domain of science (true knowledge) lies within the realm of "making," the end of which is the mastery of nature for the purpose of facilitating a comfortable life. Secondly, there is the presumption that nature is capable of being mastered because mind can, as a result of its own operations, accurately represent nature *(res extensa)* to itself. Most important, for Descartes, our capacity to mentally apprehend the principles of the natural world means that corporeal being is intrinsically conformable to the dictates of controlling mind.

Descartes's egological bias secures the foundation of his, and indeed all, variants of rationalism. But while operating within the same horizon that posits a mind/body (or subject/object) dualism, empiricism accounts for the interrelation of the two 'substances' from a perspective antithetical to that of rationalist thought. Although both approaches ultimately share an identical objective—that is, to explain the manner in which mind and matter are reciprocally related—empiricist arguments hold that the solution lies in taking the "object" as the ultimate epistemological reference point. In contrast, then, to the attempt by rationalism to perfect the mind as a mirror of the external world, empiricism claims that the mind must conform to the reality of the object.[9]

For the empiricist, mind's capacity to conform itself to the external order of things is taken as a given. Hence it is assumed that the obstacles in the path to a full understanding of nature lie not in the functioning of the intellect and its rational powers but in nature itself, in its propensity toward dissembling. For this reason the empiricist sets out to provoke nature (through repeated experimentation) into revealing its inner structure.

This disparity between approaches does not mean that rationalism in principle eschews experimentation or that empiricism abstains from rational reflection. What it does mean, however, is that the rationalist approach to empirical inquiry is performed in the spirit of confirming *a priori* theoretical deductions rather than attesting to the evidence of direct empirical observation. Contrarily, empiricism embraces reason, but it is a reason that, as Francis Bacon says, "is elicited from the facts by a just and methodical process. . . ."[10]

It was left to Issac Newton to unite rationalism and empiricism in such a way as to produce a new method for the scientific investigation of nature. The Newtonian synthesis is evinced in the extraordinary consolidation of *a priori* speculation and empirical research, whose practice led to the uncovering of those 'universal laws' that account for regularities in the behavior of observable phenomena. Modern Newtonian science, then, realizes the intent of "practical philosophy"—that is, the union of art *(technē)* and science *(logos)*—in a way which neither Descartes nor Bacon were capable of, given their predilection for subordinating matter to mind, or vice versa.

Kant regarded modern science as embodying the intellectual spirit of his age, the Enlightenment, in that science was a branch of learning that had discarded the dogmatic teachings of classical physics. He admired above all its independence of thought, an intellectual disposition he hoped one day might free all modes of rational inquiry from the bonds of "self-incurred immaturity."[11] Deeply impressed by the progress made within the natural sciences, Kant wanted to extend the scope of their success by precipitating an analogous transformation within the field of metaphysics.

We have noted in our review of Descartes's "practical philosophy" that the onset of modernity is signalled by a reinterpretation of reason's highest end. It no longer has as its objective the contemplation of the given but the understanding of natural processes for the purpose of acting on them. Thus the 'instrumentalization' of reason has been identified as a turning point in the discourse on disenchantment. We also have noted that the application of reason in modernity is premised on the assumption that the reasoning mind (the *cogito*) is distinct from that which it controls *(res extensa)*.

The reason for Kant's inclusion in this narrative becomes apparent when it is realized that his philosophical initiative involves a further entrenchment of the rupture separating mind and nature. He renders the mind autonomous by arguing, *contra* Aristotle, that rational understanding is not privy to knowledge of any necessity, such as "nature" or "the order of things," assigned to objects independent of itself. That perspective necessarily presupposes that the mind is a passive register of what lies beyond it, a view Kant squarely refutes. To the contrary, he insists that the mind, through its *a priori* principles of understanding (e.g., intuitions, categories), actively organizes the world as we experience it. This is not to say, however, that our experience of the world is determined solely by the operation of understanding. For Kant, understanding can form its concept of an object only if it first receives, through the body's sensibility, some content on which to work. Hence our experience of the world is credited both to the mind's capacity to synthesize raw sense data and its own meaning-constituting principles of understanding.

It might be argued at this point that the mind's synthetic activity attests not to the rupture but to the integration of mind and body. While there is a certain surface plausibility to such a claim, it falters when we realize that, because our experience of the world is conditioned by the *a priori* structures of the mind, there can be no direct access to the 'thing-in-itself.' In other words, Kant tells us that we can never experience the world as it is but only as it appears to us after being structured by the faculties of understanding. Because our perception of "reality" is filtered through the mind's own organizing activities, our knowledge of the world necessarily is always a knowledge of appearances or the 'for-itself.' Thus the mind for Kant is cut off from the exterior world to the extent that the experience of the latter always is mediated by the mind's own functionings.

For Kant the natural or theoretical sciences necessarily are inquiries into appearances. Consequently, what reason discovers in terms of "laws" are in fact the forms it has imposed on sense data. But one thing our understanding of natural phenomena can never reveal, not even obliquely, are the ends of human action. It is silent with respect to questions of morality, Kant says, because "from no consideration of a thing or concept . . . is it possible to know and infer what we should do, unless what is presupposed is an end, and act a means."[12] Nature, in short, offers us no clues as to how we ought to act. It is indifferent to human concerns. Here Kant adumbrates the is/ought distinction that Weber later adopts as a basic premise of his own reflections on morality.

But given nature's indifference to moral interests, the question then could be asked: Where do we look for a guide to practical action? Kant responds by saying that we must look to ourselves. He argues that since our understanding of how we ought to act cannot be drawn from our experiences within the phenomenal realm, our moral concepts must be rooted in an *a priori* rational faculty. Practical reasoning, according to Kant, presents moral agents with an autonomous moral law—the categorical imperative—whose dictates they are obliged to obey. The "rational" moral actor, therefore, acknowledges the moral law within, and acts in accordance with its directives.

In conclusion, in Kant's critical and ethical writings we witness the full impact of the egological revolution. His claim that the mind has no direct access to the world underscores the extent to which the theoretical investigation of the natural world reveals as much about the *cogito* as it does about its object. However, nowhere is the impact of this revolution more evident than in Kantian ethics, where, as we have noted, the moral will has no recourse but to will an end independent of all experience external to it.

Positivism and Anti-Positivism

If, with Kant, there arose a radical disjunction between the theoretical-scientific and practical-ethical realms, then it is equally true that modern philosophical thought is concerned in part with finding a way to reconcile these disparate realms. The work of Auguste Comte presents us with one such effort. It is of special importance to this study since the means he chooses for this resolution entail the extension of the powers of science and scientific rationality to include realms previously unincorporated.

Comte states that metaphysical questions are "outside the domain of positive philosophy."[13] True knowledge, he says, rests on observed facts. Not unexpectedly, Comte traces the scientific method—which he terms "positivism"—to the pioneering efforts of Bacon and Descartes. He regards his philosophical mission as a completion of their "vast intellectual operation," namely, to eliminate the remaining vestiges of "the superstitious alloy of scholasticism" and the ulterior motives that moved "the astrologers and the alchemists."[14]

Comte notes that positivism's maturation was a slow evolutionary process, which, during his lifetime, was only beginning to be fully actualized. From Comte's perspective, Newton and Kant were exemplary representatives of the "transitional phase" in the development of positivism, where elements both of scientism and pre-scientism (e.g., theology, metaphysics) were intermingled. There is much evidence to substantiate his claim. We see in Newton, for instance, an almost schizophrenic disjunction between his work as modernity's leading natural scientist and his equally earnest efforts in the study and practice of alchemy.[15] Kant, on the other hand, upheld a scientific understanding of nature while denying that this understanding could illuminate the realm of practical action.

This disjunction between theoretical and practical forms of inquiry troubled Comte, for in his view it bespoke a false dichotomy. Unlike Kant, he regarded the realm of practice (the "social" domain) as an appropriate object of scientific study. Consequently, any system of thought that segregated the natural from the human world Comte deemed an obstacle to what he calls "practical philosophy." The objective of this new philosophy, then, is to sustain a harmony between "the active and [the] speculative point[s] of view." He argues this can be achieved through applying positivist methodology to the domain of social interaction. Comte's ambition, in short, is to devise a natural science of society—the science of "social physics" or "sociology"—whose end is the determination of its immutable rational laws.[16]

It is not necessary for our purposes to outline the findings of Comte's new "science." Rather, it suffices to note that he believed the scientific determination of "social facts" would lead to an understanding the true order of society and the optimal configuration of the various sciences for the promotion of social utility. Thus the call for a "science of society" manifests in itself a desire to extend the range of instrumental knowledge.

If with Comte we witness the hegemony of scientism—the belief that the "objects" of scientific inquiry include both the human and non-human worlds—then its reign was short-lived. The claim that the behavior of all "facts" are explainable in terms of universal laws that account for the necessary causal connections between irreducible phenomena was soon under attack by a number of late-nineteenth-century social theorists, two of the most important being Wilhelm Dilthey and Heinrich Rickert.

What these men questioned was not the status of natural scientific reason, *per se*, but the appropriateness of its application to the study of human action. Hence the revolt against scientism is not to be interpreted as an absolute rejection of positivist methodology, but a call for its containment. In order to facilitate this end, they might have been tempted to reinvoke the Kantian distinction between the mechanistic natural world, on the one hand, and the human sphere characterized by freedom, on the other. However, as we have seen, for Kant this delimitation amounted to a shielding of the practical domain from causal explanation and, hence, from scientific knowability. This defensive rescue of the practical realm from "science" was unacceptable to both Dilthey and Rickert. They assert, on the contrary, the need to articulate a new non-mechanistic "science of man" capable of yielding knowledge of human affairs.

For Dilthey, the true object of philosophical investigation is the "human sciences," or *Geisteswissenschaften*. As with Comte before him, Dilthey wanted to emulate the success achieved by natural scientific inquiry by establishing a human science "based on experience." But in contrast to the positivist methodology of Comtean social scientific research, Dilthey's human sciences were to be based on a distinctly non-positivist but nevertheless scientific mode of inquiry. He rejects the adequacy of causal explanation to render intelligible the study of man in favor of a method founded on "understanding," or *verstehen*. As Dilthey says: "Understanding is our name for the process in which mental life comes to be known through the expressions of . . . [mental phenomena] given to the senses."[17]

For Dilthey, understanding is made possible only by "re-experiencing" the intentions, emotions, and general state of consciousness of the actor as expressed either through his actions or through artifacts. It is for this reason that one understands from the "inside" alone. Thus an analysis of an actor's "behavior" is but a requisite means of entering into his intentional world and eliciting understanding from it. Access to this world, however, is dependent upon actor and observer's sharing a common field of being. The capacity to read another's intentional world presupposes that its contents summon forth resonances within one's own experiences. We could not, in short, understand the meaning of another's actions unless we ourselves were beings capable of meaningful action.

In light of this analysis we then could pose the question: Is an understanding of the non-human natural world possible, according to Dilthey? The answer, in a word, is "no." Because for Dilthey understanding implies intentionality, the natural world necessarily lies beyond its purview. Having no "inside"—no consciousness, volition, or self-reflective rational capacity—nature can be comprehended only in the purely mechanistic terms of cause and effect. Nature therefore is regarded by Dilthey as an insensate "object" that stands opposed to the sentient "subject."

By combining some elements of positive science (i.e., empirical observation) and hermeneutical understanding, Dilthey hoped to "continue on Kant's critical road . . . to discover the laws that condition the social, intellectual, and moral phenomena."[18] This being said, it is important to note that Dilthey does not envision the practitioners of the human sciences pursuing a disinterested form of knowledge. Dilthey's claim that this knowledge will lend its possessor the "power over mental phenomena" needed to "determine human actions and thinking" reveals its utilitarian or technological impetus.[19] And so, in the final analysis, his new science of understanding is undergirt by the same ethos of mastery that guided Comte's sociological investigations. Just as the natural sciences had ostensibly laid bare the abiding infrastructure of the natural order and hence cleared the way for dominating it, Dilthey's human sciences are to perform the same function by penetrating the obscurity surrounding the coherence of human action.

Rickert shares with Dilthey an interest in establishing a typology of sciences that reflects fundamental differences in modes of rational inquiry. However, Rickert clearly disagrees with Dilthey's criterion for making such distinctions. He argues that sound reasoning demands that methodological or "formal" differences between the sciences have as their ground a "formal" distinction as well. The claim Rickert is putting forth here is very Kantian. He asserts that it is not the object of study (i.e., the natural versus human world) that ultimately dictates methodology, but the orientation the mind employs in dealing with its subject matter. Methodology is determined, he says, by the manner in which "incisions are made in the flux of reality, and the essential elements selected."[20] This separating out of essential elements from the continuum of reality is for Rickert an *a priori* mental capacity. It is the means by which we conceptualize the world as either "nature" or "history."

By conceiving the world as nature, we adopt the scientific posture to the extent that our analysis centers on its "general" aspects. Natural scientific inquiry, Rickert tells us, excludes from consideration "everything that makes any aspect of reality unique, non-repeatable, and particular." On the other hand, when we conceive the world as history, it is the "individual" or singular aspects of the world which capture our attention. The historical or cultural sciences therefore have as their subject matter everything but the common or generic elements of reality.[21]

Because the distinction between nature and history is formal, Rickert argues that the classification of the methods of natural science and history bears a logical symmetry that eluded Dilthey's formulation. Yet Rickert does not, in spite of this, abandon the notion of a material distinction between the content of the sciences. He retains an essentially Diltheyan (positivistic) orientation toward nature, stating that natural objects are devoid of value and hence can have only a "perceived" existence. In contrast, Rickert asserts that cultural phenomena are value-laden. They are, he says, either produced by man in accordance with some valued end or they are pre-existing objects upon which man confers meaning and value.[22]

The Nietzschean Critique

Despite disagreements over the criteria for establishing a comprehensive typology of sciences, Dilthey and Rickert share a common assessment of the natural sciences and the objects of their investigation. They make the claim, thoroughly Cartesian in character, that natural phenomena are mere bits of extended or disenchanted matter. Consequently, nature can be apprehended only as a mechanistic order functioning in conformity with certain universal laws that account for its regularities.

In comparison with their efforts to contain scientism, the Nietzschean critique of scientific methodology is far more radical. It can be interpreted, in fact, as a critique of disenchantment. This puts him in a unique position among those thinkers who have been cited as contributing, either directly or indirectly, to the Weberian discourse. For on the one hand, Weber co-opts certain Nietzschean themes in his writings on methodology and more substantive issues. Hence we must acknowledge its formative role. However, because Weber's articulation of disenchantment postdates Nietzsche's critique of it, we have to present reaction to the disenchantment thesis even before its full elaboration by Weber himself.

We begin by observing that Nietzsche addresses the issue of "scientific" thought—that is, virtually all philosophical thought, classical and modern, along with modern science—by probing its motivational or psychological origins. In *The Birth of Tragedy* he asks: "what is the significance of all science, viewed as a symptom of life?"[23] In other words, what does the activity of science tell us about its practitioners' general orientation toward the world? What attitude or frame of mind prompts their investigations? Nietzsche tersely responds: fear. Specifically, it is the fear of, or the escape from, "pessimism" that accounts for the scientific world view. It is rooted, he says, in a denial of the "fundamental knowledge of the oneness of everything existent, and the conception of individuation as the primary cause of evil, of art as the joyful hope that the spell of individuation may be broken in augury of a restored oneness."[24]

Modern science for Nietzsche is but the full realization of an impulse that extends back to the ancient Greeks. He interprets the latters' fondness for "logicizing the world" as an indication of their alienation from the Dionysian flow of life. Platonism, in particular, is singled out as a mode of thought sustained by an acute sense of resentment against the flux of existence. Its attempt to master the senses and the sensible world by means of "pale, cold, grey conceptual nets" is evidence of its decadence, according to Nietzsche.[25]

The scientific impulse, then, is anti-nature insofar as it rebels against the basic condition of existence—the mutability and interrelatedness of being. The misapprehension that fuels the mastery of the world is manifested not only in the effort to conceptually freeze its flux, but in the belief as well that these ideational structures are representations of the world as it really exists. Thus the "will to truth"—the will to believe that one's understanding of the world is complete or total—is likewise symptomatic of a decadent world view. It is for this reason that Nietzsche castigates men of the "objective" spirit, those who perceive the mind as mirroring the "essence" of reality and uphold the conviction that the attainment of knowledge corresponds to the transcending of "delusion."[26]

To endorse such a view is to assume a disjunction between the realm of appearances—of delusion—and a "true" world that lies behind or beyond it. It is to assume as well that the mind is capable of breaking through the veil of appearances to apprehend the "real" world that is its grounds. This world view, according to Nietzsche, wrongly presupposes that the mind is removed from the phenomenal world, that it is positioned at some Archimedean point outside the realm of appearances. He argues, in contrast, that the mind (like the eye) is fundamentally embodied and hence exists within the world of flux. As thinking beings, we necessarily confront the object of our understanding from a particular vantage point in space and time. There can only be, as a result, "perspectival" knowledge, or knowledge from a certain point of view. Moreover, because all knowledge is "situated," one no longer can speak meaningfully of a "reality" that transcends perspectival understanding, or of a "text" apart from interpretation. Philosophical expressions, such as "absolute knowledge," immediate certainty," or "thing-in-itself," are therefore vestiges of a mode of thought that vainly tries to escape the very condition of its own possibility.

For Nietzsche, then, the problem with modern science—or with most philosophical thought, for that matter—lies ultimately not in the content of its understanding but in the fact that it takes its understanding seriously, that it regards this as an accurate reflection of the true order of things. Nietzsche counters this view by speaking of a science that is an affirmation of life, a so-called "gay science" or "joyful wisdom," which adopts an ironic or playful attachment to its 'explanations.' Freed from the false consciousness that infuses metaphysical world views, the Nietzschean wise man remains open to the play of alternative interpretations while formulating his own.[27]

Summary and Conclusion

In review, we have noted that thinking, doing, and making comprise three qualitatively different sorts of enterprise for Aristotle. The "first" of the theoretical sciences (metaphysics) has as its goal reason's apprehension of first principles—the transcendental ground of being. Thus the first science is ontology. In contrast, the point of the "productive sciences" is simply to acquire knowledge of the means needed to realize the image of an artifact. Productive science therefore denotes "rational calculation" within the realm of making. "Political science," finally, is for Aristotle an inquiry into what constitutes proper order within society. Its end is determining the principles of good order.

From the perspective of this tripartite ordering, pathological states of affairs can be said to arise when these domains of activity no longer are kept distinct. For instance, with the fusion of politics and art, the master science of the good devolves into a "political *technē*."A noteworthy example of this is expressed in Hobbes's declaration that "by *art* is created that great Leviathan called a COMMONWEALTH . . . which is but an artificial man . . ." (emphasis added).[28]

The central focus of this chapter has been to clarify the theoretical and practical ramifications of the fusion of a different constellation of sciences, namely, those of theory and of art. I have stated that this fusion—initially expressed in Descartes's "practical philosophy"—had the effect of deontologizing the "first science" of modernity. By wedding theory to *technē*, the highest philosophical queries were redirected toward establishing a knowledge of those immanent "substances" that would yield to humans the power to master nature. The new foundational question became: "How is it that we know reality?," or, "What is it of reality that we know?" Modern philosophy is characterized by these sorts of epistemological concerns. The general response to questions of this sort, I have pointed out, is that knowing is conceived of as the process by which what is outside the mind is accurately represented to the mind. Hence, in order to understand how the mind comes to know the world, it is necessary to apprehend the way in which the mind is able to construct such representations. It is for this reason that modern philosophical thought can be said to manifest an egological bias.

Modern natural science is the theoretical-practical enterprise that has as its goal the attuning of mind's representations of the world (in the form of "laws of nature") to its external 'reality.' This coherence was achieved, it has been noted, by regarding natural phenomena as quantifiable generic mass, as "disenchanted." So seductive was this scientific view of the natural order that Hobbes, who, we have seen, takes politics to be an art (a form of "making"), patterns his construction of politics after the prevailing mechanistic conception of the workings of nature.

The political and ethical repercussions of scientism are evinced in Kantian critical science, as well. Kant's claim that there can only be scientific knowledge of phenomena effectively created an epistemological barrier between science and matters of moral judgment. Comte attempted to close this gap: He maintained that there ought to be a positive science of society every bit as certain in its conclusions as those attained by the natural sciences. Dilthey and Rickert also wished to establish a "human science," but they rejected Comte's positivistic route. They introduced in its stead a new mode of comprehending "social facts," namely, the science of hermeneutics. All the while, however, their allegiance to the methodology of the natural sciences remained steadfast, at least in the study of natural phenomena.

Nietzsche's comprehensive critique is directed at combatting the positivism inherent in the epistemological search to secure certain universal foundations of knowledge. A disenchanted world for Nietzsche is a world locked into a *Weltanschauung* that takes its perspectivism seriously, that is, as revealing 'reality.' Consequently, all manifestations of cognitive and moral absolutism are subject to his invective, for the attempt to stabilize meaning leads ultimately to the enslavement of man in a world other than the one in which he lives and dies. It is this will to "truth"—to attain knowledge that is free from illusion—-that for Nietzsche constitutes the prevailing ethos of a disenchanted age.

II

THE DISENCHANTMENT THESIS

You see, all mortal men are gripped by fear
because they see so many things on earth and in
the sky, yet they can't discern their causes and
hence believe that they are acts of god. But in all of
this, when we have learned that nothing can come
from nothing, then we shall see straight through
to what we seek: whence each thing is created and
in what manner made, without god's help.

Lucretius, *The Nature of Things*

It has been argued thus far that the turn toward epistemology is coterminous with a reinterpretation of reason's proper domain. The co-penetration of thinking and making has *activated* reason in the sense of having it serve as the means for attaining an exogenous end—the domination of nature. For reason to be an efficacious instrument, it had to confront an object—nature—amenable to control. But only by disenchanting nature did this goal appear realizable. Thus the turn toward epistemology can be distinguished analytically from the disenchantment of nature, but there remains a substantive link between them.

The first section of this chapter comprises an overview of Max Weber's epistemology in his methodology of the social sciences. The second section is intended to show how Weber's metatheoretical insights are congruent with his conception of the disenchanting of nature. The following section will attempt to place Weber's conception of a disenchanted nature within the wider context of the disenchantment of the world, disenchantment understood as a process of increasing societal rationalization. The chapter will close, in the last two sections, with an overview of subsequent developments within the discourse on disenchantment.

The Weberian Synthesis

Weber's interest in metatheoretical issues must be placed in its context. The simplest way to do this is to keep sight of the fact that his primary interest lay in the actual practice of social scientific research. Methodology is taken to be merely an *ex post facto* means of rendering such practices theoretically coherent. As he says: "Methodology can only be self-reflection on the means which have *proven* to be valuable to actual research. Explicit self-reflection of this sort is no more a condition for fruitful research than is knowledge of anatomy a condition for the ability to walk 'correctly'" (emphasis in original).[1] A crisis arises, however, when there is a breakdown in consensus as to what constitutes "fruitful" social scientific practice. Such a condition is analogous to the state of affairs leading up to a Kuhnian "paradigm shift," that "in-between" time when old ways of perceiving and doing things are disrupted and alternatives have yet to be established. A comparable situation existed during the *Methodenstreit*—the so-called "methodological controversy"—which dominated German social science circles during the last two decades of the nineteenth century. Focusing on Dilthey and Rickert, we have reviewed some of the leading concerns of this controversy, ones that arose primarily in response to the burgeoning of scientism.

It has been noted that whereas Dilthey had formulated a rather clean division between *Natur* and *Geist*, one which was reflected in an equally distinct division between the natural and historical sciences, Rickert's typology of methodologies narrowed the epistemological gap separating the two. For Rickert, it was the interest of the observer that determined the particular contour of reality to be worked on and hence the methodology to be employed. Thus the observer, whether a natural or cultural scientist, was said to be an "observer-participant." Weber held to this view, as well, by and large adopting Rickert's epistemological stand.

However, within the parameters of this general consensus, Weber distinguishes his position from Rickert's on at least two counts. First, he takes issue with the latter's account of the method deemed most suited to sociocultural analysis, namely, the method of individualization. As with Dilthey and Rickert, sociological investigation for Weber aims at understanding the meaning of the subjective intentions of the actor and the unique events that issue from these intentions. Yet he argues that the uniqueness of these events can be (and indeed, usually is in practice) understood in terms of specific combinations of general features or elements within the observed world. It is by working a number of these elements into a precise concept—an "ideal-type"—and then measuring a concrete act or event against it, that we can best grasp its specific content, according to Weber.

Second, and more important for this study, Weber elaborates on the status of the scientific "observer-participant" in his analysis of the value-relatedness of science. To a greater extent than Rickert, Weber stresses that knowledge of social reality is value-dependent and thus presuppositional. "Knowledge of cultural reality," he says, "is always knowledge from *particular points of view*" (emphasis in original).[2] He cautions us against assuming that these particular points of view have any kind of objective status, i.e., that they can be derived from the "facts themselves." On the contrary, for Weber it is the perceived meaningfulness of the object of study—that is, the social scientist's value orientation—that determines the "facts." This pertains to knowledge of the natural world as well: The natural scientist is no less free from values and interests than is the social scientist.

The value-relatedness of science underscores Weber's commitment to Nietzschean perspectivism. Just as "an eye turned in no particular direction" is a fatuous description of the operation of cognition for Nietzsche, so "presuppositionless knowledge" is for Weber.[3] In short, neither thinker adheres to the notion of so-called "disinterested knowledge." However, as noted, Nietzsche's brand of perspectivism is radical insofar as he claims that understanding is strictly interpretational and therefore incapable of explaining the world as it "really" is. Weber simply could not agree with this. To be sure, the scientist confronts a world framed by his interests, but for Weber his actual engagement with the world leads to results that are explanatory and not merely interpretive of that world. Thus social scientific understanding has the power to explain the characteristic traits and interrelationships between culturally significant facts as framed by the interests of the social scientist. What it cannot do is provide an explanation that yields a comprehensive theoretical overview of the whole of social reality.

What makes Weber such a compelling, if not puzzling, figure in this discourse on disenchantment is his ambiguous standing within the methodological controversy. For on the one hand he is committed to the view that the social sciences can explain adequately the coherences of the world. To this extent he aligns himself with positivist thought. But Weber distances himself from the positivist position by his claim that scientific understanding is necessarily value-related. Furthermore, Weber's neo-Kantianism prevents him from presuming that meaning (value) has objective ontological status. That is to say, for Weber the social scientist brings to phenomena a particular value-orientation which determines what in "infinite reality" is deemed worthy of being known. The world itself does not reveal or suggest to the observer its meaning. And because there are (potentially at least) as many value orientations as there are scientists, meaning is set adrift in a radical subjectivism.

The Disenchantment of Nature

It should be noted at the outset that there are relatively few places in Weber's collected works where he speaks explicitly of the phenomenon of disenchantment in general, let alone of the disenchantment of nature in particular. Aside from a small number of widely scattered remarks in the introduction to "The Economic Ethic of the World Religions" and in "The Social Psychology of the World Religions," Weber's only concerted, but nonetheless terse, treatment of the subject is to be found in "Science as a Vocation," originally presented as a paper at Munich University just two years prior to his death in 1920. Moreover, as in his remarks on disenchantment *qua* rationalization, Weber does not develop his thoughts on the disenchantment of nature in a systematic fashion. And yet his relative inattention to the notion of disenchantment is not indicative of its significance in the broad scope of issues addressed in his studies. What it reveals is simply his disinterest in making the issue an explicit object of scientific or theoretical inquiry. When Weber addresses the issue of disenchantment, he does so with uncommon passion and eloquence, revealing in the process the degree to which the subject matter commanded his intellectual attention.

Die Entzauberung der Welt—the disenchantment of the world—is the expression Weber uses most frequently to convey his vision or philosphy of history. As such, it bears a certain surface resemblance to Hegel's "phenomenology of spirit" or Marx's "dialectical materialism." However, for Weber the movement of Occidental history is best accounted for not in terms of a protracted struggle for political freedom and equality or for proletarian ownership of the means of production, but as a progressive emptying of magic from the world. Differently put, the history of the West is characterized by the world's "demagification," a term which better captures the essence of *Entzauberung* than the commonly accepted English translation "disenchantment."

What, then, does it mean to say that the world is disenchanted or without magic, and what forces contributed to this? Weber's answer to the first part of the question is seemingly straightforward; the world is disenchanted when it is assumed "one can, in principle, master all things by calculation."[4] So we can surmise that for Weber the world is disenchanted when man's bearing toward his environment—both natural and social—is informed by the belief that it can be manipulated by means of calculation. I say "belief" because Weber makes it clear in the quotation cited above that *de facto* mastery of the world is not a precondition for disenchantment. Rather, the world is disenchanted when it is perceived as a potential object of mastery, regardless of the actual level of calculative control attained by a particular social order.

It has been asserted by many observers, a number of whom will be discussed shortly, that humankind is driven by a transhistorical imperative to extend its power over nature in order to better secure its chances for survival. The species' instinct for self-preservation, they argue, manifests itself in the desire to control those variable and contingent natural processes that pose a threat to human safety. But if the desire to make the unpredictable in nature more predictable is an invariable response to our condition as earthly beings, it cannot be rightly construed as the definitive feature of a disenchanted world. Since the enchanted worlds of the past, no less than our own, were predisposed toward the control of nature, what in Weber's view distinguishes the two eras? A comprehensive answer to this reformulated question requires that we first take stock of differences in the means and extent of control in these two worlds.

Disenchantment *qua* demagification illustrates clearly the direction in which the means of control has shifted over the past twenty-five hundred years. In an enchanted world so-called "magical means" were employed to effect a measure of influence over the natural realm. Weber does not explicitly state what these means are, but given their objective—to "master or implore the spirits"—it can be inferred he had in mind various rites of appeasement, such as sacrifices, ceremonial dances, and so on. Although acts of this sort manifest the same practical impulse that propels modern science and technology, the fact that they are performed within what might loosely be called a religious or metaphysical setting is of considerable importance: In an enchanted age, unlike our own, the means of control is conditioned by the belief that the natural environment is governed by spiritual forces residing in or beyond the immanent order of nature itself. This means that the business of controlling nature is, at bottom, a matter of establishing a measure of influence over the supernatural forces that inform it. "Magic," then, is simply the name given to the art that has as its purpose the extension of power over a spiritualized natural realm.

One of the primary characteristics of magic, according to Weber, and one which distinguishes it sharply from modern technology, is its relative inability to effect real control over natural processes. Magic, in short, is an impotent art. Its successes are largely fortuitous and its failures conveniently interpreted by its practitioners as signs of impending success. There are, of course, reasons why the use of magic to control nature invariably yields poor results. Chief among them is the fact that in an enchanted world the will to command nature's obedience is checked by an opposing will, the will of nature, or, more precisely, the will of the spiritual forces that oversee its operation. As F.M. Cornford has noted in reference to the magical world view, and in general agreement with Weber's thesis, the degree of autonomy possessed by these spiritual powers is a function of their perceived otherness. The more they recede from the realm of the human and familiar, the more they become, in his words, "divine and mysterious."[5] Consequently, their actions and motives for action progressively elude human comprehension and calculability. And as the spirits go, so goes their domain. The ways of nature in an enchanted age are equally mysterious and incalculable, thus rendering them impervious to human mastery.

It was noted earlier that for Weber the world is disenchanted when one can, in principle, master all things by calculation. If we bracket for the time being the meaning of "all things" and continue to focus on the realm of non-human nature, we see that in an enchanted age nature is incalculable because its mind or soul shares with the human mind the capacity to function in unpredictable and unconditioned ways. It follows, then, that the disenchanting of nature signifies in part divesting the natural world of its uncertainty. Disenchantment *qua* demagification, on the other hand, informs us that this same process, when viewed in terms of the transhistorical impulse to control nature, is characterized by a corresponding change in the means of control.

Weber is quite clear as to the direction of this change. In a disenchanted world, he says, "[O]ne need no longer have recourse to magical means in order to master or implore the spirits, as did the savage, for whom such mysterious powers existed. Technical means and calculation perform the service."[6] Stated differently, we could say that in a world where nature is perceived as devoid of mind—as mere *res extensa*, to use Cartesian phraseology—science and technology replace magic as the preferred means of control.

Unlike the practice of magic, where a mysterious and impenetrable factor (i.e., the will of the spirits) interposes itself between the human and the natural realm, modern science confronts its object directly. The magician's current counterpart no longer operates under the assumption that nature is alive and in possession of an unfathomable life-force. Rather than viewing it as some kind of recalcitrant benefactor who has to be cajoled into dispensing a few meagre offerings, the modern scientist regards nature as an impersonal order whose obduracy is an illusion created by human ignorance of its ways.

The repercussions of this shift in perception of the extent of human control over nature are dramatic. As long as the natural order was thought to be alive with mind, the most the practical impulse could have hoped for was to achieve a measure of control over nature. What is meant here by "control" is best understood if we first note that the word literally means to work "against" *(contra)* the "wheel" or "roll" *(rotulus)*. Thus we could say in reference to our specific concern here that the practitioner of magic performed his functions knowing that the roll of nature—the flow of its processes—ultimately is shaped by a force transcending and overpowering the merely human. All that can be expected in such a situation is to check this superhuman power by seeking concessions from it that further the material interests of the community.

When nature is stripped of mind, however, this same flux is perceived as an immanent and self-generating process. Man no longer has to contend with a fickle third party in his dealings with the natural order. This opens up the possibility that the human mind can come to know nature on its own terms. This means, in principle at least, that the roll of nature can be made an object of understanding, and, correspondingly, that this understanding can be utilized in such a way as to press human designs on nature's flux. Here control transforms itself into mastery.

How this alteration in perception actually leads to an amplification of real existential power over the world is not yet clear. In addressing this issue, perhaps it is best to restate the fact that for Weber we moderns are standing at the endpoint of a millenia-old process which has transformed dramatically both our understanding of, and interaction with, the natural world. He refers to this process as "intellectualization" or "intellectualist rationalization." Weber goes on to say that it is through science or "scientific progress" that our understanding of nature has been intellectualized.

Obviously, by scientific progress Weber does not have in mind the advances made by the modern natural sciences alone, since the origin of the disenchantment process antedates the birth of modern science by over two thousand years. Evidently, by "science" Weber means that tradition of rational inquiry which had its inception in the thought of Thales, the ancient natural philosopher who took the first tentative step toward conceiving nature without reference to the supernatural. Thales's rational temperament is revealed in his rejection of mythological accounts of the origin and status of the natural world and in his attempt to comprehend its essence on its own terms. But the boldness of this move could not dislodge traces of a lingering metaphysics in his thought. The claim that "the nature of things"— that which sustains the world of nature—is the suprasensible substance "water" reveals the extent to which the natural realm for Thales remained enchanted.

Athough Thales's speculations constitute a clear example of a quasi-intellectualized understanding of the natural world, the mode of inquiry he initiated soon gave rise to descriptions of the order of things in which all traces of the supernatural had been extirpated. In the writings of thinkers such as Leucippus, Democritus, and perhaps most of all, Lucretius, we find articulations of a world where, as one commentator put it, the "gods and the immortal soul have vanished in a dance of material particles."[7] It is in their so-called "atomic" theories of nature that we find the truest expression of pre-modern account of a disenchanted world.

As Lucretius unequivocally states in this chapter's opening quotation, an intellectualized approach to understanding the ways of the world means uncovering the "true" causes of natural events. These true causes can be discerned, he goes on to say, only if we see "straight through to what we seek," that is, only if we first cut through the mystifying dogma surrounding the supernatural and realize that the world functions "without god's help."[8] Interestingly, Lucretius's soulless universe is not disenchanted in the strict Weberian sense of the term. There are at least two reasons why this is so, and, relatedly, why a despiritualized natural world is a necessary but insufficient condition for disenchantment. First, as noted, for Weber the natural order is disenchanted when it is perceived to be free of mysterious, incalculable forces. Lucretius's account of nature in *The Nature of Things* certainly appears to meet this criterion. A thoroughgoing materialist, he argues that the natural realm is solely composed of atoms and the void. In so doing he consciously attacks the Roman religion for its leading role in perpetuating the myth that natural events are divinely willed. Such an understanding, Lucretius asserts, only serves to breed fear in men's minds over causes unknown. It is far better to realize, he adds, that nature is mere unconscious 'stuff' and thus indifferent to human concerns and interests.

Despite having taken the mystery out of nature in this manner, Lucretius's cosmos retains an element of incalculability, which prevents it from being what a disenchanted world must be in principle at least—knowable and predictable. In his effort to account both for the creation of the universe and for change within it, Lucretius was compelled to adopt the Epicurean teaching that atoms, "at uncertain times and at uncertain points," swerve from their regular patterns of motion.[9] It follows that the present configuration of the universe is for him a product of chance, and that, despite its propensity to sustain its current form, unexpected alterations within the given order are a constant probability. With the principle of unpredictability firmly established in this way, the Lucretian world retains an element of mystery, which places it beyond complete rational comprehension.

There is, however, a second and more profound reason why Lucretius's atomic theory of nature failed to generate a technological or disenchanted world view. This pertains to the way in which the premodern natural scientist chose to react to the perceived indifference of his worldly surroundings. Before reviewing the Lucretian alternative, it bears repeating that the modern scientific intellectualization of the world, beginning in the sixteenth century, precipitated a philosophical defense that underscored the project of mastery. As stated in our first chapter, Descartes is perhaps the most influential spokesman for a new world view where recognition of nature's indifference to the human condition was coupled with a challenging response that raised "practical philosophy" to the rank of most noble endeavors. The Lucretian response, in contradistinction, eschews mastery altogether. It does so in part for the reason already stated concerning the practical impossibility of mastering that which is susceptible to unpredictable change. But beyond this, Lucretius puts forth the essentially moral argument that the attempt to master nature would be undesirable because it would require the unlimited development of the practical arts, which, in turn, would aggravate the desire for new and unnecessary things—the source of all human strife. Aware of such propensities, the wise Epicurean wishes only to live in accordance with the modest demands of nature and to seek freedom from bodily pain and mental anxiety.

This detour by way of Lucretius has been taken to illustrate why a world divested of mind is not, in itself, a sufficient condition for undertaking its mastery. The case of Lucretius shows us that while the despiritualization of nature is a precondition of the mastery of nature through science, its realization as a sociological and material fact requires the presence of additional stimuli. What these might be one would be hard-pressed to say definitively. However, I already have suggested that we may look to Descartes's valorization of practical philosophy as one possible stimulus, for it denotes an abrupt change in Western thought which until then had subsumed utilitarian concerns under those related to contemplation (philosophical or religious) or to politics. In other words, with Descartes we witness the philosophical endorsement of the implicit power held within the scientific world view, an authorization which appears in part responsible for unlocking this power.

There is at least one other potential trigger mechanism that must be taken into consideration at this point. Weber asserted that the intellectualization process which eventually led to the world's disenchantment is multifaceted. So far I have concentrated on giving an account of only one side of this process—the progression of natural scientific thought. This particular emphasis has been warranted both with respect to the topic at hand—the disenchantment of nature—and to the fact that although it comprises only a fraction of the intellectualization process, it is "the most important fraction," in Weber's estimation.[10]

Be this as it may, Weber unambiguously states that science is but one of the contributing forces to the intellectualization process.

Neither it nor any other single causal factor is solely responsible for the emergence of our disenchanted world. On the contrary, it is only by means of a confluence of mutually interactive intellectualizing forces that this outcome has occurred. In an effort to determine which forces contributed to the release of science's potential for mastery of nature and how they actually effected this, it is necessary to broaden the scope of the analysis by formally introducing the notion, "the disenchantment of the world."

The Disenchantment of the World

Weber uses "the disenchantment of the world" to signify that modernity is distinguished by an understanding that assumes "all things," and not just non-human nature, can be mastered through calculation. In other words, the 'object' of mastery in a disenchanted world includes both the natural and the human domain.

The question that must be asked is: What intellectualizing power, aside from that of science itself, is responsible for the realization of the ethic of domination in human–nature relations, and what connection, if any, does this have with disenchantment on a more comprehensive scale? In answering this question one must first take note of what initially might appear to be a logical inconsistency in Weber's treatment of the disenchantment problem. As we have seen, the very person who states that scientific progress is the most important element in the intellectualization of the world remains curiously silent on the issue in a substantive sense. Why is this? I would argue that it has to do with the simple fact that as a sociologist Weber is naturally drawn toward understanding why individuals in a given setting act as they do. Thus if we were to approach the topic of disenchantment with the interests of a sociologist in mind, we would find that the most captivating question is not, "How did science disenchant the world?" but "How is it that human beings have come to act as if the world is disenchanted?"

Because Weber appears to have been primarily concerned with questions of the latter sort, his research led him to explore those forces in society which have the ability to substantively reinforce or alter patterns of human behavior. Neither philosophy nor science figure prominently in this regard, for the transformational power possessed by each is restricted to the few who traditionally have been willing and able to receive it. In contrast to the limited sociological impact of rational discourse, the power of religion—precisely because of its affective appeal—historically has been of great importance in shaping the attitudes and actions of the many.

It was suggested previously that at least two factors acted as release mechanisms for science's latent powers of mastery. One of them, to repeat, takes the form of Descartes's apology for the modern scientific project. Yet we now see that as important as this development may have been in terms of signalling a major shift in the way philosophy received the demystifying powers of science, it itself did not have the capacity to translate this disenchanting force into a sociological reality. According to Weber, we have to look to religion or to some religiously inspired motive to find a mechanism capable of bringing the idea of disenchantment down to earth.

It should come as no surprise to learn of the significance of religion to Weber's philosophy of history if we note that for him the rise of world religions—e.g., Christianity, Buddhism—comprises an element in the multifacted intellectualization process. Along with science, religion served to rationalize and ultimately erode the magical-mythical world view. This was achieved, Weber argues, by religion's demand for a more coherent and meaningful justification of human suffering, and, most important, by its enumeration of directives outlining the way of life most likely to win salvation from this suffering.[11] He claims that the "Protestant ethic" emerged as the most influential Occidental response to this salvific challenge. Here disciplined action, not leisure or contemplation, came to be interpreted as a sign of God's glory. No longer, as in the Western classical or medieval eras, was labor perceived as a mere means to satisfy the immediate material interests of the individual and his community. Rather, worldly activity of this sort was ennobled and given a sense of inner dignity when, in the Calvinist mind, it was seen as a visible confirmation of one's faith. Significantly, for Weber the "work ethic" outlived its formative stage and persists in modernity in a wholly immanent or secular form. That is to say, disciplined ascetic action has come to be regarded in modern society as an activity of intrinsic worth, as a good in and for itself. When the value of worldly activity has been firmly established in this way, all means that have the capacity to effect real change in the world are implicitly sanctioned. In this setting science is no longer perceived, *pace* Lucretius, as a means to an extra-scientific end—as a means of justifying a particular moral stand—but as an inherent good that, in principle at least, establishes mastery over the world.

The natural sciences, of course, constitute just one among many means of mastery. And the disenchanted nature they preside over is just one of the world's domains amenable to intellectualization. We have seen that the rationalizing influence of religion—of Protestantism—created a cultural milieu that could embrace the *end* of science and thus facilitate the realization of its instrumental essence. But for Weber the rationalizing influence of religion also contributed to the formation of a worldly attitude that advanced the intellectualization of all domains, extending beyond the natural and into the human. "The disenchantment of the world," then, is the expression Weber uses to describe intellectualization on this more comprehensive scale.

In order to make sense of Weber's somewhat convoluted theory of rationalization, especially as related to the linkage between the two disenchantments—of nature and of the world—it is important to note that the many strands of the intellectualization process issue from a common source. This is to say that the various intellectualizations are instances of a single mode of rationality. The mode of rationality that underlies a disenchanted world is best seen in the context of the tension between what Weber calls "formal" and "substantive" rationality, or *Zweckrationalität* and *Wertrationalität*, respectively.[12] Formal rationality, on one side, refers to the reasoning process that determines the means necessary to attain a given end. It is formal because it denotes an intellectual operation focusing exclusively on the calculation of means. Formal rationality, then, is strategic thinking. Its sole aim is to find a way to get from one point to another, not to determine whether the endpoint is a goal worth pursuing or reaching. Formal rationality, in other words, is indifferent with respect to ends, values, or the question of content. It is not intrinsically directed toward any particular purpose. For this reason we could say that it is a value-neutral, instrumental, or technical intellectual operation. Thus we find Weber employing a wide variety of descriptive terms in referring to it, such as "purposive rationality," "instrumental rationality," "means-ends rationality," and "technical rationality."

Substantive rationality, on the other hand, refers to the value of ends as perceived from a particular point of view. An ascetic, for example, perceives his continent existence to be a rational end, given his commitment to the value of asceticism. For Weber the actions of an ascetic constitute "value rational" behavior because they flow from a conscious belief in the intrinsic worth of this way of acting.

Weber argues that both formal and substantive rationality are subjectively defined. This is obvious in the case of the latter, given what we know of his epistemological convictions. The ascetic, to return to our example, assumes his way of life is rational—he assumes it makes good sense—because he believes it to be of value. Here the reasonableness of one's actions is directly associated with the missing component in formal rationality—subjectively held values. That formal rationality also is grounded for Weber in the subject is not as self-evident, however.

In defense of his assertion that calculative reasoning is subject-driven, Weber argues that the process of determining the means needed to attain a given end does not necessarily mean that the most effective or efficient means to do so is in fact chosen. An individual, in other words, might reason that means X is the best way to achieve a particular end, yet in fact might not have selected the most appropriate means under the circumstances. He might, in short, have made an error in strategy. Determining the technically most effective means to a given end is achieved through the employment of what Weber calls *objecktive Richtigkeitsrationalität*, or "objectively correct rationality."[13] In contrast, to calculate means without the aid of objective or scientific knowledge is simply to reckon from the subjective expectation of the results of one's action.

As noted, a disenchanted world is a world where it is assumed all things can be mastered through calculation. What has to be clarified at this point is what Weber means by "calculation." Does he take it to be a form of reckoning where one's subjective evaluation of the appropriateness of the means chosen is paramount? Or does he mean by calculation what we might call "objective reasoning?" Although there is to my knowledge no direct textual evidence to support either interpretation conclusively, there are nonetheless good reasons to believe that Weber tended to identify calculation—i.e., formal rationality—with scientific or objectively correct reasoning. I say this in part because it is difficult to imagine how the world could be seen as an object of mastery, even in principle, without utilizing a form of rational calculation that can produce results that positively reinforce the expectation of mastery. Certainly, at the very least, within the realm of man's interaction with the natural world this expectation has been met most effectively by technically correct rationality. Moreover, since, as Weber observed, science is the most important fraction of the intellectualization process, a claim could be made that the mode of reasoning most appropriate to it is likely to have a disproportionate influence on the rationalization process as a whole. If this interpretation is sound, then, while certainly not discounting the subjective component in the equation, a case could be made that calculative reasoning in a disenchanted world increasingly adopts the mantle of technical correctness. The term "technical rationality" therefore could be said to convey more accurately than other descriptive titles the essence of modernity's pre-eminent mode of reasoning.

A disenchanted world, then, is one in which all domains within society are restructured in accordance with the demands of technical rationality. What this reorganizing process has yielded in a substantive sense for Weber will be discussed shortly. Of more immediate concern is his understanding of these domains in relation to the disenchantment process itself.

We begin by recounting the fact that in an enchanted world the presiding supernatural forces rendered the course of natural and human events meaningful, if not fully intelligible. Weber argues that in such a world all aspects of human conduct, be they political, esthetic, or economic, were informed by a single overarching order of meaning. Thus it makes little sense to speak of these realms of conduct as if they were truly distinct, as if they functioned in accordance with separate norms or logics.

However, all this changes upon the disenchantment of the world. This development brings with it a breakdown in the unity of meaning that prevailed within magical-mythical societies. The old cosmos of meaning is replaced in modernity with its acosmic configuration, typified by the emergence of differentiated "value spheres" (e.g., economic, political, scientific, esthetic), each possessing its own immanent norm (e.g., profit, power, knowledge, beauty).[14] And it is precisely because these value spheres pursue discrete ends that Weber drew the conclusion that they stand in "irreconcilable conflict" with one another.

Weber first raises the issue concerning the irreconcilability of value spheres in support of his claim that the social scientist, in his capacity as a teacher, ought to refrain from promulgating personal points of view. He is constrained from doing so for the epistemological reason that it is impossible to rationally defend a value preference. But beyond this Weber argues the impossibility of 'scientifically' pleading for interested stands, on the grounds that even if one were to uphold the 'truth' of a particular position, this would not in itself constitute a defense of other aspects of its value, such as its goodness or beauty. Thus a kind of polytheism is said to prevail in a disenchanted world. As Weber points out, it is as if the gods who populated the enchanted worlds of the past have died only to be resurrected in the form of incommensurable value spheres.[15] In this qualified sense, at least, the contemporary world remains enchanted.

The only significant difference between the two epochs lies in a change in "the bearing of man," one which has resulted in the impersonalizing of the conflict. But, of course, this is a significant development, the impact of which should not be underestimated. In an enchanted world, conflicts between the gods did not undermine the coherency of the cosmic order. If anything, these struggles reinforced it to the extent that they were attempts to rectify perceived transgressions of the established order. In contrast, the appearance of these transmogrified gods in modernity signals an era of unresolvable tension between competing value spheres. And to the extent that Weber takes this tension to be eternal and irreconcilable, the future of our disenchanted world holds for him no promise of value reintegration, no respite from its "ethical irrationality."

The picture of disenchantment emerging here itself rests, it seems, on a fundamental tension, if not contradiction. For on the one hand Weber claims that disenchantment has produced a kind of ethical schizophrenia, where, apart from the subjectivizing of the valuing act itself, entire sectors of social life are set adrift in pursuit of their own distinct normative logics. Yet he also argues that disenchantment produces a counterforce—technical rationality—which infuses these disparate value spheres and restructures them according to a single unifying principle. In what sense, then, if any, are these two impulses themselves compatible? Is the scenario presented by Weber an either/or one? Is it a matter of deciding whether a disenchanted world is either fundamentally at war with itself or a well-oiled mechanism whose integrated parts serve to realize a single end—mastery? Or does Weber see these two seemingly antithetical impulses co-existing in a disenchanted world?

Before addressing this important matter, a review of the other half of Weber's characterization of disenchantment is in order, that is, his account of the rationalization of value spheres. As stated earlier, by "rationalization" Weber means something like technical reasoning, a kind of calculative thinking whose end is the determination of the most effective means to attain a given objective. It is a mode of reasoning concerned with process and thus utterly indifferent to the value of the ends it strives to attain. When value spheres are rationalized, according to Weber, action within these various domains is likewise formalized and instrumentalized. That is to say, action is restructured in accordance with the principles of goal-directedness and technical correctness. Hence, for instance, the rationalization of the economic order in a disenchanted world has produced, in capitalism, a system premised on the deliberate and calculating pursuit of self-interest, free from the constraining values of tradition and sentiment, e.g., the religious ethic of brotherliness.[16]

The contemporary legal order, on the other hand, has evolved into a complex body of abstract legal maxims, which, precisely because of its involution, tends to lose sight of those substantive ends that ground it and lend it meaning. Likewise, the rationalizing of human interaction within the public sphere has produced the modern bureaucracy with its impersonal formalism, efficient structuring of channels of communication and command, and growing demand for "technical expertise" from those "specialists without spirit" of whom Weber speaks.[17] Even the arts, as witnessed in a number of esthetic revolutions during the early part of this century, turned in on themselves to display a similar fascination with form at the expense of content.

All of these developments indicated to Weber the loss of spirit within the social realm. They point to the loss of any value or vision within society capable of leading it beyond its own parameters—to self-transcendence. As a consequence, the disenchanted world retreats within itself and fixes its attention on matters related to its own self-management.

It has been argued that one of the distinctive traits of a disenchanted world is its apparent contrariety. We have seen, for instance, that with respect to values and ends this world is typically heterogeneous and conflictual. But when this same world is perceived in relation to means, it presents a homogeneous face where action across all value spheres is informed by a single mode of rationality. What then, to repeat a question already asked, does Weber have to say about the disenchanted world's paradoxical core? It appears from all indications that he simply accepts it as a given. He seems to hold to the notion that the rational superstructure of the disenchanted world rests on the shifting ground of distinct and often conflicting valuations among both persons and value spheres. In other words, Weber sees the business of calculating the means to action—the 'end' of technical reasoning—as superimposed upon a fundamentally unrelated operation that selects the end these means are to realize.

This is not to say, however, that Weber was unaware of the propensity in modernity to subsume ends under means. His references to the "loss of freedom" in a disenchanted world indicate to us how serious a threat Weber took this development to be. Yet beneath his gloomy prognostications about life in the "iron cage"—about a world locked into its own technological imperative—there remains in his thought an element of optimism that offsets this otherwise dire forecast.

His guarded optimism originates from two sources. The first pertains to the incommensurability of the operations of reasoning and valuing. Weber, as we know, assumed the two are distinct, and this allowed him to conclude that no matter how pervasive the realm of means becomes, the human capacity to articulate ends remains intact. The second and related conviction is that there continues to exist in modernity the potential for a truly heterogeneous mix of articulated ends. Both these persuasions suggest that Weber would not be party to any argument predicting the inevitable collapse of the means-ends distinction.

Nowhere is Weber's resistance to the subsuming of ends to means more vividly expressed than in his discussion of the limits of modern science in "Science as a Vocation." In this essay he makes it abundantly clear that one of the central problems confronting the disenchanted world is that its inhabitants act as if the tension between means and ends were non-existent. Weber argues that most of us do so when we erroneously believe that science is more than a mere ensemble of technical means. We falsely assume that the extent of control it has afforded us is an indication of its capacity to be more than a mere instrument. We presume, in short, that science can tell us something about the meaning of the world in which we live.

This Weber vehemently denies. While it may help us in our bid to master all things by calculation, it can not, he says, tell us whether "it ultimately makes sense to do so."[18] Thus Weber wants to impress upon us the problematic nature of science's worth. Granted, it may be "of value" in that it assists us in our effort to master the world, but use-value is not to be confused with "value" in the deeper sense of the term. For instance, were Weber alive today, he would most assuredly acknowledge the fact that recent developments in the study of quantum mechanics have helped us understand better the behavior of subatomic particles. However, what he would not assert is that this knowledge brings us any closer to understanding why these particles behave as they do. Science, in short, remains silent on questions of meaning. Weber eloquently summarizes his position on this matter when he observes that the "fate of an epoch which has eaten of the tree of knowledge is that it must know that we cannot learn the *meaning* of the world from the results of its analysis, be it ever so perfect. . ." (emphasis in original).[19]

It is evident from this statement of Weber that he believes we have had to strike a Faustian bargain in return for our newfound mastery. What we have gained in terms of knowledge of and power over the world we have lost with respect to its meaning—to our ability to rationally determine its value. This state of affairs Weber stoically accepts. It is a consequence of the "fate of our times," as he puts it. Yet this predicament need not lead to despair, in Weber's opinion. What is truly frightening about the new world, in his view, is not its supposed meaninglessness, but its blissful neglect of the question of meaning as witnessed in a popular culture that tends to measure the value of an end in terms of its use-value.

Weber tries to counteract this cultural disposition by stressing the importance of injecting meaning or value into the world. The question that now must be asked is: Where do we look for meaning in a disenchanted world? We now know that for Weber one cannot look to science or reason for guidance because they have lost their power to illuminate the meaning of the world. He therefore was led to the Nietzschean conclusion that meaning must be imputed to the world by ascribing value to it. Meaning, in other words, must be willed into existence by those who have the capacity to create and sustain it.

We have seen that for Weber the intellectualization process has resulted in the flight of meaning from the world in that the intellect has lost the ability to determine the world's value. By acknowledging the fact that scientific understanding and technical rationality are not privy to matters of ultimate meaning, Weber believed he could clear the path for acts of authentic valuation within the social order. Ideally, if the realms of means and ends could be neatly distinguished in this way, then the means that science presently commands could be made to serve the ends articulated by those capable of doing so, such as political leaders or artists. Herein for Weber lies the only hope for escape from modernity's iron cage.[20]

That Weber remains hopeful in view of the draining of meaning from the world is evidenced in his treatment of science and technology as a sociological datum. As he relates in an interesting passage from "Science as a Vocation," not only is science unable to inform us about meaning, it cannot even supply us with increased knowledge of the conditions under which we live.[21] By this I take it he means that in the world that science has built, the technological milieu we have created for our convenience has become so complex that those who rely on it for their daily existence have virtually no knowledge of its operation. Although Weber himself does not use the term, we could say that our technological environment has acquired "magical" qualities to the extent that we count on processes whose behavior we are at a loss to explain. This is in stark contrast to the so-called "primitive," who, precisely because of his lack of technological sophistication, has a nuanced and immediate grasp of his tools and their use.

What Weber chooses to stress is yet another limitation of science. After arguing elsewhere that science is not privy to matters of ultimate meaning, he tells us here that it has not even been able to perform the ancillary task of informing the general public about the functioning of its own creations. What Weber could have chosen to comment on, but tellingly did not, are the potential consequences of living in a world that is both technogically powerful and enigmatic. If he had, he might have come to the conclusion that our disenchanted world is in danger of becoming re-enchanted. Only this time the "gods" would appear not in the form of the supernatural but in the immanent guise of technology itself. That he did not choose to seriously consider this possibility—as we will see others have—does not mean that Weber's disenchantment thesis dismisses this out of hand. On the contrary, I argue here that it is his tacit recognition of precisely such a threat which in part prompted Weber to articulate his critique of science in the first place.

Lukács and Instrumental Rationality

The importance of Weber's "disenchantment thesis"—the generic expression used here to describe the disenchantment of both nature and the world—lies in the clarity with which it discloses the effect modern science has had in shaping our understanding of human–nature and interhuman relationships. It has been noted that for Weber this impact can be traced to the use of reason as a technical tool. The question that needs to be addressed at this point is: For whom is disenchantment an issue? According to Weber's own assessment, it is certainly not a concern for those "big children" who further the ends of the natural sciences. Neither, one could argue, are the masses unduly concerned with their fate. To be sure, they may live in the grip of modernity's iron cage, where they are forced to perform tasks over which they have little or no control. Still, there is a measure of solace to be found in this world to the extent their technological milieu compensates them with distractions from boredom.

Georg Lukács, more explicitly than Weber, argues that the disenchantment of the world—which he redefines as "reification"—penetrates to the very core of human consciousness. He does so by offering a Marxist interpretation of the genealogy of modern rationality. As an introduction to Lukács's reformulation of disenchantment, we begin by placing his thought within the context of our extended discourse.

Lukács's personal and professional affiliation with Weber was close indeed. Between 1912 and 1915 he was an active and highly respected member of Weber's "Sunday circle," an eclectic group of scholars who established, in the study of Russian mysticism and literature, a common basis for discussion. It also provided a focal point around which its members could rally a critique of Western capitalist culture. It was this general concern for the "crisis of culture" that had befallen the rationalized, disenchanted, capitalist Western world that originally drew Lukács to Heidelberg and the Sunday circle.

An interest in rehabilitating an authentic culture was a guiding theme in Lukács's intellectual endeavors. It meant for him redemption from alienation, the restoration of a world where people's actions are directed toward ends that facilitate mutual support and interdependence. Lukács's early (pre-1918) writings were characterized by an attempt to isolate the source of the alienation that hampered such a reconciliation. He was led to conclude at this time that the tension between the intransigent reality of an inauthentic capitalist world (the "is") and authentic cultural values (the "ought") was all but unresolvable. As a result of this "tragic antimony," Lukács, like Weber, resigned himself to the 'fate' of modernity. Yet whereas Weber in his lectures on the vocations of politics and science rescued at least partial meaning from and hope for the world as it was, Lukács's original reaction was to retreat from the world entirely. Thus we witness him admonishing his colleague Paul Ernst: "Go back inside yourselves! The outside cannot be changed. . . ."[22]

However, by the time of his writing *History and Class Conscious-ness*, Lukács's first mature work as a self-conscious Marxist, the posi-tion he adopts with respect to the crisis of culture is charged with renewed vigor and optimism. He now argues that the crisis of culture is the crisis of "reification." Simply put, reification for Lukács is the phenomenon whereby human relations take on the form of 'laws of nature' and thus become objective 'things' that stand opposed to an otherwise mutable social reality. It is, in short, a freezing or objec-tification of the contingent and fluid movement that typifies all non-pathological social relations. In order to better understand what is meant by the reification of social relations, we must investigate that which Lukács likens it to, namely, the laws of nature as articulated by modern science. This, in turn, calls for a more thorough under-standing of his views on the status of scientific knowledge.

With respect to these related issues, Lukács criticizes (in a thorough-ly Weberian manner, one might add) the positivist assertion that scien-tific knowledge can be elicited simply from a reading of the "facts themselves." He is well aware that a descriptive account of so-called "facts" already implies an interpretation and hence presupposes a his-torically conditioned framework of understanding. But Lukács, like Weber, is equally aware that a hermeneutical conception of knowlege is not an integral part of the self-understanding of Western science. On the contrary, modern science, in its blindness to what we may call, along with Weber, its "value-relatedness," operates under the illusion of objec-tivity. Thus by presupposing the objective validity of its truth claims, science presents them as immutable "givens" or "laws."

Lukács claims that the propensity of modern science to reify con-cepts is rooted in the capitalist conquest of nature. As a materialist, he attributes the drive to dominate nature not to some progression within the realm of 'ideas,' but to the concrete intentions and actions of certain individuals. But the endpoint is the same as that reached by non-capitalist critiques of the domination of nature: The natural world is perceived as a mere 'thing' to be utilized in furtherance of the inter-ests of man.

For Lukács the capitalist domination of nature that precipitated the reification of natural scientific concepts is mirrored in the process whereby the capitalist productive process comes to be viewed as an in-dependent and immutable 'thing' by the worker. As Lukács notes in an elaboration of Marx's theory of commodity fetishism, the modern labor process alienates the worker from his creations to the extent that it progressively eliminates "the qualitative, human, and individual at-tributes of the worker."[23] In place of an organic relationship between worker and product, the laborer in the modern workplace is subjected to "abstract, rational, specialized operations," which he takes to be the 'natural laws' of capitalist production. His fate therefore appears to him to be determined by these so-called "objective laws."

Commodity fetishism and the attendant process of reification is for Lukács a "specific" problem of the age of modern capitalism because only here has it become "the universal structuring principle" of society.[24] To a greater extent than Marx, he is convinced that the repercussions of fetishism are manifested in all aspects of society, not merely in the economic sector. To be sure, the source of reification lies within the economic sphere, but for Lukács reification has expanded beyond the bounds of its original context and penetrated the very core of consciousness in modernity. The crisis of capitalism therefore is seen by him as a general crisis of the culture itself. He characterizes this crisis as a passive acceptance of the reified 'natural order' (the *status quo*), an order that for the members of society takes on the appearance of a "second nature."

Lukács's critique of reification includes as well the claim that the rationalizing of the world leads to the objectification of the temporal dimension of human existence. Historical consciousness, or consciousness of temporal continuity, he says is replaced by consciousness of the discontinuous facticity of the "given." The political or social ramifications of this mode of consciousness are inherently conservative in that it promotes aquiescence before the 'laws' of the existing social order—the so-called "powers that be." And since the *status quo* is capitalism, the propensity in modernity is toward continued deference to the 'laws' of capitalist production and, it might be added, to the dictates of positivist natural science.

The picture painted here by Lukács would be at least as bleak as Weber's were it not for his marginally more optimistic outlook on the possibility of an escape from modernity's iron cage. According to Lukács, escape is contingent upon subjecting the law-like character of modern society to what he calls "historical and dialectical examination." It is not necessary for our purposes to discuss at length Lukács's proposal for the dissolution of reification. It only needs to be said that overcoming alienation, the demystification of reification, and hence the reestablishment of authentic culture, lies within the power of the proletariat's class consciousness. Accomplishing this, which for Lukács is by no means historically predetermined, would result in the practical mediation of such "bourgeois" antinomies as subject and object, spirit and nature, freedom and necessity.

By recasting the disenchantment problem in terms of a Marxian analysis of the crisis of culture, Lukács obviously changed the tenor of the debate. But its central and defining characteristic remains unaltered. Both he and Weber were intent on accounting for and critiquing what they took to be the essential meaninglessness of action in contemporary society. And despite their different approaches to this common problem, they agree that the solution must be "political" in nature. For Weber, as we have seen, this means individuals must take upon themselves the challenge of articulating the ultimate goals of their actions. Lukács, on the other hand, places his faith in the power of the proletarian class to dissolve reification. In this latter instance, then, we witness what might be called the more unambiguously political of the two solutions to the disenchantment problem.

The year that witnessed the publication of Lukács's *History and Class Consciousness* (1923) also marked the founding of the Institute for Social Research in Frankfurt, the "Frankfurt School." The varied interests of its members—the most notable for our purposes being Max Horkheimer and Theodor Adorno—did not vitiate their basic commitment to the "critical approach" to existing society. "Critical theory," as it came to be known, garnered much of its intellectual strength from its opposition to the "scientific," or positivist approach to social research, in both its non-Marxist and Marxist variants. Hence, Weber's non-Marxist quasi-positivist account of the methodology appropriate for the social sciences and vulgar Marxism's adumbration of the 'laws' of class struggle were viewed with suspicion.

The impact of Lukács's writings on the Frankfurt School has never been adequately assessed.[25] The lack of scholarly research on this issue, however, should not hinder efforts to reach general conclusions concerning the extent of his influence on Horkheimer and Adorno. Doubtless it was the spirit of Lukács's defense of Marxism— its presentation as a critical method of socioeconomic analysis rather than as an outline of the "laws" of societal development—that must have struck a responsive chord with the Frankfurt theorists. To be sure, Lukács's claim that the working class was the "subject/object" of history and hence the only potential force capable of de-reifying social reality was not supported by Horkheimer and Adorno. However, in the main, such differences did not detract from the latters' indebtedness to his critical approach to sociological analysis or from the relevance of a number of his central concepts (reification, fetishism, etc.) to their specific concerns.

The reformulation of these concepts was not undertaken exclusively within the Marxist paradigm, however. This is especially true of the writings of interest to us here, namely, those written during and after the Second World War. It is at this point in their careers that Horkheimer and Adorno begin to distance themselves from the Marxist tenet that upholds a view of humans as essentially productive beings.

To adopt such an outlook, they argue, is to uncritically accept the rationale underlying the productive process. Specifically, it is to presuppose the validity of technical rationality and the disenchantment of nature. It is precisely these presuppositions that Horkheimer and Adorno expose to scrutiny. Hence an analysis of the "crisis of culture" ultimately calls for a broader examination of the conditions that resulted in humans' estrangement from their natural environment and the establishment of their rational powers of domination.

Horkheimer and Adorno adopt a Nietzschean strategy toward this end. Moving beyond Weber's descriptive examination of disenchantment and purposive rationality, they seek to uncover the motivation that underlies them. What accounts, they ask, for reason's predisposition toward mastery and control? Horkheimer, for one, responds by asserting that "reason was born of man's urge to dominate nature."[26] But it is not merely modern rationality which is said to evince a predatory relationship toward the natural world. Rather, reason *per se* is so disposed. It is the character of Western rationality, then, that leads Horkheimer, along with Adorno, to argue that disenchantment is intrinsic to the logic of Occidental rationality. This account itself is limited, however, in that it leaves unasked the secondary question regarding reason's need to dominate nature. Horkheimer responds, again echoing Nietzsche, by claiming that "fear" fuels the urge to master nature. More specifically, it is the fear of the unknown and the alien, even, he says, of "the mere idea of outsideness."[27]

The first step whereby the fear accompanying the primal experience of an immediate and undifferentiated nature is appeased is taken during the cognitive revolution that results in the separation of object and its concept. Horkheimer and Adorno argue that the formation of the concept, which is at once identical to and distinct from its referent, represents the initial phase in the "spiritualization" of nature, and, conversely, the alienation of object and concept. They claim as well that at this early stage the benefit accruing from this development outweighed its cost, for humans' alienation from the natural world is in fact a precondition for their feeling "at home" in the world. That is to say, the world can be divested of its alien character and made "one's own" only by investing it with meaning—a process coextensive with its mediation via concepts about it.

This movement from a pre-animist to an animist level of consciousness is then accompanied by increasing levels of differentiation between object and concept, of heightened degrees of "abstraction." One such advancement in abstraction is manifested historically in the formulation of the Olympian deities, who, unlike the autochthonic spirits of animism, are no longer identical with various natural elements but instead *signify* them. Here Horkheimer and Adorno argue, once more, that human ratiocination is sustained by a desire to control nature. At this level, however, the desire is expressed vicariously through the powers of the gods. They function as intermediaries between man's perceived helplessness in the face of nature's forces and those forces themselves. By seeing in the gods the embodiment of various aspects of human essence (spirit), the forces governing the behavior of natural events in the domains over which they preside are rendered intelligible, if not entirely controllable. The consolidation of the objectifying power of human conceptualization in the classical world is witnessed in the Platonic 'ideas,' according to Horkheimer and Adorno. They conclude, again in agreement with Nietzsche, that the Platonic mode of thinking is the highest expression in the premodern world of man's alienation from the Dionysian flow of existence, an alienation said to be psychologically rooted in resentment against life and expressed in the attempt to master it conceptually.

To be sure, Platonism represents to Horkheimer and Adorno the endpoint in classical times of a process by which intellect (reason, mind) distinguishes itself from sensuous experience in order to subjugate it. Yet they find Homer's portrayal, in the *Odyssey*, of Odysseus' struggle against the Sirens to be of greater interest because here the actual *agon* between the ego (reason) and nature is depicted. By the time Plato had arrived on the scene the play between the forces of a dynamic nature and those of a static rationality had been all but arrested in favor of the preeminence of the latter. Platonism in actuality builds upon this victory. However, in the passage from the *Odyssey* we witness a mythological portrayal of the decisive event itself, of the moment when the play of forces was arrested. The richness of the authors' interpretive analysis of this event warrants a brief review.

For Horkheimer and Adorno the genealogy of Western rationality—or the dialectic of enlightenment—is the history of renunciation. What sets off these "introversions of sacrifice" is the progressive denial of man's embeddedness in nature. The *mis-en-scène* of this unfolding drama reveals two principals. On the one hand, we have the enchanting power of nature personified by the Sirens and their "liquid song." This natural force is said to account for the human propensity to indulge in pre-rational pleasure, to lose oneself in a rapturous communion with nature.[28] On the other hand, we witness the ingenuity and cunning of Odysseus and his men.

With the assistance of the goddess Circe, Odysseus and his crew renounce nature's seductive call by devising various means of resistance. Through the technical ploy of stopping their ears with wax, the oarsmen manage to deny themselves the deadly pleasure of hearing the Sirens' song, and, consequently, avoid being drawn to their certain 'death'—an undifferentiated union with nature. Odysseus cheats a similar fate by binding himself to the ship's mast, a tactic that enables him to experience nature's allure without having to succumb to it.

According to the Frankfurt theorists, the kernel of wisdom contained in Homer's portrayal of this episode is that the renunciation of pleasure and the mortification of the passions is the price to be paid for the security of the self, for self-preservation in the face of a hostile and enchanting natural order. Most important, they argue, is the fact that Odysseus was able to preserve himself by virtue of his cunning and wit, that is, by means of his capacity to reason calculatively. According to this reading, then, instrumental reasoning is intimately related both to the constitution of the "self"—to Odysseus' "homecoming"—and the self's alienation from nature.

But for Horkheimer and Adorno the trade-off in this instance between estrangement from nature and self-constitution results in a net loss. As they say: "Everyone who practices renunciation gives away far more of his life than is given to him."[29] One could add in this regard that Odysseus' disassociation from nature and from his natural passions is a foreshadowing of the loss of meaning which is endemic to modernity and which expresses itself ultimately in the usurpation of ends by means. The preservation of the self has been secured at the cost of disenchantment.

If we witness in Homer's depiction of this Odyssean adventure a "moment" in the dialectic of enlightenment, then for Horkheimer and Adorno it is only with the Enlightenment itself that the dialectic is fully realized—that the world becomes fully disenchanted. Because disenchantment means disillusionment, knowledge of the world as it "really is," post-enchanted thought is necessarily self-conscious about the distinction between illusion (myth) and reality. Its consciousness of myth as illusion means that it necessarily places itself beyond illusion. To be beyond illusion with respect to an understanding of nature is to realize that the propensity in mythological thought to anthropomorphize nature leads to a mistaken view of the world, that it is in fact merely an unconscious imputation of the self into the world. Demythologized or disillusioned consciousness, then, is free from the illusion that nature possesses any "hidden qualities," forces that transcend its material being.[30] So whereas mythical consciousness alleviated humans' fear of the world by seeing in it a reflection of their own essence (mind, spirit), 'enlightened' consciousness reaches the same end by opposite means, by taking the natural world to be a mere 'thing' and hence benign with respect to human designs.

Only when nature is conceived in this way is the potential for human mastery over it fully realizable. Having been denied a life of its own, nature, *qua* extended matter, is reduced to a quantifiable mass. Hence the historical significance of the discipline of mathematics in a disenchanted world, a discipline whose power, Horkheimer and Adorno note, has enabled man to construct a "schema of the calculability of the world."[31]

Due to its unparalleled success in erasing all traces of otherness in nature, Enlightenment thought is said by Horkheimer and Adorno to be "mythic fear turned radical."[32] This is most clearly manifested in positivism, a method of rational inquiry that marginalizes everything that is not reducible to quantitative measurement and susceptible to the leveling power of abstraction. The end product is the so-called empirical "fact" that positivism takes as its raw material and which proves to be in truth anything but "objective" (i.e., unmediated by the ego) and "concrete."

Confronted with a disenchanted world, mind is forced to fall back on itself in an attempt to recover meaning. Relegated to this tactic, the *cogito* secures meaning in the only avenue remaining open to it, that is, in the assurance of its own continued existence. Thus the principle of self-preservation becomes the canon of positivist thought, and reason the means to its attainment. As a result, Horkheimer and Adorno uphold the Weberian identification of modern rationality with instrumentality. "Subjective" reason, as Horkheimer refers to it, has as its 'end' the determination of the most efficient means to realize ends that are "taken for granted and are supposedly self-explanatory." What distinguishes this assessment from Weber's, which at face value appears to be virtually interchangeable, is the connection they draw between technical rationality and man's comportment toward nature. Specifically, they argue that subjective reason is an outgrowth of the "revenge of nature." Nature, in effect, is said to retaliate against the power that disenchants nature by emasculating that power. It makes sure that the mind is able to master the world only by "imitating its rigidity and by despiritualizing itself in turn."[33] Hence the payment that is exacted for the disenchanting of nature is the disenchanting of mind, the routinizing of thought processes.

Horkheimer and Adorno argue that thinking of this sort is "totalitarian" because it consists merely of the instantiation of particulars under predetermined principles. The grounding of all knowledge on these predetermined principles ensures that modern reason can know only that which it constructs in its conceptions since it is incapable of telling us anything about the world that it has not already imputed to the world. Consequently, reason in modernity is said to be "tautological" and science a "self-activating" analytical procedure. Modern science, in short, is a law unto itself (literally "auto-nomous"), or, as Horkheimer and Adorno prefer to say, "a system of detached signs devoid of any intention that would transcend the system."[34] In the final analysis, enlightened or disenchanted thought never manages to resist the allure of myth. Whereas mythic consciousness alleviated its fear of nature as "other" by attributing to nature a reflection of its own essence, modern consciousness realizes a similar end by disenchanting nature. In each instance the result is the same, the putative 'human–nature' dialogue reveals itself to be an egological monologue.

As already stated, Weber does not seriously question the status of the modern scientific enterprise, save to point out its limitations in articulating the ends of existence. In contrast, as we have seen, the critique of disenchantment by Horkheimer and Adorno is more far-reaching. As a result, their program for recovery is more radical. They maintain that any attempt to reconstitute the present must begin by recapturing the spirit of the "classical requirement of thinking about thought."[35] They point out that this mode of thought issued in a conception of reason—referred to as "objective" reason—that informed the whole of the classical conception of 'reality.' But as successful as classical reason was in establishing a "cosmos" within which man could order his existence, the authors insist that the remedy to our present condition cannot be found in a reactionary and essentially romantic return to some form of rational objectivism. They claim that objective reason often results in ideological (read: uncritical) dogma, a definite *faux pas* for a method of inquiry that espouses a "critical" bias.

At the time of writing *Dialectic of Enlightenment*, Horkheimer and Adorno speculate that a possible alternative to either objective or subjective reason might be found in the middle ground between the two. They argue, rather vaguely, that the determination of this course would facilitate the emergence of a more rational society. Just what they meant by a more "rational society" is not altogether clear, for neither author at this point was particularly rigorous in detailing the substantive content of their proposed reformulation of reason. Only in subsequent writings were they able to articulate with greater precision their respective solutions to the disenchantment problem.

Horkheimer, for one, states in *Eclipse of Reason* that the aim of critical theory is to precipitate a "mutual critique" of the main variants of reason with the end in view of reconciling the two in reality. However, he thinks a complete reconciliation is neither possible nor desirable. As Horkheimer notes perspicaciously, even a claim for the primacy of nature hides within itself a dominance of the ego. For, he says, "it is spirit that conceives this primacy of nature and subordinates everything to it."[36] The way out of this impasse is to realize that the dualism of subjective and objective reason (like that of spirit and nature) is merely an "appearance," albeit a necessary one, he adds. Thinking becomes derailed, then, not when it posits these concepts but when it exalts either of them to the exclusion of the other. Hence critical theory's positive program, according to Horkheimer, is to comprehend the mutual interplay and interconnection of intellectually distinguishable antinomies, such as spirit and nature, or subjective and objective reason.

Horkheimer does not provide us with a full description of the contours of such an understanding, nor tell us how it may serve to effect concrete social change. Adorno's program for recovery, on the other hand, while not wholly satisfactory in itself (for reasons to be discussed in Chapter Four), does provide us with a more substantive account of an alternative relationship between humans and nature. For this reason it merits closer attention.

As noted, for the Frankfurt School theorists it is rage against the externality of the natural world that drives forward the process of disenchantment. Adorno explicitly renounces the domination of the object by the subject and in its stead introduces the concept "negative dialectics," a notion that acknowledges "the preponderance of the object," as he puts it.[37] However, Adorno, like Horkheimer, does not advocate a return to man's original embeddedness in nature, even if this were self-consciously realizable. Recovery from disenchantment cannot be had by returning to the golden era of a mythopoeic experience of nature. Both "pure immediacy" (the negation of the subject–object dichotomy) and "fetishism" (subjective reason's reification of its conceptual 'objects') are equally unappealing, in his view. The objective, therefore, is to articulate what he refers to as a "non-regressive" overcoming of the subject–object dualism, one that avoids the pitfalls associated with either the underdeveloped ego (as in animism) or the overdeveloped ego (as in modern consciousness).

The details of Adorno's account of how such an outcome may be accomplished are lengthy and complex and need not concern us at this point. Suffice it to say he argues that by liberating historical consciousness, by realizing that the triumph of subjective rationality in modernity (where calculative reason holds sway over a disenchanted world) is not "second nature" but a human construct, one may be able to reactivate long-repressed memories of a vital mode of interaction between humans and nature. Specifically, Adorno, following Walter Benjamin, stresses the importance of recovering man's mimetic experience of the natural world, an experience characterized by the human capacity to find non-sensuous similarities between the self and the natural order. It is through an analysis of art that Adorno believes we can gain entry into this way of experiencing the world, and to realize in the process that it is possible to know the world in such a way as to have conceptual domination kept in check by sensuous receptivity. In short, for Adorno the esthetic experience provides us with a model of a relationship between self and nature that is far less conflictful than the one which currently prevails.

It is precisely because the ego functions as a mouthpiece or agent of the object in the genuine esthetic experience that art for Adorno possesses the capacity to captivate or enchant. Here the self is, quite literally, held captive by the object and hence de-centered with respect to its relationship to the object. It is for this same reason that art, within the context of a thoroughly rationalized and disenchanted world, often is viewed as a profoundly irrational, romantic, and even childish enterprise. The commanding ego of the modern age cannot easily account for a self that is not a self—an ego not wholly in control of its relationship with the world. That artists are an anomaly in contemporary society does not mean that their work is to be regarded as frivolous or a source of amusement. Genuine art does not merely entertain, according to Adorno. Rather, ideally it serves to subvert the prevailing technical ethos by revealing the fundamental irrationality of that ethos. As Adorno says: "The irrationality in the principle of reason, as evidenced in its fetishization of means, is unmasked by art with its overt irrationality. . . ."[38] Authentic art, therefore, possesses for him a capacity to illuminate the covert irrationality of a seemingly rational world. To this extent it serves as a latter-day gadfly to the technological society.

In review, we see in the late critical theory of Horkheimer and Adorno the identification of a condition originally articulated by Weber, namely, the disenchantment of the world and the concomitant instrumentalization of reason. However, they part company with Weber on at least two counts. First, they account for this condition by incorporating into their exegesis certain Nietzschean themes, the most salient being the linkage between the drive to master a disenchanted nature and the fear of nature as "other." Second, and as a consequence of the first, they claim that the challenge of disenchantment can be adequately met only by rethinking the human–nature relationship.

In concluding this section I would like to address a possible objection to my treatment of Horkheimer and Adorno. It could be considered an oversight that I have allowed to go unchallenged their claim that modern rationalism is a mere extension of ancient rationalism. Let it be said at the outset that the debate over the nature of the relationship between ancient and modern rationalism is highly charged, and, judging from the literature on the issue, shows no sign of imminent resolution. One thing is clear, however. Horkheimer and Adorno agree with the Nietzschean assessment that Occidental rationality is a manifestation of the will to power and that it has progressively demythologized the world and eventually rendered the world an object for mastery.

According to this reading, ancient Greek rationalism, while still partially embedded in a pre-philosophic or religious world view, managed to take an important first step toward the complete emancipation of man's rational/critical faculties from the strictures of myth. The strength of this interpretation, as I see it, is that it enables one to contrast our modern disenchanted world with the ancient Greek era, yet at the same time prevents us from assuming that these worlds are incommensurable and hence represent alternatives to each other. The difference between them, I would argue, is one of degree (albeit extreme), rather than of kind. Consequently, I do not see any inconsistency in the claim made initially in Chapter One that, on the one hand, an understanding of the ancient world view can serve as a means to bring into relief the modern condition, and, on the other, that the ancients set into motion a force (rationalism) that eventually destroys the old order completely.

Systems Theory

Horkheimer and Adorno share an aversion to the consequences of a mode of reasoning that sanctifies the subject and its determining role in establishing the grounds for 'knowledge' of the natural and social orders. In their divergent ways they attempt to redress this epistemological imbalance, and, in the process, to at least disrupt the disenchanted world. Systems theorists argue that efforts of this sort are futile. What is at issue here, they say, is not the status of reason as a faculty of the subject. Nor, from within this perspective, are questions concerning its intersubjective truth content said to be of any ultimate consequence. Presumptions of this kind, it is claimed, result in the misconception that a symmetry exists between knowledge of the whole and of its parts, that, for instance, the mode of rationality operative in a given social order is a macrocosmic replication of its expression at the level of the subject. From the system theorists' perspective, a conjecture of this sort leads to the simplistic and erroneous belief that societal reordering can be effected through the manipulation of the individual actor's experience of reason or of the world. But this is not possible, it is argued, if the contour of the prevailing social order and the mode of rationality that informs it are conditioned by the logic of the order itself.

This general approach borrows from the sociology of Emile Durkheim, who, in his *Rules of Sociological Method*, claims that society is not merely an aggregate of individuals, but a system with its own specific reality and its own particular characteristics.[39] It is this emphasis on the independence of the "system" that differentiates the system theorists' orientation from that of Lukács, Horkheimer, and Adorno, and draws it toward (and ultimately beyond) Weber's portrayal of modernity as an iron cage.

The systems approach to social and political analysis builds upon insights from the sciences of physics and biology, the most significant of these being the principle of entropy. This principle describes the propensity of natural processes to move from more ordered to less ordered forms of organization. Thus the natural world is said to "run down" over time. An explanation of the phenomenon of life therefore necessarily entails an account of the manner in which entropy is arrested, or at least temporarily forestalled. In nature, the combatting of entropy is achieved by means of negative feedback. It is through feedback that an organism is able to adapt to environmental "noise" (disorder) and hence maintain a homeostatic relationship with it. The maintenance of life, then, is dependent upon the continual flow of messages (information) between a given organism and its environment, and upon the organism's ability to adjust itself positively (negentropically) in response to any increase in the disorder of its environment. Moreover, the capacity of the organism to adapt positively to environmental noise is said to be a measure of its "rationality."[40]

The rationality of a system does not have to be set by the indeterminacy of nature's disquiet, however. The science of cybernetics has as its end the making of the indeterminate more determinate. This it does by solving the problem of control and communication. The solution, it is argued, lies in attaining knowledge of the operation and the interrelation of those mechanisms that enable an organism to maintain itself in its environment. The objective of the science of cybernetics is none other than to acquire knowledge of the means to facilitate the maximizing of a system's rationality. Such knowledge then will permit the creation of second-order systems that are more efficient (or "rational") than those found in nature itself.

The appropriateness of the science of cybernetics as a tool for social understanding (or social engineering) rests on whether or not the contemporary social order exhibits the properties of a cybernetized system. Most systems theorists think it does. One of the best representatives of this school of thought is the French sociologist Jacques Ellul, for whom the rationalization of the social domain is seen as a manifestation of an increased capacity for system self-management. To understand better what Ellul means by this, it is necessary to outline his account of the genealogy of "technique."

Ellul is well aware (along with Heidegger) that technique—understood as *technē* or technical know-how—preceded modern science chronologically. What distinguishes it from modern technology is that, in its initial, pre-modern configuration, technique was contextualized within—and hence constrained by—a comprehensive background of meaning. However, upon the dissolution of its ontological ground, technique began to assume an autonomous status. Its disengagement from the realm of final causes facilitated its transformation into the dyad of *technē* and *logos*. It is in this manner that technical know-how was "rationalized" and its rationalization in turn radicalized, a process that resulted in the "extreme development of means" so characteristic of modernity.[41] Understood in this way, technique is Ellul's answer to Weber's technical rationality.

It is interesting to note that despite the Weberian tenor of Ellul's description of autonomous technique, not to mention their agreement over the suppression of substantive meaning in modernity, Ellul explicitly denies having been influenced by Weber's sociology.[42] He admits certain obvious parallels in their thought, yet stresses differences in approach as well. The latter is certainly true in one important respect. As we have noted, Weber wanted to impress upon his readers the fact that technical reason is a neutral tool to be used to further subjectively held ends, the status of which cannot be determined rationally. He emphasized this point to warn us of the possible consequences of living in a world that mistakes the realm of means for an end in itself. Ellul concurs with Weber's general assessment of the growing technologizing of society. However, he differs from the latter with respect to the severity of the crisis. That is to say, Ellul is convinced that modern society is all but locked into the technological ethos and that our actions within it are ultimately determined by the demands of what he calls technical "efficiency."

Because Ellul tends to view the rationalization process as unavoidable, he is understandably less optimistic than Weber about the chances for recovery from the ill effects of disenchantment. His pessimism rests on the conviction that the value-neutral character of technique does not in the long run ensure its immunity from value considerations. The situation now exists, he says, where subjects and their subjectively held value preferences no longer posit the end(s) to which means are applied. Rather, for Ellul, technique has become an end in itself disguised as means. In the absence of external constraints, self-engendering technique is said to be "no longer conditioned by anything other than its own calculus of efficiency."[43] Thus technique carries with it its own positive momentum, one which pervades and animates all realms of modern conduct.

In order to understand why for Ellul technique has filled the void created by the erasure of substantive ends, and has not, as Weber hoped, remained a mere means, it is necessary to refer to a central aspect of Ellul's philosophical anthropology. Ellul concurs with Weber, Horkheimer, and Adorno that technique has effectively demythologized and disenchanted the world. The invasion of technique, he says, "desacralizes the world. . . . For technique nothing is sacred, there is no mystery, no taboo." He goes on to say that people living in this technicized realm, who know very well that "there is nothing spiritual anywhere," are at the same time psychologically unable to live in the harsh light of this reality. Therefore they impute a sense of the sacred to the prevailing ethos, that is, to scientism and technique itself. In deference to Horkheimer and Adorno, we may say that as a consequence of *"the revenge of the sacred,"* technique itself takes on the characteristics of that which it negates. Technique thus is rendered "a god which brings salvation."[44]

We could surmise that technology for Ellul has become a new god in part because Weber's wish to resuscitate an autonomous realm of ends failed to materialize. The growing imbalance between technological and valuative imperatives which concerned him is no longer an issue for Ellul, since the scales now appear to have tipped decidedly in favor of the technological. So the objective of the contemporary social critic is not, as it was for Weber, to warn us of the impending loss of "values," but to announce the repercussions of that loss. Nor for Ellul does it make sense to speak of the limitations of science and technology when they have so thoroughly insinuated themselves into the fabric of everyday life. As argued earlier in this chapter, Weber could still interpret our ignorance of the technological order as an indication of science's limits. Ellul, in contrast, interprets this same phenomenon as proving precisely the opposite claim. He maintains that ignorance of the forces that create our technological environment only serves to illustrate how powerful these forces have become. Our lack of understanding of these technologies only reinforces their hold on us by lending to them and their products a magical aura. Although Ellul himself does not say as much, we could conclude that the world thus portrayed is immanently re-enchanted.

Because the world has become a self-enclosed system, according to Ellul, the scope of human action is necessarily constrained by the system's exigencies. This is to say that man is now relegated to the role of the system's caretaker or custodian.[45] But in depicting humans as merely keepers of the system, Ellul is not implying that they lack all freedom. He does not deny, for example, the tremendous space for lateral movement within the system, a space so intoxicating in its possibilities that it gives the impression of boundlessness. But he does say that given the technological system as an ensemble of means, such freedom remains confined within the parameters of technique. Thus, from the point of view of the self-maintenance of the system, this freedom is merely peripheral.

Interestingly, from the perspective of systems analysis, the conditional character of human freedom within technological society is an indication of its highly rational organizational structure. The proliferation of technique in modernity has resulted in so thorough a mediation of the natural and social environments that its control over these realms is in principle fully established. The social order, therefore, is in possession of the means needed to sustain a homeostatic relationship with its environment: It is truly rational. If, however, the ambit of human freedom were to include non-technological (inefficient) modes of action and social interaction, then the system's range of control would shrink correspondingly. Disorder would infiltrate the system, thereby reducing its capacity to adapt positively to changes within the environment. For this reason, the sanctioning of absolute freedom of action within the system would be counterproductive.

The German sociologist Niklas Luhmann shares with Ellul a "systems" bias, as witnessed in Luhmann's reference to his own method of social analysis as a "general systems" approach.[46] As in all approaches of this sort, human action is taken to be organized into "systems," that is, into patterns of interrelationships between actors. The goal of these systems is said to be self-maintenance. In other words, the goal of all social systems is to sustain basic configurations of interrelationships between actors. As noted, most systems analysts utilize analogies drawn from biology (i.e., the "organism") to schematize the functioning of systems. Consequently, they generally assume that social systems maintain themselves in the way non-human biological organisms do, i.e., through processes that function in such a way as to differentiate systems from their environment. The task that systems analysts set for themselves, then, is to show how these processes facilitate this end. That is to say, their objective is to describe how societal entropy is forestalled.

The approaches which Ellul and Luhmann adopt in their systems analysis of society differ only with respect to the means deemed best able to account for the system's capacity for self-maintenance. Ellul's response, as noted, was to see in technique the ultimate weapon in the battle against societal entropy. It is through the perfection of the science of control that the system for Ellul has been able to adapt more effectively to changes in response to its environment. Hence an analysis of society based upon a systems approach presupposes in Ellul's case a world view that takes nature—both human and non-human—to be disenchanted.

Luhmann's position on this issue is somewhat more difficult to ascertain. On the one hand, the processes he sees as central to the self-maintenance of social systems are said to be common features of all organic life, both human and non-human. Hence, by drawing together the domains of the natural and the human, Luhmann dissuades us from concluding that the relationship between the two is characterized by humans' domination and control of nature. On the other hand, the perception of nature and natural processes to which Luhmann subscribes, and upon which he models the functioning of social organisms, is grounded in a scientific reading of organic life. To this extent it remains unclear as to whether or not Luhmannn's analysis of social systems is immune from the effects of disenchantment.

Nonetheless, as stated above, Luhmann suggests there exists a natural proclivity in all biological systems toward self-maintenance by means of processes that operate in accordance with a single underlying principle. Specifically, this drive toward self-maintenance is said to be sustained by "mechanisms" that function in such a way as to reduce the complexity within a system. These mechanisms are necessary, Luhmann argues, because all systems exist within a multidimensional environment that provides an inexhaustible supply of stimuli—information—to which an organism potentially may respond. Were a system not able to respond selectively to the full range of environmental stimuli, it would run the risk of merging with its environment. Therefore these mechanisms perform the vital function of filtering out and selecting, from the complexity and randomness of environmental noise, certain stimuli to which the system then is primed to respond. In so doing, these mechanisms create pockets of reduced complexity (i.e., systems) within a more complex informational field. They function, in short, as the means by which a system differentiates itself from its environment, or as the means by which order is drawn from disorder.

Luhmann extends his analogy to biology when he claims that, like non-human biological systems, social systems progress as they become increasingly differentiated from their environment. This is said to include the increasing differentiation of social subsystems from their environment (i.e., other social subsystems) as well as the differentiation between the overarching societal system and its larger environment. By increasing differentiation, systems are able to respond to environmental stimuli in more numerous and nuanced ways. Hence this development assures greater flexibility in the relations between system and environment. This is considered an "advance" because an increase in response flexibility enhances a system's level of adaptation and therefore its capacity for self-maintenance.

Luhmann enumerates three types of functional mechanisms which further the end of system self-maintenance. The first, referred to as the "mechanism for variation," allows increased differentiation within the system and thus new patterns of interaction among subsystems and between the societal system and its environment. This mechanism is said to inhere in the process of "communication," which Luhmann defines as the transmission of symbols, patterns of symbols (i.e., codes), and patterns of codes (i.e., media) between actors. Its primary function as a mechanism is to reduce complexity by delimiting the range of possible discourses in which actors might engage. However, because of the binary, dialectical character of its elements, communication allows for the introduction of new meanings and ways of action. As a result, there is built into the structure of communication a capacity for increasing complexity.

Yet Luhmann is equally aware that an increase in complexity is not, in itself, an indication of a system's evolutionary advance. It just as easily could signify the reverse, for increased complexity may stand for mere increased randomness. For this reason Luhmann introduces a second mechanism, which he calls the "mechanism for selection." This mechanism is roughly analogous to the process of natural selection within the biological world. Only those symbolic (as opposed to genetic) mutations that increase the system's ability to adapt successfully to changes in its environment are thereby "selected" as new features within the evolving system. For instance, Luhmann regards the creation of the medium of "truth in science" to be one example of what is called a communicative "success." This medium functions in such a way as to simplify the understanding of a complex universe. And its success in reducing complexity in our understanding of nature grants it an ongoing role in the contemporary social order.

Lastly, the "stabilization mechanism" denotes for Luhmann the process by which the products of communicative success are entrenched within the structure of a system. This process normalizes new media through the formation of supporting subsystems. Thus, for instance, the introduction of the medium of truth in science is normalized, or stabilized, by establishing agencies and organizations (governmental, economic, social) which function in such a way as to reinforce its role within the life of society.

Because the communicative act holds within itself the capacity to generate new meanings, complexity-reducing mechanisms produce, over time, increasingly complex and differentiated societal systems. There arises in these systems greater numbers of subsystems, with more complex forms of organization within each of them, and hence greater and more varied possibilities for subsystem interrelation. This in turn results in greater complexity in the relationships between the societal system and its environment. As already stated, this increase in complexity results in a corresponding increase in the system's level of adaptibility, for the system now has at its disposal a greater range of possible responses to its environment. There is, however, a down side to this increase in system complexity. For with increased differentiation there arises as well an increased probability of maladaptive decisions being made concerning the optimal relationship between system and environment. Thus an increase in a system's level of adaptibility is accompanied by a potential increase in its instability.

This propensity of evolving systems toward destabilization must be checked if system overload is to be averted. Yet it cannot be won at the expense of a reduction in the system's complexity, for that would undercut its highly evolved capacity for self-maintenance. The solution, then, can not lie in the retrogressive move towards reduction of differentiation within modern social orders. Rather, Luhmann argues that differentiated societies can reduce complexity (and hence increase order) by developing what is called codes of "differences." In other words, order is regained in factionalized societies by establishing codes, interpretative frameworks, which provide a means of creating order out of differences. For instance, Luhmann takes the articulation of the ideological distinction between "progressive" and "conservative" politics to be a code that provides a means of accounting for differences in political vision. Thus the danger that imperils a political system characterized by value fragmentation is checked by the introduction of a code that the factions utilize to structure their differences.

By comparing the systems theories of Ellul and Luhmann, we see how differences in their understanding of the mechanisms that combat societal entropy lead to radically different understandings of the systems themselves. For Ellul, a societal system ordered by technique is a monism in the sense that a single principle—the principle of efficiency—dictates its operation and future development. For this reason nothing really new occurs within the technological system because genuine novelty by definition is inefficient and hence excluded from the realm of acceptable alternatives. Luhmann, on the other hand, reaches a very different set of conclusions. This rests, ultimately, on his claim that all social systems are sustained by communication. It is because communicative acts are structured in such a way as to allow for generating new meanings and actions that Luhmann regards systems, including the overarching societal system, as dynamic and progressive. Hence, unlike Ellul's portrayal of the contemporary social system as a self-sustaining monism, Luhmann presents us with a view of society that underscores its mutability.

So, from a Luhmannian perspective, modernity's propensity to view nature as disenchanted is merely a manifestation of a particular expression of complexity-reduction. There is nothing in Luhmann's account of the evolution of societal systems that precludes the possibility of new forms of complexity-reduction in our knowledge of nature from displacing old ones.

But this is not to say that the system's mutability is unrestrained, for as stated there exist mechanisms that routinize certain modes of discourse and action. Hence, according to the implications of Luhmann's own view, the symbolic mutations within a societal system where certain media (e.g., truth in science) have stabilized will most likely not produce substantive changes. We can conclude, then, that the distance separating Ellul and Luhmann on the propensity of the current societal order to maintain its present trajectory is less apparent in fact than in principle.

Summary and Conclusion

Our investigation in this chapter has led us across the variegated terrain of the disenchantment thesis. We began with Weber, for whom modernity is characterized by the technical rationalization of personal, societal, and human–nature interactions. The post-Weberian discourses on disenchantment examined in this chapter react to Weber's description of the modern condition in either one of two ways. The first interpretational camp includes those arguments that respond to the disenchantment problem by calling for a fundamental reconsideration of the modern, beginning with a critique of technical rationality. It has been argued here that the Frankfurt School theorists offer the most penetrating critique of this sort. While not abandoning their critique of bourgeois culture, Horkheimer and Adorno strayed from the orthodox Marxist path (and deepened the investigation considerably) by boldy arguing that the disenchantment of the world lies within the very impulse of Western *logos*. Consequently, they asserted that any corrective measures necessarily would entail an equally daring reinterpretation of the meaning of reason and rationality. As noted, among the critical theorists, Adorno's attempt to realize a non-repressive mode of rationality seems to offer the most promise as a potential antidote to the instrumental rationalization of the world.

The second interpretational camp, on the other hand, contains arguments that take disenchantment to be a datum of the world whose facticity all but precludes the possibility of effectively transforming the *status quo* through non-systemic means. Within this grouping we have witnessed two very different kinds of evaluative responses to this acknowledged 'fact.' Ellul, for one, does not revel in the *Zeitgeist* of modernity. On the contrary, it is a matter of great concern for him insofar as the technological system appears irrevocably committed to the project of mastery for its own sake. As he sees it, the fate of modern society is sealed if it is in truth a closed "universe," for then there can be no vantage point outside the system that might serve as a standard for evaluation or critique. Despite Ellul's portrayal of technological society as a system, in the final analysis it does not constitute for him a universe, that is, a closed system of meaning that does not admit of alternative or unconditioned world views. As a Christian, he maintains that belief in the Kingdom Of God provides one with the needed extra-systemic vantage point from which to appraise and resist the kingdom of means.[47]

Luhmann, as we have seen, argues precisely the opposite. The system-environment monad for him is a universe because it contains within itself all the possiblities of experience or knowledge. Since this monad has no 'outside,' criticisms of the system are necessarily generated from within its evolving parameters. Furthermore, the measure of a critique's 'truth,' as with any other symbolic mutation, is determined by the extent to which it enhances the system's powers of adaptability. Therefore those critiques that would undermine the system's ability to maintain itself would be rejected out of hand by members of the system. Because technology has proven to be a highly effective means of augmenting society's powers of adaptability, it is inconceivable, according to Luhmann, that a fundamental reconsideration of the technological ethos would be considered. It makes little sense, then, to say that his systems approach to social understanding can be construed as a vindication of modernity. The contemporary social order is no more in need of defense than is a tree or any other system. It is apparent that for Luhmann all that remains to be done is to provide a description of the system.

PART TWO

THE JOURNEY HOME

III

MODERNITY VINDICATED

> One could say that, by inventing the airplane,
> man corrects the "error" of Nature, which
> created him without wings. But that would only
> be a metaphor: to say that is to
> anthropomorphize Nature. Error, and hence
> truth, exists only where there is language *(logos)*.
>
> Alexandre Kojève
> *Introduction to the Reading of Hegel*

In this chapter attention will be focused on arguments which react to disenchantment in a manner other than that taken by either the Frankfurt School or systems theorists. Neither strictly condemnatory of technical rationality nor dispassionately supportive of the *status quo*, they defend the Enlightenment project by calling for the release of the emancipatory powers of science and technology. Of the two arguments under consideration here, the one presented by Hans Blumenberg in *The Legitimacy of the Modern Age* is the more dubious, in that it does not deal squarely with the kinds of questions that preoccupied Weber, Lukács, Horkheimer, and Adorno concerning disenchantment and the status of technical rationality. Hence, from the perspective of this study, his defense of modernity is somewhat questionable due to its uncritical reception of the technological ethos. This being said, Blumenberg's argument in favor of the continued development of productive forces within society is sufficiently intriguing to merit its inclusion in our investigation.

Jürgen Habermas's defense of modernity, on the other hand, can be viewed as the more sophisticated of the two, for the following reason. Like Blumenberg, Habermas vindicates the modern age to the extent that he upholds its basic commitment to the project of mastering nature. In so doing he sanctions a perception of nature as disenchanted. However, to a greater degree than Blumenberg, Habermas regards disenchantment as an enabling, empowering phenomenon that has yet to be fully actualized. The challenge facing Habermas, then, is to identify and remove that which has prevented a disenchanted world from empowering humans with its potential. Briefly stated, Habermas argues that the solution lies in recreating a balance of forces between technical rationality and a consensual form of reasoning which he refers to as "communicative rationality." This corrective measure, it will be shown, represents the end point of Habermas's longstanding attempt to isolate and offset those forces that have encumbered modernity.

In order to arrive at a fuller understanding and appreciation of the scope of his efforts in this regard—culminating as it does in Habermas's "dialogue with Weber"—it is necessary to trace the progression of his thought on the issue of disenchantment. For purposes of clarity this will be presented in two stages. The first is an analysis of his earlier writings, including such texts as *Theory and Practice, Toward a Rational Society, Knowledge and Human Interests,* and *Communication and the Evolution of Society.* The relevant arguments of his more recent writings will then be reviewed, the central text being *The Theory of Communicative Action.*[1]

Blumenberg and the Legitimacy of Modernity

Blumenberg launches his defense of modernity by censuring one of the most influential arguments in the post-World-War-II era against the legitimacy of the modern age. In *Meaning and History,* Karl Löwith contended that the pathology of modernity is attributable to its "secularization" of the eschatological pattern set up by the Christian religion. As he says: "The modern overemphasis on secular history as *the* scene of man's destiny is a product of our alienation from the . . . supernatural theology of Christianity" (emphasis in original).[2] Eric Voegelin later reiterated the same theme when he wrote: "The attempt at constructing an *eidos* of history will lead to the fallacious immanentization of the Christian *eschaton*."[3] The implication is that modernity is in need of redemption and that this can be realized only by recapturing the spirit of a past age.

Such a view—the "secularization thesis"—devalues modernity, according to Blumenberg, in portraying it as the 'fallen' progeny of an authentic cultural tradition. An interpretation of this sort underplays historicism and historical discontinuity, in Blumenberg's view, and has had the effect of robbing modernity of its substantive cultural presence. The result is the conception of modernity as "a remainder, a pagan substratum, which is simply left over after the retreat of religion into autarkic independence from the world."[4]

Yet in assailing the secularization thesis, Blumenberg does not want his readers to conclude that modernity is unrelated to and unconditioned by what preceded it. Thus, for instance, he chastises as presumptuous the Enlightenment claim that modernity is wholly distinct from the classical and medieval eras. The "reality of history," Blumenberg says, means that it can "never begin entirely anew."[5] But he infers from this that whatever it is that modernity inherits from history, it cannot be something that was originally Christian.

His argument in support of this claim runs as follows: the Christian interest in eschatology could not have been the starting point of modern historical consciousness, because if it were, modern consciousness would have been characterized by a continued concern over matters related to teleology, albeit now expressed in an immanent form. Blumenberg asserts that no such interest in teleology exists in the modern age. He therefore concludes that the dispute between the ancients and the moderns is not over the ontological status of ends but "the status of permanent prototypes as obligatory ideals [ends]."[6] In other words, for Blumenberg the bone of contention between the two epochs is over the very existence of ends as binding norms of conduct. Weber, as noted, had argued along similar lines when he distinguished the pre-modern from the modern era on the basis of the modern dissolution of rationally determinable ends. Modernity thus was defined as an era in which 'ends' are taken to be the product of non-binding acts of human self-assertion and will.

The transition from an adherence to the "obligatory ideals" of the ancient world to the principle of "human self-assertion" that epitomizes modernity was not, for Blumenberg, the work of an 'external factor' that somehow managed to pervert the authentic substance of eschatological ideals to further its own purposes. Rather, modernization is said to be the result of an immanent cultural development. As he puts it, "eschatology historicizes *itself*—not, however, by transforming itself and continuing a false 'incarnation' but rather by enforcing the reoccupation of its position by heterogeneous material" (emphasis in original).[7] This statement warrants elaboration. The use of the phrase "heterogeneous material" in reference to modernity and its displacement of the 'old' world may appear to contradict Blumenberg's previously stated views on the continuity of historical development. The confusion is dispelled, however, once it is realized that the continuity underlying the transition to the modern age is said to be a continuity of problems rather than of solutions. In order to probe more deeply into Blumenberg's rather complex reading of the historical transition to modernity, we will investigate a concrete and, for our purposes, very pertinent manifestation of one such "problem."

"Self-preservation" for Blumenberg is a transhistorical human concern brought on by the impotence of our power in the face of the vagaries of nature's forces. In contrast to the constancy of this particular challenge, the method of coping with it—in other words, the shape of the problem's solution—has changed dramatically over time. For instance, he argues that prior to modernity humans' relationship to the natural environment was conditioned by an understanding of our embeddedness in natural processes. Hence technique was used primarily to supplement and assist nature and its ways, to aid in the execution of its ends. At this point it was conceived as a means to facilitate the proper functioning of an extra-instrumental end—the natural order itself.

However, with the dissolution of the pre-modern order of ends— which Blumenberg refers to as the "disappearance of order"—self-preservation became the theme of human self-comprehension. That is to say, the collapse of technique's meaning-constituting ground had the effect of redirecting attention to technique in isolation. Modern technique, thus understood, is qualitatively different from its pre-modern counterpart, according to Blumenberg. Freed from external constraint, it now is amenable to refashioning in terms of "technology." This process is synonymous with a re-evaluation of the meaning of reason as well, as noted in the first chapter. Indeed, this newly developed conception of what it means to think and reason comprises the "heterogeneous material" that is said to reoccupy the void created by the dissolution of pre-modern consciousness. Technology has become the new locus of humans' self-understanding.

The upshot of Blumberg's view is that the problem of self-preservation has acquired a new dimension of meaning because now it is conditioned by a qualitatively different mode of consciousness. This in turn results in a revised solution, one for which modern science and technology are the means. It could be argued at this point that Blumenberg's defense of modernity is no more than an elaborate justification of the "Cartesian revolution," grounded in Blumenberg's idiosyncratic interest in refuting the secularization thesis. But it is more than this, in fact. Not only does Blumenberg sanction the intrinsic validity of modern science—that "great instrument of self-assertion," as he puts it—but he goes on to say that it possesses as well the capacity to "surpass the character of pure self-assertion."[8] Because science and technology in his view are not bound by any self-referential dynamic (e.g., the will to power), they are said to have the potential to transcend their own limitations.

Interestingly, this strong defense of science and the modern project is underscored by Blumenberg in his response to Nietzsche's critique of both. It has been said that for Nietzsche freedom from the straitjacket of modern science is to be found in the mobilization of art and the esthetic experience against the domination of positivist consciousness. His objective was to resist the entrenchment of any 'truth' that would arrest the free play of interpretations. In order to facilitate this end, says Blumenberg, Nietzsche had prescribed that the human will "should consist in imputing the least possible binding force to reality, so as to make room for his [man's] own works."[9] But in Blumenberg's view, Nietzsche overlooked the possibility that modern science itself may possess such a "nonbinding force," a force that for Nietzsche animated only a joyful wisdom. Because for Blumenberg there is no necessity in modern science's adherence to the *telos* of nature's domination, it has the potential to break out of competition with nature's accomplishments and present itself as "authentic reality." One condition must be met before this end can be realized, however. The securing of modern science's authentic reality is for Blumenberg contingent upon retrieving the presently obscured motives of modern science and subjecting them, he says rather cursorily, to "man's purposes in relation to the world," as defined by his self-interest.[10]

There are a number of difficulties associated with Blumenberg's defense of modernity, a few of which should be touched upon at this point. First, the portrayal of modern science as unbounded by its present limitations only seems to reaffirm his faith in the liberating powers of technical rationality. I use the word *faith* deliberately here, for Blumenberg appears unable to give reasons for his assertion that modern science need not remain an instrument of domination. Yet reasons seem required, given the fact that nothing in the current state of affairs indicates that the grip of technical rationality on modernity is loosening appreciably, if at all. As it stands, Blumenberg's claim that modern science possesses a non-binding force reveals simply his hope that science is capable of performing a final act of overcoming, namely, self-overcoming.

A second difficulty arises with his statement that optimally self-interest directs the modern scientific project. The problem here is that Blumenberg neither hints what these interests might be nor adequately accounts for the process by which science is to subordinate itself to them.

Lastly, also troubling is the eschatological imagery Blumenberg employs in his description of the future of modern science, as when he speculates on the possibility of it gaining an 'authentic' reality. Evidently, he fails to see the irony in upholding a view of contemporary science as a mere prefiguration of what it might become, while admonishing those who conceive of modernity as a pale reflection of what it once was.

Habermas: Early Works

As noted in Chapter One, the study of metaphysics was a nobler activity than politics for Aristotle because its "object" was nobler. And because the objects of theory and practice were taken to be qualitatively distinct, neither activity was thought to infringe upon the jurisdiction of the other. Thus, for instance, a person's ability to philosophize had no bearing on his capacity to be a good citizen. On the other hand, the activity of some in 'making' was for Aristotle regarded in part as a means of liberating certain other individuals from the necessity of the production-consumption cycle, thereby providing them with the leisure to pursue more fully such human activities as politics or philosophy.

It was noted as well at the beginning of this study that the activation of reason in modernity altered drastically the relationship between thinking, acting, and making. Politics, for instance, came to be viewed as an object of theoretical knowledge. The assumption here was that it was possible to gain scientific knowledge of politics in the same way that the natural scientist gains an understanding of the workings of the material universe. This is turn facilitated the treatment of politics as an object of control, just as scientific knowledge of nature is utilized for the purpose of mastering it. The upshot of this development is that in modernity the practical science of politics eventually gave way to discourses on "political technology."

Weber was highly critical of the wholesale technologizing of politics—of politics *qua* administration. Politics could be revitalized, in his view, only if the apparatus of the state were guided by an individual or a group of individuals whose range of action was not delimited by the imperatives of the technological order. These outstanding personalities are leaders, who, by definition, would rather articulate and act in accordance with their own ends than submit to the will of others. They are, Weber adds, "men with the politician's sense of responsibility, not the bureaucrat's sense of duty and subordination . . . proper in its place but pernicious in political respects."[11] Hence it is by means of their passionate yet sober commitment to a personally held political vision that these "guiding spirits" can direct the 'system' to an end that transcends its internal momentum. If, however, Weber indeed looked to individuals of this sort to free us from modernity's iron cage, he must have assumed that the political leader is impervious to the technological ethic that he admits envelops the contemporary social order. His antidote to political and bureaucratic legalism would be ineffectual if the ethos that pervades it were to infiltrate and mold the perceptions of political leaders themselves. For then the steering mechanism itself—the personal political vision— would be tainted by the force it ostensibly can contain.[12]

It was Horkheimer and Adorno who exposed this potential oversight by tightening the connection between disenchantment and the rationalization of all forms of human thought and action. Hence politics for them is more firmly committed to the task of controlling human beings than Weber had previously assumed. Ellul took the argument one step further by claiming that political domination is not rooted in the anthropocentric desire for control—although this once may have been the case—but in the technological system's own internal set of demands. From this perspective, politics is seen to be firmly embedded within the web of technological imperatives. No longer conceived as a distinct "value sphere," it functions solely as a means to facilitate the needs of the overarching system. Hence the ethical and political agendas are said to be conditioned by the exigencies of technology itself.

Habermas concurs with the general observation that the disenchantment of the world, as manifested in the proliferation of technologies of control, has had an enormous impact on social and political practices. However, the consequences of this development have been mixed, in his view. On the positive side, disenchantment has fostered what he calls the heightening of the productive forces of society. That is to say, the rationalization of the political, legal, and administrative orders has resulted in an increase in the powers of control within these domains. But it is precisely this augmentation of power which has produced as well those "unplanned sociocultural consequences" that he says arise whenever the "power of technical control over nature made possible by science" is applied to society.[13] Disenchantment, therefore, also advances new types of difficulties, i.e., those normally associated with overly complex systems. However, what is truly problematic in all of this, according to Habermas, is not that rationalization brings with it certain unforeseen consequences. An indictment of this sort, after all, can be leveled against all strategems of action. Rather, Habermas censures the prevailing view that takes rationalization to be an unqualified good in its being simply emblematic of a practice's increased enabling power.

In his early writings, Habermas addresses this issue in reference to a discussion on the meaning of "enlightened action." It is important to note at the outset Habermas's choice of words here. When one speaks of "enlightened action" there is an immediate and implied reference to its antithesis—"unenlightened action." As the latter term connotes, to act in an unenlighted manner is to be blinded by ignorance or misinformation. Just as enchantment refers to illusion, unenlightenment conjures up images of self-delusion and deception. Thus Habermas's call for enlightened rational action as an antidote to the blind self-directedness of the contemporary social order is very much in line with a basic tenet of the Enlightenment. And despite the fine-tuning of his thesis over the years, there remains throughout a conviction that true "progress" within the societal order can be realized on the condition that only certain obstacles to its realization be removed. Habermas's faith in the founding spirit of modernity remains unshaken throughout.

In *Toward a Rational Society*, Habermas states that the potential for enlightened action is not to be confused with the capacity for control made possible by the empirical sciences. Because technology is said to be restricted solely to the "scientifically rationalized control of objectified processes," it does not extend into the sphere of *praxis*, which for Habermas is a realm of activity that is as distinct from technology as politics was from *technē* for Aristotle.[14] The rationale behind his argument in support of the incommensurability of control and action is undeniably Weberian. Like Weber, he sees a radical disjunction between knowledge of ends and of means. As he says in *Knowledge and Human Interests*: "Scientific theory gives rise to technically exploitable knowledge, but not to normative or action-orienting knowledge."[15] Again, like Weber, he asserts that awareness of the distinction between the realms of ends and means—or of *praxis* and *technē*—is obscured in the minds of the average citizen in contemporary society. They have lost, in his view, the capacity to distinguish practical from technical power, or "action" from "control." It is Habermas's contention that by regaining this insight we will regain as well a sense of what it means to act in an enlightened manner.

Habermas is well aware that his effort to establish the autonomy of *praxis* can be misread as an attempt to rekindle a division similar to that outlined in classical political theory. In a general sense at least, the potential for confusion is not altogether unwarranted, for his understanding of "action" is comparable to what the ancient Greeks took it to mean, namely, the activity most appropriate to the *bios politikos*. However, what initially attracts Habermas to the Greek model is not the practical wisdom *(phronēsis)* that informs the virtuous activity of the good citizen. Although he admires its "practical orientation," he thinks it to be too soft a science, possessing none of the "rigor of [modern] scientific knowledge."[16] It is the "irreversible achievement of modern science," Habermas goes on to say, that all reflective thought—including reflection on *praxis*—retains a methodological precision. The ancient art of practical wisdom, in his view, is simply too intuitive an operation to accept as viable in an age characterized by systematic reasoning. So, in the final analysis, his partiality toward classical politics pertains solely to its perception of action as distinct from *technē*.

As already noted, for Weber the proliferation of purposive rationality and purposive-rational action in modernity signals the ascension of "value freedom" in the sense that no thought or act is regarded as being intrinsically directed toward the fulfilment of a specific human end or good. Rather, any meaning it may possess must necessarily be imputed to it. Habermas concurs with this assessment, and argues that should this insight continue to be overlooked, there exists the very real possibility that society—as a consequence of its passivity with respect to the act of valuation—will accept unconditionally the dynamic of instrumental reason and technique, i.e., the principles of efficiency and economy. He admonishes us, therefore, to reclaim the realm of "ends" (politics) from the demands of technology.

Habermas realized this would be a daunting task. The pervasiveness of purposive rational thought and action in modernity, he notes, all but renders "any theory that relates to *praxis* in any other way than by strengthening and perfecting the possibilities of purposive-rational action . . . [as] dogmatic."[17] If theories of action that do not conform to the ethos of technology are to be consigned to the scrap heap of mere "valuation"—to the repository of unverified and hence unsubstantiated 'theories'—then it stands to reason, according to Habermas, that the recovery of politics demands that we find a way to account for action within the context of a non-technological mode of rationality.

As Habermas sees it, there are only two possible orientations toward *praxis* within the prevailing paradigm, neither of which are particularly appealing, in his estimation. Either one reduces practical problems to technical ones or one adopts the Weberian stance whereby practical problems are dealt with according to a plan based upon a commitment to subjectively held values. The choice is between acting in conformity with the objectivity of technical rationality, on the one hand, or in conformity with the subjectivity, and hence the irrationality, of value preferences on the other. That there is no middle ground between these extremes indicates to Habermas the need for a new paradigm of rational action. He does not, however, call into question the status of technical rationality in his effort to redefine the autonomy of *praxis*. As noted earlier, the problems besetting modernity are said by Habermas to lie in our inability to distinguish between technology and politics, and not in any inherent shortcomings in science as a productive force.

Science in itself is not a problem, according to Habermas, because the methodological commitment that constitutes "empirical-analytic inquiry" is rooted in the very structure of human existence. Far from being a merely conventional practice, he argues that science is deeply rooted in the human species' interest in its self-preservation and reproduction. Hence science and scientific knowledge are supported by what he refers to as a "technical cognitive interest."

But by claiming that technical knowledge is grounded in an abiding interest of the human species, Habermas, it can be argued, employs a form of transcendental idealism to shore up his defense of modern science. He anticipates this charge and responds by asserting that the species' technical cognitive interest is not grounded in an *a priori* transcendental consciousness. Rather, it is derived from what he says is the invariant relation of the human species to its natural surroundings.[18] In other words, for Habermas the technical interest that sustains science and technology is a material and not an ideal interest. Like Blumenberg, Habermas seems to be suggesting that the human species is constituted in part by a transhistorical interest in its own material self-preservation. And like Blumenberg, he agrees that this end can be realized best—that is, most rationally—through technical manipulation of the natural environment.

Restated in Weberian terms, the problem for Habermas is not that nature is, as he concedes, correctly perceived to be disenchanted and hence amenable to domination, but that human actors falsely take their social and political environment to be disenchanted as well. The point Habermas wants to stress—one with a distinguished history in the modern German philosophic tradition, beginning with Kant and reappearing in the neo-Kantianism of Dilthey and Rickert—is that the action domains of the natural scientist and the moral-political actor are fundamentally incommensurable.

In *Toward a Rational Society* Habermas refers to these disparate realms of technology and politics as "work" and "interaction," respectively. Some three years later, in his *Legitimation Crisis*, they are relabeled "system" and "lifeworld." Despite the fact that the new terminology is meant to reflect more accurately the true nature of the discrepancy between the two domains, the core distinction between them remains virtually unchanged throughout Habermas's mature writings. By *system* he means that field of relations characterized by purposive-rational action, that is, action governed by technical rules based on empirical knowledge of the natural world. It is a mode of action informed by what Weber had called "technically correct rationality." As such, it is synonymous with the realm of science and technology. The term *lifeworld*, on the other hand, signifies the realm of communicative, symbolic action and is said to be governed by binding consensual norms. In contrast to purposive-rational action, Habermas takes communicative action to be grounded in what he calls a "practical cognitive interest." Secured within in a distinct interest, communicative action has its own purposive function, namely, the mutual understanding of the actors' symbolic or cultural universe.

Whereas rationalization within the "system" is a matter of increasing technical control over nature, "communicative rationalization" for Habermas describes the process in which symbolic interaction becomes disengaged from the distorting influence of the technological ethic, i.e., control. Habermas maintains that "progress" within the lifeworld extends the cooperative search for standards of action and manifests itself in the articulation of the "rational will" of those participating in the communicative practice.

Now it is possible to assess the meaning and import of the call for enlightened action. We began by noting that for Habermas action that is not enlightened is informed by the technological ethos; the ideological nucleus of unenlightened action is centered on the blurring of the distinction between technology and practice. Hence, for the technocratic mind, all domains of human endeavor are taken to be structured in accordance with the imperatives of purposive rationality. This is the ethos of the modern age outlined by Habermas in his early writings. And, as noted, its shortcoming is not that it is inimical to human interests *per se*, but that it is not reflective of and responsive to the totality of human interests.

Enlightened action is meant to counterbalance this one-sidedness. By claiming that the successful maintenance of the human species relies upon satisfying a number of interests, Habermas is able to argue that practical concerns are qualitatively distinct from technical ones and thus must be addressed in an equally distinct manner. He therefore claims to defend the integrity of politics against the prevailing conception, which tends to view interpersonal relations as a subset of purposive rational modes of behavior.

This freeing of *praxis* from the gravitational tug of the technological ethos opens up a new realm of possible relationships between them. It will be argued more fully in the following section that Habermas himself seems to favor a view that sees the "lifeworld" as a potential steering mechanism for the system. In this configuration, the system would be guided along a path between the logic of its own order (as systems theorists argue) and one determined by the wholly subjective intentions of those at the controls of the technological apparatus (as Weber might say). Conceived in this manner, enlightened action for Habermas is very much in the spirit of the Kantian pronouncement equating enlightenment with thought's escape from its self-inflicted immaturity. But whereas for Kant the goal was to free metaphysics from its blind adherence to the premises of classical and neo-classical ontology, Habermas's intention is to liberate *praxis* from its role as the handmaiden of technology. Upon completing this task, the lifeworld would be free to exert its influence on the system by extracting from it those potentials it deems salutary. As Habermas puts it:

> This challenge of technology cannot be met with technology alone. It is rather a question of setting into motion a politically effective discussion that rationally brings the social potential constituted by technical knowledge and ability in a defined and controlled relation to our practical knowledge and will.[19]

For Habermas the "mythic spell" that envelops the social system—as manifested in the hegemony of scientism—can be broken only by mobilizing "practical knowledge" in the manner described above. Only practical knowledge has the power to disenchant fully that force—science—that putatively disenchanted the world but that in truth never completed the task. Science's failure, then, is said to lie not in its power to lay bare the workings of the natural world, but in its having eluded self-conscious and rational control. Thus Habermas refers to science pejoratively as a "halfway rationalization." In the process he alludes to the fact that in order to finish the task science has begun—that is, in order to rationalize fully the world and to escape the mesmerizing allure of the "new witch doctors"— science must be subjected to the emancipatory power of the lifeworld.[20]

In conclusion, we recall how Weber faced squarely the "ethical irrationalism" of our age, and argued that, given the situation, the best that could be hoped for was to inculcate strong commitments to, and responsibilities toward, subjectively held values. Habermas, although profoundly influenced by Weber's descriptive analysis of the modern condition, could not endorse this stance of stoic resignation before the given. This to him was a response born out of decadence and world-weariness: "The process of enlightenment made possible by the sciences is critical, but the critical dissolution of dogmas produces not liberation but indifference. It is not emancipatory but nihilistic."[21]

What, then, is to be done? Curiously enough, we know that, although for Habermas the disenchantment of the world leads to nihilism, an escape from nihilism cannot be grounded in a critique of its source. Science breeds nihilism and a perception of nature as disenchanted, to be sure. But because science is a "given," rooted in an invariable human interest, Habermas is forced to conclude that its undesirable consequences are, in some sense, natural and inevitable. This is why he is compelled to treat science (technology), not as a threatening force which needs to be reassessed at its root, but presents it optimistically as a challenge, one whose disabilities, if met head on, can be overcome by rendering it a genuinely salutary force in human existence. And it is only by recreating *praxis* (enlightened action) within an autonomous lifeworld that the system can be made to comply with those extra-systemic directives that only non-coercive dialogue can formulate.

Habermas: *The Theory of Communicative Action*

Neither brevity nor ground-breaking originality are to be counted among the virtues of Habermas's *The Theory of Communicative Action*. The text's primary strengths lie elsewhere, namely, in its skillful synthesis of ideas previously developed by the author, and in their further elaboration and refinement. What makes the text an especially interesting work from the perspective of this study is that the repackaging of his critical theory of society accords Weber's theory of rationalization a central position within it.

A number of observations can be drawn from Habermas's focus on the Weberian problematic. First, and most obviously, it explicitly affirms the centrality of Weber's theory of societal rationalization to Habermas's own presentation of it. Second, it provides him a framework within which to examine and critique the ways in which the Weberian problematic has been addressed by a variety of subsequent authors. Finally, and most important, the results of this analysis serve as a foil against which Habermas presents his own theory of societal rationalization. That is to say, he confirms the validity of his theory by showing how it averts certain deficiencies that he argues are intrinsic fixtures of all previous critiques of technical rationality. Thus he aims to reconstruct Weber's theory of rationalization with the "improved conceptual tools" furnished by the insight gained from Habermas's own understanding of communicative action. An analysis of this last issue will constitute the core of this section's investigation. In order to facilitate such an inquiry, I begin by reviewing Habermas's critique of Weber's remarks on the disenchantment of the world, and its impact on human action.

Habermas argues that the concept of purposive-rational action—or "action theory," as he calls it—is the key to understanding Weber's complex theory of rationality. He claims that as with any sociological action theory, Weber's variant can be analyzed from three different theoretical perspectives. The first is referred to as "metatheoretical" and is said to pertain to the framework of a theory of action "conceived with a view to the rationalizable aspects of action." Here the determining criterion of rational action is the pre-theoretical conceptual filter through which, from a complex of potential elements, certain characteristics are selected as meaningful. At the second or "methodological" level, there are the criteria of rationality determinative of the actor's self-understanding of the reasonableness of his actions. Lastly, action can be analyzed at an "empirical" level, where the reasonableness of social and political configurations is measured in terms of certain pre-established criteria.

Habermas subjects Weber's action theory to this multiperspective theoretical analysis and arrives at the following conclusions: First, Weber assumes that only action embodying a means-end or purposive rationality is "rational" *per se*. Consequently, Habermas notes, from this perspective "all other actions can be classified as specific derivations from this type [i.e., purposive rational action]." Second, for Weber an actor understands a plan of rational action in terms either of its perceived ability to achieve a given end or of its "technically correct" capacity to do so. In other words, an individual's actions are taken to be rational to the extent that they conform to the canons of *Zweckrationalität* and technical correctness. And finally, for Weber the instrumentality of rational action, as revealed at the metatheoretical and methodological levels of analysis, is given empirical expression in bureaucratic forms of social organization. In this latter regard there exists an isomorphism between the activities of individuals and those of bureaucratic organizations, the latter being seen as the former writ large.[22]

An analysis of Weber's action theory from these three perspectives illustrates forcefully, in Habermas's view, its disenchanted character. For it reveals the extent to which the rationality of modern action is determined independently of value considerations. But the problem in complex societal systems is that the weight of the realm of technical means is so great that it restricts individuals' capacity to set for themselves the ends of their actions. The result, as both Weber and Habermas are well aware, is that the rationalization of society leads to a loss of freedom. However, Habermas is quick to point out that for Weber this loss is conceived strictly in terms of action theory, that is, solely with regard to the obstruction of individuals' ability to determine the ends of their actions. Habermas concludes that this orientation necessarily conditions the corrective measures Weber proposed to rectify the situation, i.e., the reliance on "political" leadership.

Because Weber conceives of action in terms of the purposive rational behavior of individuals, he is, according to Habermas, unable to conceive of a societal means of restraining the prevailing technical order. By viewing the rationalization of society solely from the perspective of the purposive activity of the isolated actor, Weber fails to take into account "the mechanisms for coordinating action through which interpersonal relationships come about."[23] As we will see, Habermas argues that only by relying on and utilizing these mechanisms for coordinating action can the technical order be contained.

In order to appreciate fully the sophistication of Habermas's reworking of Weber's theory of societal rationalization, it is necessary to outline the highlights of his commentary on the latter's interlocutors. We begin by noting that, according to Habermas's conception of the genealogy of modern rationality, Weber's analysis of societal rationalization was detached by Lukács from its "action-theoretic framework" and transposed to the "anonymous process of capital-realization within the economic system."[24] Thus the relationship between the acting subject and his worlds (natural, social, and subjective) is said by Lukács to be "prejudiced" to the extent that it takes on the properties of a reified commodity. Habermas refers to this process as "the reification of the lifeworld."

From Lukács's perspective, Habermas tells us, Weber errs when he idealistically assumed the disenchantment of the world to be the product of the dissolution of a unifying world view, and when he implied as well the irrevocability of this fragmented state of affairs. We know Lukács did not endorse either postulate. However, this did not absolve him of theoretical error, in Habermas's estimation. His mistake, Habermas asserts, is that Lukács holds on to the Hegelian belief that "the process of the reification of consciousness had to lead [by its very nature] to its own overcoming in proletarian class consciousness."[25] This in turn rests on a more fundamental, and possibly a more erroneous, presupposition, namely, that for Lukács there exists a facet of human nature impervious to the powers of reification.

Regardless of the plausibility of these assumptions, Habermas is convinced that Lukács places unsatisfiable demands on his theoretical proposal to re-establish authentic culture. He argues that Lukács's "decisive error" was his attempt to pawn off the concept of the so-called "realization of history" as the "revolutionary actualization of philosophy." By doing so he overstepped the bounds of acceptable thought, according to Habermas. For if such an accomplishment were possible, it would have to grasp not only "the totality that is hypostatized as the world order," but also "the world-historical process" of which the proletarian revolution is the capstone.[26] This it cannot do, since, for Lukács, the totalizing or objectifying suppositions constitutive of such knowledge would be incompatible with Lukács's adherence to the post-Weberian notion concerning the impossibility of establishing such objective knowledge.

The incompatibility between Lukács's theoretical intentions and the suitability of the means he uses to reach it is reflected, in Habermas's view, in the tension within Lukács's thought between certain Hegelian and Weberian themes. As noted, for Lukács "the reification of the lifeworld" (to borrow Habermas's phrase) calls for its dismantling through the reconciliation of humans and their created environment, their "second nature." Lukács appropriated the basic concepts of Hegelian logic as the means to facilitate this reconciliation. However, because, in Habermas's estimation, Lukács adopted the Hegelian method "unanalyzed," there arose a number of unanticipated theoretical difficulties. The first of these concerns the disparity between the endpoints of Lukács's and Hegel's dialectics. Hegel's dialectic led to the 'ideal' reconciliation of subjective and objective reason in the form of Absolute Spirit. But as Habermas tells us, and this surely must have been realized by Lukács as well, a reconciliation in thought alone merely leads to the reproduction of the reified structures of consciousness in the sense that it "constrains us to adopt a contemplative relation to the world that we ourselves created."[27] Consequently, Habermas points out, Lukács must give the Hegelian dialectic a "Young-Hegelian twist," if he wants to use it to explain the coming-to-be of the desired reconciliation in both thought and action.

Another major difficulty facing Lukács stems from the fact that his proposed reconciliation rests within the Weberian discourse on the dissolution of the substantial unity of reason. For Weber, and *prima facie* for Lukács as well, there can be no theoretical re-establishment of objective reason at the level of philosophical thought, let alone at the level of *praxis*. Lukács is well aware of this limiting condition. He skirts around it by driving a wedge between the rationalization of action systems, on the one hand, and the fragmentation of reason, on the other. Specifically, he argues that the unity of reason can be regained at the level of *praxis* even if it cannot be achieved at the level of "cultural interpretive systems" or world views. For Lukács, the theoretical incapacity for reconciliation does not mean the foreclosure of the prospects for political redemption.

Lukács's defense is unsound in Habermas's view, for it effectively strips the revolutionary capacity of the bourgeoisie of any coherent rational justification. In the final analysis, then, Lukács is unable to meet the challenge that his proposal demands. He cannot provide a conceptual vantage point from which the totality of the world-historical process can be grasped, nor, for this very reason, does he have the rational capacity to determine who constitutes the potential redeemers of history.

According to Habermas, not only does Lukács err in a general theoretical sense, he also (as alluded to above) committed a serious interpretive misjudgment with respect to the revolutionary potential of the proletariat. Horkheimer and Adorno were the first to capitalize on this error. In Habermas's opinion, their considerable achievement was to put aside "Hegel's logic" and to "explain empirically" the evidence that refutes Lukács's claim that there exists within humans an inner resistance to reification, and that this capacity necessarily is expressed in the revolutionary potential of the proletarian class.[28]

Disappointment over the prospects for revolution in the decades between 1920 and 1940 led Horkheimer and Adorno to reconsider the standard Marxist interpretation of the theory of reification. Their deliberation resulted in the assertion that the rationalization (or disenchantment) of the world is not, as Lukács believed, only "seemingly complete," but in truth a *fait accompli*. As stated, this radical reinterpretation is based on the claim that reified structures of consciousness did not emerge out of capitalist relations of production but instead are rooted in reason itself. The disenchantment of the world is said to be grounded in the dynamic of the Occidental *logos*, which from its inception has been characterized by its predatory relationship to the natural world. Hence the source of the reified structures of consciousness is attributable to the pathology of the human–nature relationship, and not to distortions among subjects as they act and speak.

Horkheimer and Adorno argue, in effect, that impaired interpersonal relations are epiphenomena of a more fundamental disturbance and therefore should not be confused with their cause. Habermas concludes from this that, whereas for Weber "loss of freedom" is characterized by the impoverishment of action, Horkheimer and Adorno understand it primarily in "psychoanalytic" terms, that is, in terms of the structural deformation of rational consciousness, a deformation grounded "in the anthropological foundation of the history of the species. . . ."[29]

Although Habermas takes their critique to be an improvement over Lukács's, in that it represents a theoretical adjustment to the empirical reality of the times, it is not without difficulties of its own. He uncovers them in the same way he exposed the shortcomings of Lukács's thought, namely, by bringing to the reader's attention the philosophical context of the critique of instrumental reason and by determining whether or not it can satisfy its objective within these limiting conditions.

Habermas observes at the outset that Horkheimer and Adorno are theorizing from the Weberian assumption that knowledge of means is unrelated to knowlege of ends. This rift is symptomatic of the disintegration of reason's totality, of being "the whole of what is," he remarks. As a result, their appeal to critical reflection "cannot be understood as a disguised call to retreat to a Marxistically restored Hegel. . . ."[30] It cannot, in other words, be understood as the dialectical working out of a lost totality, as the reconciliation of pure with practical reason. Philosophical enterprises that have as their desired end the restoration of totalities of this sort are identified by Habermas as belonging to the era of "great" philosophy, an age that perished along with the dissolution of religious-metaphysical world views—the central contributing factor to the world's disenchantment.

Yet, as Habermas sees it, the radical claim Horkheimer and Adorno make concerning the completeness of the rationalization process in
modernity presupposes just such a religious-metaphysical world view.
Their assertion demands, in his words, "a conceptual apparatus that
will allow them nothing less than to denounce the whole as the un-
true."[31] The problem then becomes one of determining the means to
legitimately acquire such an apparatus.

Habermas is very clear as to the kinds of schemes that do not
work. The "Weberian thorn" in the side of critical theory is a continual
reminder of the fact that the required conceptual framework cannot
be constructed simply by renewing the pretensions of the claims of the
great philosophical tradition. Not retaining a measure of integrity
with respect to one's time and place would render dubious any attempt to recycle dead world views as a ground for contemporary critiques. On the other hand, an immanent critique of science does not
necessarily prove to be a suitable alternative either. Horkheimer and
Adorno's critique of rationality is proof that even within this realm of
discourse there exist the totalizing pretensions often found within the
tradition of great philosophy.

For Habermas, the incongruity between Adorno and
Horkheimer's intended objective (i.e., a critique of technical
rationality) and their inability to provide a defensible rational account of it jeopardizes the legitimacy of the entire project. He further charges Horkheimer and Adorno guilty of philosophical sleight
of hand to the extent that they fail to address this inconsistency. As
he says, their efforts to overcome instrumental reason by returning
to its origins and revealing its pathology are merely an attempt to
"outdo objective reason," that is to say, to know the 'truth' about the
true conditions of Western *logos*.[32]

Habermas argues that this misguided endeavor only can lead to
paradoxical results. For if reason was instrumental from the beginning, then the reasoning that uncovers this insight would, as a consequence of its understanding, then shed its purposive character. In
other words, by virtue of being an "instrument of reconciliation" (between reason and nature), such reasoning no longer would be informed by instrumentalism. This leads Habermas to conclude, rather
ironically, that the critique of instrumental rationality would clear the
way for the establishment of a "counter-rational" mode of reasoning,
by which he means a mode of reasoning that functions as an alternative to the rationalism of domination that has prevailed throughout
the course of Western civilization. The problem with this 'solution,'
Habermas notes, is not that such an alternative is wholly devoid of
meaning. Rather, the difficulty lies in its incapacity to render this
meaning intelligible in a discursive manner.

As we have seen, the mimetic or esthetic experience for Adorno represented an authentic mode of knowing and an alternative to technical rationality. His *Aesthetic Theory* was an attempt to map out the contours of this alternative mode of understanding, to give a rational account of it. But Habermas is unimpressed by Adorno's effort. It amounts, in his view, to the abdication of discursive reason in favor of mere speculation. This alternative mode of knowing, he says, "seals the surrender of all cognitive competence to art in which the mimetic capacity gains objective shape."[33] To this extent the mimetic experience eludes logical or discursive clarification. It is a mere "impulse" which reawakens one's empathetic sense of union with the natural world. Consequently, any attempt to produce a "theory of mimesis" is doomed to failure in Habermas's estimation. And so he concludes that the dialectic of enlightenment is a paradoxical affair: "It shows the self-critique of reason the way to truth, and at the same time contests the possibility that, at this stage of complete alienation, the idea of [discursive] truth is still accessible."[34]

Habermas contends that a survey of the development of critical theory from its inception to the late writings of Adorno illustrates the degree to which it has betrayed its original ambition, i.e., to critique the given order and to reconstruct it in light of this criticism. It in fact has withdrawn behind the lines of discursive thought to the "mindfulness of nature," a view which he perceptively recognizes as coming "shockingly close" to Heidegger's "recollection of being."[35] In the final analysis, then, Habermas castigates Adorno for returning to the world-denying repose of contemplation, to theoretical musings divorced from practical realities.

It has been said that Horkheimer and Adorno are guided in their critique of instrumental reason by the idea of a reconciliation between reason and nature. And yet, Habermas argues, they are averse to establishing the theoretical grounds of this reconciliation for fear of falling back into metaphysics. So strong is this antipathy, he adds, that Horkheimer and Adorno forego all attempts to provide a rational defense of it.

Habermas maintains that the *aporias*—the impasses or paradoxes—to which all previous critiques of rationalization have led can be accounted for by their adherence to a common cognitive paradigm. This conceptual horizon, which he calls "the philosophy of consciousness," is said to be rooted in the experience of the subject as a thinking substance.[36] Here the subject is posited as standing over against the object in the same way as the Cartesian *res cogitans* confronts *res extensa*. Because mind is taken to be opposed to, or alienated from, the truth content of its object, the overcoming of alienation necessarily requires a reconciliation of their respective truth contents. This, Habermas asserts, is an impossibility because reasoning predicated upon the alienation of subject from object is by definition incapable of bridging this epistemological impasse—of thinking beyond the very condition of its possibilities. Therefore, the only viable option for the post-Weberian critical theorist who remains committed to discursive reasoning is to abandon the prevailing and ineffectual paradigm.

Renouncing this paradigm would mean, within the context of the critical theory of Horkheimer and Adorno, foresaking the supposed inherent linkage between human ratiocination and the desire to control nature. It likewise would entail discrediting the effect this orientation has had (through nature's revenge) on reasoning—its reification. This move does not lead Habermas to repudiate outright the dialectic of enlightenment, however. For there remains within the dialectic a valid and valuable insight, namely, Adorno's notion of "mimesis." The problem is that its rational core is obscured as a result of its expression in the language of the philosophy of consciousness. Thus Habermas takes upon himself the task of elucidating the central meaning and significance of mimesis to circumvent the difficulties in its presentation by Adorno. This Habermas does by interpreting the concept in the context of the linguistic philosophy of intersubjective communication. As he says:

> Adorno cannot elucidate the mimetic capacity by means of an abstract opposition to instrumental reason. The structures of reason to which Adorno merely alludes first become accessible to analysis when the idea of reconciliation and freedom are deciphered as codes for a form of intersubjectivity . . . that makes possible a mutual and constraint-free understanding among individuals. . . .[37]

Habermas, then, extracts the rational core of Adorno's conception of "mimesis" by applying it to intersubjective (as opposed to subject–object or human–nature) relations.

This paradigm shift from the philosophy of consciousness to linguistic philosophy is to occur within action theory. But this is not to be confused with the "action theory" articulated by Weber. It was noted that Habermas criticized Weber for conceiving action only in terms of the purposeful activity of the isolated actor. Action, thus conceived, was informed by a mode of rationality "restricted to the cognitive-instrumental dimension" and grounded in "subjective self-assertion." By adhering to such a premise, Habermas maintains that Weber was bound to interpret bureaucratic phenomena in terms of "the subsumption of acting subjects under the objective force of an apparatus operating autonomously above their heads."[38] For Weber the pathologies that arise from this condition were twofold. First, as previously stated, actors experience a loss of freedom to the extent that purposive rational modes of social organization frustrate their capacity to act in accordance with self-posited ends. Second, Weber maintained that actors also endure traumatic psychological effects as a consequence of living in a rationalized, means-oriented social order. This "one-sided style of life," as Habermas refers to it, contributes to a perceived "loss of meaning" by actors within contemporary society. Together, these developments precipitated the so-called "paradox" of societal rationalization, where the heightened powers of societal control are conjoined with a sense of personal powerlessness.

Despite Habermas's objections to the specifics of Weber's description of social pathologies, he is sympathetic with the general thrust of the Weberian analysis. He explicitly acknowledges the fact, for instance, that Weber's theory of rationalization "still holds the best prospect of explaining the social pathologies that appeared in the wake of capitalist modernization."[39] However, in Habermas's opinion, its full potential as an explanatory theory remains unrealized as long as the meaning of action is interpreted along Weberian lines. He asserts that only by reinterpreting our understanding of what constitutes action can Weber's initial diagnosis be made fruitful. This he does by defining action as communicative interaction among persons who have as their objective not "control" (as do purposive-rational actors) but "consensus." Consensus among actors, then, can be likened to the mimetic experience within the paradigm of the philosophy of consciousness in that both have as their end a non-coercive or dialogic understanding of the "other." Action is "enlightened," to use Habermas's now out-dated terminology, when it operates according to this principle.

It was mentioned in the previous section of this chapter that Habermas's turn toward communicative action did not necessitate rejecting purposive rational action. His critique of Adorno's understanding of mimesis illustrated the extent to which he viewed as errant the objective outlined in *Dialectic of Enlightenment* concerning the need to displace technical rationality with a more salutary mode of reasoning. By contrast, the paradigm shift he himself espouses is meant merely to supplement the cognitive-instrumental aspect of reason and action with a more encompassing communicative rationality. Habermas supports this strategem by adopting a key Weberian insight, namely, that technical rationality is an appropriate means of controlling a contingent environment. Hence he argues that an increase in cognitive-instrumental rationality leads to "a greater independence from limitations imposed by the contingent environment on the self-assertion of subjects acting in a goal-directed manner."[40] But this increase in control is not accompanied by added insight into the nature of the ends of control. Habermas here concurs with Weber's assessment of the non-teleological character of instrumental reason. He also agrees with Weber's observation that, by overlooking the value-neutral character of instrumental thought and action, the "realm of means" has all but become an end in itself. Both individuals, in short, fear that the goal of human existence is being increasingly identified with the furtherance of mere material self-preservation.

As previously stated, during the pre-modern era the means to material self-preservation were contextualized within an overarching "order of things," which had the effect of devaluing the productive enterprise. With the dissolution of this old order, the activity of 'making' was liberated, so to speak. Habermas is acutely aware of the effect that the decontextualing of *technē* had on human self-understanding. Like Blumenberg, he claims it has extended our capacity to secure human self-perpetuation to such an extent that it now is perceived as the sole end of human existence. As Habermas puts it: "Objectifying thought and purposive-rational action serve to reproduce a 'life' that is characterized by the knowing and acting subject's devotion to a blind, self-directed, intransitive self-preservation as his only 'end'."[41]

Although he accedes to Blumenberg's view that the concept of self-preservation has altered dramatically upon the enervation of the religious-metaphysical world view, he cautions that it changes "not only in the respect emphasized by Blumenberg." Habermas maintains that Blumenberg's understanding of self-preservation is limited because he, along with Horkheimer and Adorno, operates within the context of the philosophy of consciousness. By perceiving the subject in terms of human "self-assertion," he conceives the act of self-preservation only in physicalistic terms, that is, in relation to a power struggle between man and nature. But as Habermas tries to show, when our understanding of rationality expands to encompass its communicative component, the concept of self-preservation takes on a more nuanced meaning. For not only does it signify the physical reproduction of the species—an end for which technical rationality serves as the most appropriate means—it includes as well the reproduction of social life, whose success is dependent upon the flourishing of uncoerced action supported by communicative rationality. Habermas therefore concludes that "the social-life context produces itself both through the media-controlled purposive-rational actions of its members and through the common will anchored in the communicative practice of all individuals."[42]

Habermas then applies this critique to Weber's theory of rationalization. Habermas argues that, because Weber failed to take into consideration the dual mechanisms by which social life reproduces itself, he mistakenly attributed the source of social pathologies to "conflicting action orientations," or to the tension between the valuing subject and the value-neutral technological and bureaucratic orders. In short, Habermas faults Weber for his one-dimensional account of societal rationalization. In Habermas's view the complexity of the process can be captured only by moving from an analytical approach that concentrates on conflicting action orientations to one that articulates the opposition between what he calls "principles of societal integration."

Before reviewing the repercussions of this shift in focus on the theory of societal rationalization, it bears repeating that despite Habermas's reworking of the Weberian problematic, the aim of his analysis is consistent with Weber's to the extent that they both wish to account for the one-sided style of life that prevails in contemporary society. Where they part company, however, is over their description of what constitutes this one-dimensional mode of existence, and what forces are responsible for its development.

We have seen that for Weber this one-sided style of life is a consequence of the pervasive and intractable presence of rationalized forms of action within various social institutions. This phenomenon, in turn, is said to be attributable ultimately to the dissolution of great religious and philosophical world views—the disenchantment of the world. Habermas counters by arguing that the source of social pathologies is better explained in terms of the outcome of a contest between two equally viable mechanisms through which the social order or lifeworld is able to reproduce and integrate itself—the so-called "dual mechanisms of sociation."

One of these mechanisms is non-normative and non-linguistic. Here the claim is made that certain actions within the lifeworld can be integrated by "media-steered" (or "objectivating") means, such as power or money. Action-coordinating mechanisms of this sort are said to integrate the lifeworld systematically and to enhance its "material reproduction." The bureaucracy and the economy are the most prominent examples of institutionalized media-steered systems. According to Habermas, their primary end is to enable actors to intervene in the world to realize their ends in a purposeful manner. The second mechanism of action integration is linguistic, and pertains to those actions that rightfully can be coordinated only by means of consensus arrived at through communicative interaction. This process, designated by Habermas as "social integration," serves the need of the lifeworld to reproduce itself symbolically, and lies at the heart of what in his earlier writings he referred to as "practice" or "politics."

What Habermas brings to our attention is that a more precise understanding of social pathologies within contemporary society demands a reinvestigation of the process of societal rationalization within the context of the lifeworld/system distinction, or, more specifically, within the parameters of the tension between the lifeworld's dual mechanisms of sociation. If we adopt this strategy, he argues, it becomes apparent that purposive rational modes of action coordination do not, *per se*, pose a threat to the freedom of the acting subject, but in fact can facilitate such freedom. Habermas's analysis of the phenomenon known as the "mediatization of the lifeworld" illustrates this point well. The evolution of societal rationalization, he claims, has led to the formation of a "technicized" or "mediatized" lifeworld in that the coordination of action within it has shifted increasingly from a linguistic to a non-linguistic format. This development reveals what he takes to be an important trend in the growing rationalization of the lifeworld. And it is important to note that he views it as salutary, in that it provides the means for actors to reproduce their material needs. For Habermas, increased reliance on bureaucratic and economic mechanisms of action-coordination only furthers the individual's capacity to achieve desired personal aims.

As already stated, it is Habermas's contention that Weber's limited understanding of action prevented him from recognizing the emancipatory force behind purposive rational institutions and practices. Now we are in a position where we can see more clearly why this (from Habermas's perspective) "thin" conception of action also accounts for Weber's inability to locate the true source of social pathologies. For if, as Habermas claims, we can no longer identify routinized practices as the source of modernity's ills, then we are led to conclude that pathologies arise only when mechanisms of system integration are employed as a means of coordinating the lifeworld's symbolic practices. As he says, the lifeworld's "symbolic reproduction cannot be transposed onto foundations of system integration without pathological consequences."[43] The "mediatization" process violates the integrity of the lifeworld only when that process crosses the "threshold" that leads to the lifeworld's internal colonization.

Habermas's thesis, then, can be summarized in the following manner: Although communicatively structured domains of action can be reintegrated along systemic lines, this conversion process is achieved at a cost. The price paid for such a conversion is the reification of action domains, a process that Habermas describes as "the bureaucratic disempowering and desecration of spontaneous processes of opinion and will-formation," or, stated more economically, "the distintegration of socially integrated contexts of life."[44] He realizes the conditions that set the stage for the structural violation of the lifeworld are the same ones responsible for its emancipatory potential as well. Therefore he must account for certain ironies in the unfolding of the logic of societal rationalization, as Weber had tried to do (unsuccessfully, in Habermas's opinion). But this is not to say that for Habermas societal rationalization contains a paradoxical core, as Weber had claimed previously. For Habermas, it is not the case that a rational social order must produce an impoverishment of freedom and meaning. That this has occurred within contemporary society Habermas does not deny. But that this is an integral component of the logic of the rationalization process he most emphatically denies. Thus in order to defend the claim that Weber's understanding of the rationalization process is misguided, Habermas has to convince us that the emancipatory potential of a rational social order has been undermined by Weber. He must show us in addition the manner in which this subversion has taken place.

For Habermas the presence of social pathologies within the modern social context can be accounted for by examining the bifurcated differentiation process that characterizes its development. On the one hand, he claims that societies evolve in accordance with a first-order process of differentiation in which the lifeworld and the system and subsystems all develop according to their own distinct inner logics. The lifeworld, for one, is said to become increasingly "rational" to the extent that action oriented to mutual understanding gains greater independence from normative contexts (e.g., tradition) and becomes ever more the product of self-reflective discourse.[45] Habermas maintains that the rationality of the system, in contrast, is measurable in terms of its increased complexity. Utilizing insights gained from his reading of Luhmann, he identifies system rationality with adaptability, arguing that the more differentiated a system is, the more successfully it can accomodate itself to contingencies within its environment.

Habermas notes, in addition, that societal rationalization is characterized by a second-order differentiation process. Here "system" and "lifeworld" are said to become increasingly differentiated from each other, or "uncoupled." He takes this uncoupling process to be the means by which the lifeworld has reintegrated itself in response to certain tensions that have arisen within it. These tensions arise in response to the fact that a communicatively rationalized lifeworld historically has been unable to cope with increased demands placed upon mutual understanding to coordinate action. As a consequence of the overloading of this capacity—that is, of "politics"—there has arisen a breakdown of sorts within the communicatively structured lifeworld. This dysfunction has been compensated for, Habermas claims, by the introduction of systemic action-sociating media into the lifeworld, such as power and money. Hence he argues, in effect, that it has been the incapacity of communicative practice to meet the challenges brought on by its own success (through rationalization) that has triggered the separation of subsystems from the societal components of the lifeworld.[46] These subsystems filled the void created by the inability of the lifeworld to coordinate actions communicatively. When, however, the sociating power of these subsystems begin to infiltrate domains of action not amenable to media-steered coordination, we have a situation where the "independent imperatives" of these subsystems turn back "destructively upon the lifeworld itself." This process can so disrupt the lifeworld that in a highly rationalized social order the colonized lifeworld itself "seems to shrink to a subsystem," to a mere adjunct of the domain of purposive rational action.[47]

Habermas provides a concrete example of the pathological effects of lifeworld colonization in his discussion of the "juridification" of communicatively structured action. He defines this phenomenon as the tendency toward an increase in "the legal regulation of new, hitherto informally regulated social matters."[48] Thus "functional disturbances" are said to arise within the lifeworld when administrative and judicial controls no longer merely "supplement" socially integrated contexts with legal institutions, but convert them to the medium of law. In jurisprudential terms, juridification denotes a shift by which the law no longer regulates social practices but actually constitutes them. In the former, non-pathological instance, the law codifies existing social practices that are communicatively structured, and so merely supplements them by adding to these practices the authority of law. In the latter instance, however, administrative and legal controls intervene in existing social contexts and actively reconstruct them in accordance with a rationale not agreed upon by the actors within the context. By identifying juridification as pathological in this way, Habermas underscores the normative claim (grounded in an invariable human interest) that systemic controls ought to be supportive of the existing contours of communicatively structured practices. Should they transgress these boundaries, they run the risk of deforming, and hence violating, these contexts of social life.

Although, Habermas notes, the juridification of lifeworld practices often is advanced with good intentions by political and judicial administrators—who characteristically legitimate such changes in the name of 'justice,' 'human rights,' etc.—this does not alter the fact that it constitutes the erosion of its communicative infrastructure. Thus, when we as a society relinquish our responsibility for coordinating actions communicatively, we subject ourselves to new forms of sociation and control, which Habermas, like Weber (although for different reasons), regards as inhibiting our capacity to act.

In conclusion, we have seen that Habermas is critical of Weber to the extent that his theory of societal rationalization posits an autonomous subject in opposition to the "objective force" embodied in economic and state structures. According to Habermas, one-sided styles of life cannot be ascribed to the irreconcilability of differen-

tiated cultural value spheres or to the tension between the valuing
subject and the value-neutral administrative apparatus. He argues instead that the bureaucracy and the economy are subsystems that
have been filtered out of the societal components of the lifeworld and
can serve the legitimate function of materially reproducing the social
order. Therefore these subsystems are not, *contra* Weber, invariable
obstacles to human freedom and meaning. They become sources of social pathology only when they infiltrate and restructure a domain of
action that Weber was unable to account for, namely, the domain of
communicatively integrated social practices. According to Habermas,
Weber (along with Horkheimer and Adorno) misread the true nature
of social pathologies because he failed to identify the second-order differentiation process that characterizes societal evolution. In short, he
was unable to see the rationalization of the social order in terms of the
uncoupling of system and lifeworld. For this reason he was not in a
position to conclude that social pathologies arise when mechanisms of
system reproduction reconstitute domains of action best integrated
through communication and consensus.

Summary and Conclusion

In light of the preceding commentary on Habermas's critique of
Weber, Lukács, Horkheimer, and Adorno, a number of final observations can be made. First, Weber's theory of societal rationalization
constitutes the focal point of Habermas's *The Theory of Communicative Action* in that Weber's theory provides the seminal argument explaining the loss of faith in Enlightenment reason and progress. It
consequently has become a foundation for the argument of those who
have come to regard modernity as inherently problematic.

Because, as we have seen, Habermas does not adhere to this view,
Weber is targeted as his most formidable intellectual adversary.
Habermas therefore sees to it that he constructs his theory of societal
rationalization upon what he regards as the ruins of Weber's theory.
Second, it appears that the power of Weber's analysis is such that,
despite its reformulations in the hands of Lukács, Horkheimer, and
Adorno, none were able to escape the prevailing Weberian
paradigm—the philosophy of consciousness. Consequently, as we have
seen, Habermas maintains that their respective efforts were bound to
fail because they demanded of reason what it cannot possibly supply
in our post-metaphysical, disenchanted age. So he concludes that the
aporias to which the previous formulations of societal rationalization
lead illustrates the need to rework the theory from within the context
of an alternative paradigm of action theory. This shift in focus

facilitates the ongoing task of constructing a critical theory of society, one which Habermas maintains was "interrupted" with the critique of instrumental rationality.

It should be mentioned in closing that it has not been the aim of this overview of the theory of communicative action to recount the universal conditions—i.e., validity claims—that Habermas argues are required for the possibility of unimpeded human communication. These conditions he lays out in detail in the reconstructive science he calls "universal pragmatics," whose particulars are not within the purview of this investigation.[49] What has been of importance, however, is to show that the shift toward communicative action has radically altered the meaning of rationalization for Habermas. In short, within the context of Habermas's reconstructive science, this means the overcoming of systematically distorted communication. Progress in this regard is to be measured against what he calls an "ideal speech situation," in which consensus between participants is reached on the basis of the recognition of certain validity claims set in the general structure of possible communication. Habermas thus assumes that non-coercive and non-distortive communication is built into our everyday, pre-theoretical interactions. Only by rooting out those destructive forces that impede genuine discourse will our communicative potential be realized.

IV

MODERNITY RECONSIDERED

Naturam expellas furca, tamen usque recurret.
(You may drive out nature with a pitchfork,
but she will always come back.)

Horace

The aim of this penultimate chapter is twofold. The first objective is to evaluate Habermas's conclusions with respect to the disenchantment debate. Is the disenchantment of the world, as articulated initially by Weber and reformulated by the critical theorists, in fact a misreading of the pathology afflicting contemporary society, as Habermas asserts? Is the purported phenomenon an artifact of an intellectual paradigm—i.e., the philosophy of consciousness—that is unable to account for or cope with the pressures the technical ethos exerts on the contemporary social order? In short, are previous discourses on disenchantment inadequate, as Habermas maintains? If so, is his reinterpretation of the rational core of disenchantment persuasive? Does it satisfy some of the basic concerns that are central to this investigation, such as the notion of domination? Questions of this sort need to be addressed in order to establish a critical framework with which to reassess the issue at hand. It is this latter undertaking—the rethinking of disenchantment in light of an evaluation of Habermas's critique—that comprises the second major objective of this chapter.

The first of the chapter's three divisions is given over to an appraisal of Habermas's commentary on the disenchantment thesis. The subsequent sections then begin the task of reconsidering the issue in the context of the previous analysis. At this point I will have put forth an argument that calls to question Habermas's claim that the shift from a philosophy of consciousness to a paradigm of linguistic philosophy—from consciousness *qua* thinking substance to intersubjectivity—obviates difficulties inherent in the Weberian interpretation of disenchantment. To the contrary, I argue that Habermas's proposed solution to the disenchantment problem creates a new set of concerns that are as troublesome as those he ostensibly overcomes.

Hence it is apparent that the discourse at that juncture can move in only one of two possible directions. Either we concur with Habermas's critique of previous accounts of disenchantment while rejecting his reformulation of it, or we adopt a more radical stand and dismiss his contention that the impasse to which the philosophy of consciousness leads can be circumvented only by abandoning it. Following the first path is difficult, I would argue, on the grounds that it is hard to imagine how a challenge to disenchantment could be sustained if one were to renounce both the philosophies of consciousness and intersubjectivity. The second course of action, therefore, appears to be the more promising. This is the route followed in the final two sections of the chapter. Of these, the first deals, in more detail than accorded it, with the viability of mimesis as an effective response to the technological ethos. Contrary to Habermas, I argue that Adorno's esthetic theory contains the key to solving the conundrum that confronts us at this point. This defense hinges on countering Habermas's claim that Adorno's alternative to the rationalism of domination is not discursively intelligible.

The segue from Adorno to Merleau-Ponty in the final section can be viewed as broadening the scope of our new course of investigation. I attempt, for instance, to illustrate the manner in which Merleau-Ponty's phenomenological description of perception incorporates certain elements of Adorno's esthetic theory in its rendering of the human–nature relationship. Most important, the impact of the "ontological turn" in Merleau-Ponty's mature writings is addressed in the context of a revitalized discourse on disenchantment.

Habermas Appraised

The strength of Habermas's critique of disenchantment rests in part on the credibility of his claim that the autonomy and directive power of the communicative lifeworld can be sustained in the manner he suggests. I will put forth here that even if one concedes to Habermas the validity of his proposal to overcome the colonization of the lifeworld, which is a generous concession, its enactment merely would reinforce the technological character of the comprehensive societal order. It would redouble the disenchantment of the world, for his reliance on communicative action and rationality as an antidote to system imperatives only serves to breathe new life into the phenomenon that he ostensibly tries to contain. That is to say, Habermas actually rationalizes the need for an expansion of our powers of control and domination by insisting that the system's instrumental capacities ought to be used to further those ends that participants in the lifeworld articulate by means of uncoerced communicative interaction.

Yet Habermas insists on such a solution because for him a societal order propelled by cognitive-instrumental interests alone is effectively condemned to the satisfaction of its desire for mere physical, material reproduction. The claim that system-skewed configurations of this sort are actuated by "blind, self-directed, intransitive self-preservation" only serves to underscore his basic agreement with Weber's view that instrumental rationality has no *telos* other than that of control.[1] Consequently, liberation from this blind self-directedness is contingent upon setting instrumental rationality (and its appropriate domain, the system) "in its proper place as part of a more encompassing communicative rationality" [and its appropriate domain, the lifeworld].[2] Habermas, as noted, justifies this assertion by claiming that the reproduction of social life is insufficiently supported by cognitive-instrumental interactions between humans and nature or amongst human beings. It requires as well the production of value consensus.

Habermas argues that communicative action is a crucial mechanism for social integration, since in its absence the lifeworld is relegated to purposive rational means of reproduction alone. Here only the material needs of society would be satisfied. This is clearly insufficient, however, since Habermas maintains that the needs of society extend beyond the merely material to encompass symbolic practices as well. It is because these practices are becoming increasingly mediatized—i.e., restructured by system imperatives—in contemporary society that he argues we must reclaim for them their appropriate integration mechanism—communicative action. Only in this manner can the lifeworld be decolonized and made to satisfy needs beyond those associated with system imperatives. Only then will the bonds be broken that subordinate the lifeworld to the systematic constraints of material reproduction.

Habermas's theoretical objective is to present an argument in support of a communicatively rationalized lifeworld. He acknowledges, in contrast, that virtually all lifeworld practices in the modern state are infused with system imperatives. These imperatives are, by his own account, non-normative in nature and hence grounded in the dynamic of power and control. The task of liberating the lifeworld from this sociating mechanism therefore requires that the lifeworld regain a normative function. Only then, Habermas says, can the inner logic of media-steered subsystems such as power and money be properly limited.[3] One could say, then, that the measure of a revitalized lifeworld lies in its capacity to steer, rather than be steered by, technically rationalized subsystems.

It should be noted that Habermas's position on this issue is similar to Ellul's call for the containment of the technological system. In formal terms, both argue that technical-rational modes of action are now out of control and thus in need of some restraint. Both realize as well that this objective cannot be achieved through technological means. Rather, the solution hinges upon mobilizing an extra-systemic force within society capable of subverting the intrusive presence of technical rationality in all aspects of conduct in the lifeworld. In short, the solution requires the disengagement of technical modes of action from other forms deemed distinct. Habermas and Ellul share the conviction that the efficacy of such a force ultimately rests upon its capacity to assign to technically rationalized practices a more circumscribed function than they presently command.

This process involves reorienting the public's understanding of the meaning and role of purposive modes of action. It sets out to demythologize them by revealing that they constitute a mere ensemble of means. Bureacracies, for example, are generally perceived as effective means of processing the vast amounts of information needed to facilitate the proper functioning of complex societal orders. However, if understood accurately, it will be apparent that they serve only this purpose. Because bureaucracies are mere instruments, they require normative guidance, a need that they themselves are incapable of supplying.

Having established this shared perspective, the difference between the positions of Ellul and Habermas stands out clearly. For Ellul, revealed religion supplies the ends for which to steer technological practices; Habermas remains more neutral with respect to the substance of these ends when he asserts simply that they must be formulated through rational and uncoerced production of value consensus within the lifeworld. Notwithstanding this tension between their views, both individuals generally agree that modes of action based on the ethic of control need not be debilitating if perceived as mere means.

However, to do otherwise—to conceive purposive rational action as an end in itself—is to misconstrue it as technology. It is necessary, then, when referring to Habermas especially, to enclose the term *technology* within single quotation marks in order to denote his ironic attachment to the phenomenon, for 'technology,' in its strict etymological sense, denotes the conjoining in the real world of making and knowing. As we have noted, it is this very union that leads to the one-sided style of life that Habermas claims can be corrected by steering purposive rational modes of action in accordance with ends determined through communicative action. Thus the system for Habermas is to be understood as the domain of *technē*, not of 'technology' as expressed in

the union of *technē* and *logos*. Taken as a mere ensemble of instrumental means, the devitalized system can then be steered in conformity with those ends that the participants in the lifeworld have
freely approved. In other words, for Habermas, communicative imperatives lend the system its *telos*—its normative compass. Insofar as
these imperatives constitute the system's *telos* or rationale, they can
be said to supply it with its *logos*.

That a non-pathological societal order must keep distinct the
realms of means and of ends is axiomatic for Habermas. For this
reason it can be surmised that the process whereby the societal order
is brought under the control of ends determined through communicative action presupposes a de-technologized system. The system must
undergo, in effect, a "logosectomy" if it is to be rendered a mere ensemble of means as Habermas desires.

There are at least two issues that remain problematic vis-à-vis the
proposed transfiguration of the relationship between the main societal
subsystems. The first is a pragmatic concern. The empowerment of communicative practices which Habermas advocates appears unlikely to
materialize in an age where all indicators point to their increasing ab-
sorption by the mass media. One would be hard-pressed to find any
evidence suggesting sustained and substantial gains for communicative
practices in this regard. Even hopeful developments, such as growing
public interest in the so-called "green movement," seem doubtful at best,
given the fact that the media that disseminate the 'message' simultaneously propagate the 'counter-message,' the allure of consumerism.

This concern aside, there is an underlying aspect of Habermas's
thesis which from the perspective of this study is far more worrisome.
This pertains to the fact that even if one were to concede the possibility that the system can be de-technologized in the desired manner, this modification would not alter the technological character of
the social order taken as a whole. For although communicative action
prevails in an ideal Habermasian social order, it is, as the source of
the system's *logos*, the locus of its mastery as well. Hence, when
viewed from the perspective of their dynamic interrelation, the "system–lifeworld dyad" manifests the conjoining of *technē* and *logos*.
What the system loses in terms of its cybernetic quality, the "system-
lifeworld" gains. (See Fig. 1.)

Thus Habermas's argument in support of the need for a division of
function between systemic and communicative modes of action presents us
with an outstanding difficulty. Rather than providing a definitive
analysis of the issue, his claim that such a configuration is non-pathological illustrates his bias concerning the criterion for determining
what constitutes a pathological social structure. Habermas's pre-
scriptive conclusions do not alter the fact that, in formal terms, the

COLONIZED LIFEWORLD

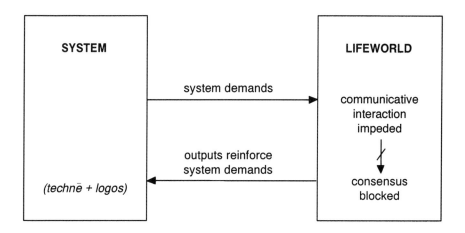

DECOLONIZED LIFEWORLD

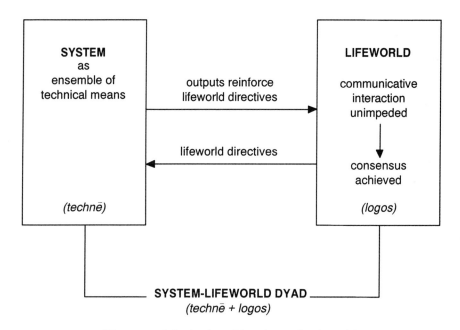

Figure 1. Colonized and Decolonized Lifeworlds

relationship between systemic forces and communicative imperatives is characterized by the control of the former by the latter. Thus the system–lifeworld dyad exhibits the same kind of "subject–object" relationship that characterizes human–nature interactions within the system. Moreover, because Habermas advocates reversing the seat of control in the power relationship between the domains—i.e., by transposing it to the communicative lifeworld—it can be argued that his ideal social order is as infused with the forces of domination as the one that he attempts to set aright.

That the technological impetus persists and even flourishes in Habermas's schema, means, from the perspective of this investigation, that the challenge of the disenchantment thesis has not been adequately met. Habermas has not so much resolved the question concerning domination as displace it. Having established the apparent futility of redressing the issue of domination within the human–nature relationship, he relocates it in the tension between the two societal arenas. By reformulating the question concerning domination in this manner, Habermas concludes that the solution lies in the containment of the system, or, what amounts to the same thing, in its devitalization. He assumes that the realm of purposive rational action constitutes a force essentially neutral with respect to ends and therefore amenable to control by extra-systemic imperatives.

The question must now be asked: Is it reasonable to assume that the domain of purposive-rational action can be controlled in this manner? That Habermas thinks so is illustrative of his skepticism toward the possibility of, and thus the need for, a rational and immanent reconciliation between reason and nature within the prevailing paradigm of the philosophy of consciousness. Consequently, as we have seen, Habermas abandons this ill-fated project and turns toward linguistic philosophy as a means to establish a discourse on what he deems to be the rational core and main insight of Horkheimer and Adorno's critique of instrumental reason. What is especially questionable about this line of reasoning is that it suggests there is a qualitative difference between human–nature and interhuman relationships. The person who, for Habermas, toils with nature as "object" must establish simultaneously a dialogic, non-coercive understanding of his fellow human being as "subject." But again, one must question the premise upon which he rests his conclusion. Do the 'objects' of these relationships (i.e., nature and human beings) warrant such distinctive treatments?

Certainly, at an ontic level of analysis—i.e., the level of real being—there exist differences between the existence of humans and non-human nature which may account for differences in our handling of them. But these differences recede when the being of man and nature is viewed ontologically, that is, from the perspective of the Being of their being. Here all human and non-human worldly existence shares a common presence. This commensurability transcends and dissolves the strict division between the two domains. It shores up the ground for arguments claiming a reciprocity between our treatment of humans and non-human nature, arguments that do not have to rely at all on a "mystical" reunion or on "oceanic" feelings of oneness. It also supports the validity of such notions as "the revenge of nature," which otherwise may appear to be more a product of whimsical speculation than genuine critical insight.

If one upholds the validity of this fundamental linkage between human and non-human existence, then an analysis of the origins of pathological social relationships cannot take place in isolation from an investigation of humans' comportment toward their non-human environment. Clearly, Habermas rejects any claim in support of the linkage between human and non-human existence. As cited in the previous chapter, he does so because the relationship between humans and nature in his view cannot be accounted for discursively or rationally, which amounts to the same thing in his opinion. Of course, for those who uphold the traditional identification of reason with *logos qua* speech, a rational account of this relationship cannot possibly be given, because nature does not speak. Habermas doubtless would agree with Plato's observation in the *Phaedrus* that the lover of "rational learning" *(philomathes)* avoids the "trees and open country" because they do not give lessons.[4] According to this understanding, reason's proper domain is the human or intersubjective world alone. From this it follows that thought which explores the linkage between the human and non-human worlds can only be a kind of speechless intuitionism. Although it still may be possible to speak about matters of this sort, the claim would be made here that such speech is *alogon*, that is, talk that merely points to what is at bottom a fundamentally mysterious phenomenon.

There are at least two conceivable reactions to this critique. First, one could agree with its premises but take issue with the conclusion Habermas draws from it. In other words, one may begin by upholding the identification of reason and speech and argue that the kinds of intellectual discourse that Adorno—and later, Merleau-Ponty—embark upon are not, strictly speaking, rational. But one could conclude from the above, *contra* Habermas, that the value of this "poetic" mode of thought to our functioning as rational beings traditionally has been overlooked and that this neglect has led to the estrangement of reason from its theater of operation—the world. The solution to the disenchantment problem in this instance would be to repoeticize the world, and not, as Habermas argues, to reclaim for reason its proper place and dignity within the social order.

The other option is more ambitious. Here one would uphold the rationality of thinking about the interconnection between the human and non-human worlds. This option is ambitious, because it necessarily rests on an understanding of reason that runs counter to its traditional association with *logos* as speech.

It is not within the scope of this study to investigate at length the meaning of reason along the lines adumbrated above. However, it is important that we set the stage for a reading of esthetic theory by at least responding to Habermas's critique in a positive, if cursory, way. The first thing we can say with certainty in this regard is that esthetic theory does not pertain primarily to the intersubjective world. Art, and especially the art form of greatest interest to Adorno and Merleau-Ponty—painting—is inspired by an extra-linguistic or mute form of communication between humans and the world. Thus this 'dialogue' is beyond the bounds of rational discourse as usually defined. Do we conclude from this that the experience is in fact extra-rational? Do we allow the traditional understanding of reason to go unchallenged? Certainly, apologies need not accompany an argument that stresses the importance of a more poetic understanding of the world. However, as noble an assertion as this may be, attributing the adjective "poetic" to discourses on the human–nature nexus automatically relegates them, in a disenchanted age, to the status of mere subjective value preferences. It thus seriously compromises these discourses' perceived capacity to reveal the true conditions of worldly existence. If the objective is to restore this capacity, then it seems to me it can be done best by arguing that such accounts are rational in the revised sense that they reveal- -or at least have the capacity to reveal —what it means to exist as worldly beings. The fact that this understanding does not issue from communicative intercourse between subjects need not mean it is necessarily beyond reason. But what that most assuredly indicates is that the experience rendering it intelligible is fundamentally at odds with the one typically associated with discursive reasoning.

John Caputo, in his book, *Radical Hermeneutics*, depicts this tension brilliantly and to good critical effect. He describes modern rationality as the process by which an interrogating "subject" demands that "reasons" be brought forth from the "object." Following Heidegger, Caputo claims that this so-called rational exercise is a decadent refiguration of an original experience where reason (*logos*) meant quite literally the opposite, that is, the "letting-be" of the object. Here a truly rational understanding of the world is acquired, not by asking why it is the way it is, but simply, he says, by "linger[ing] in its own emergent *physis*."[5]

I submit that the kinds of experience Adorno and Merleau-Ponty reflect upon in their analyses of art and esthetics are precisely those that have at their core the rational experience of letting-be. The esthetic encounter, we shall see, is premised upon an openness to those paths of communication which link the world to humans and sustain our capacity to receive its 'language.' Because there can be no answer (for nature does not speak) to questions such as, "Why do these paths of communication exist?," or "For what purpose do they exist?" there is no way to defend the reasonableness of the experience in the traditional sense of the term. All I can suggest, in conclusion, is that we approach Adorno and Merleau-Ponty's reflections on esthetics with the same sense of openness that the authors exhibited toward their subject matter.

Adorno Revisited

The claim was made in Chapter Two that Horkheimer and Adorno radicalized the notion of disenchantment by arguing that the pervasiveness of technical rationality in contemporary society cannot be directly ascribed to the rise of modern science in the sixteenth century but to the actualization of the dialectic of Western rationality *per se*. A disenchanted world therefore is characterized by the realization of reason's *telos*—the mastery of the world, both human and non-human. Given this understanding, Adorno and Horkheimer concluded that a less directly manipulative mode of reasoning ought to supplant the existing one. It has been suggested here that, of the two authors, Adorno's account of mimesis represents the more cogent of the arguments in support of such an alternative mode of reasoning.

Adorno is well aware that a critique of Western rationality ought not mean the wholesale abandonment of critical thought. Fully cognizant of being within the Western philosophical tradition, he neither thinks it possible nor desirable to re-enchant the world by simply returning to a mythopoeic experience of nature. Rather, Adorno seeks middle ground in his articulation of a counter-Enlightenment mode of thought, one which avoids the failings associated with relapsing into *mythos*, on the one hand, and endorsing technical rationality, on the other. To appreciate fully the implications of Adorno's esthetic theory for our renewed investigation of the disenchantment problem, we reopen our examination to analyze it more thoroughly.

In his *Diaries*, the Swiss painter Paul Klee remarks: "The artist's power should be spiritual."[6] Adorno unquestionably would agree. The preparatory task of reviewing some of the more fundamental aspects of his esthetic theory will enable us to understand the sense in which Adorno sees the creative act as primarily spiritual.

According to Adorno, the artist's power lies in his ability to represent nature's appearance in a sensuous form. But a faithful representation of nature demands an openness to the essential quality of that which is to be represented. For Adorno, this entails a receptivity to the world's mysterious and enigmatic appearance. More precisely, it involves an ability to respond to that part of nature that "says more" than what is revealed to an artist's senses. The artist's objective, then, is to represent in sensuous form nature's mystery as revealed by its "plus of appearance"—its "beauty."[7]

The term *beauty* for Adorno defies simple description precisely because nature's surfeit of meaning is extra-sensible. Adorno nonetheless attempts to define the ineffable by likening nature's beauty to its "atmosphere" or "aura." One experiences the beauty of a particular natural setting in the act of apprehending the atmosphere that emanates from its appearance. In short, nature for Adorno is evocative, and what an observer educes from it is its mood or sense of place.

A second major aspect of nature's appearance is the indeterminateness of its beauty. Here Adorno claims that because the "plus of appearance" is characterized by its "indefinability," it eludes simple delimitation. Of course, he does not mean by this that understandings of what constitutes beauty cannot and have not been articulated. Rather, he simply is alluding to the fact that these conceptualizations are necessarily conditioned by the sensibilities of the particular social order from which they issue.

The reason why nature's beauty is indeterminate—why for Adorno it has so many faces—is that it emerges from a background of silence, or, more specifically, "meaningful silence."[8] Because nature is mute, because it cannot speak to us discursively, it is we who necessarily must speak for it if it is to speak at all. And the fact that we have the capacity to speak for nature means that nature's silence must be meaningful. For if it were merely mute, we would only be able to speak about nature. It is clear, then, that for Adorno nature retains, despite its silence, a genuine capacity to 'speak' to man. We, in turn, are endowed with the power to 'read' nature's language, and to creatively re-present it, even though the medium of intercourse is extralinguistic. Yet it is precisely because the medium of interchange is non-linguistic that the meanings we draw from nature are necessarily more equivocal than those emanating from speech.

It is important to note, when accounting for the process by which nature 'communicates' with man, that the atmosphere a particular setting may evoke is not, in a literal sense, contained in either its constituent parts or in their assemblage. One cannot say, for instance, that the aura of melancholy that may accompany the sight of a field lit by a late autumn sun is reducible simply to the natural environment itself. It makes no sense, save for aficionados of purple prose, to speak of a 'melancholy field.' But we cannot draw from this the opposite conclusion that one's melancholia is wholly unrelated to nature's appearance. That would be equally absurd. The truth of the matter, according to Adorno, is that the "plus of appearance" is distinct from that present before us but is nonetheless mediated by what we see.

Adorno argues that the task of artists is to imitate or represent the beautiful in nature rather than nature itself.[9] They appropriate the "plus" from its contingent setting in nature and sensually recreate it in a determinate fashion in a work of art. The artists' power, then, is said to reside in their capacity to "objectify" the evanescence of natural beauty.[10]

Adorno goes on to say that the "plus" of an artwork's appearance comprises its spirit. Artists, therefore, have as their objective the imitation of nature's beauty, as spirit. If they capture it, the work of art will yield a spirit that, as with nature's beauty, transcends the material of its appearance, yet remains mediated by it. The artist will have created a work of art whose spirit, Adorno tells us, "dwells in particular objects," yet "shin[es] forth through appearances."[11]

One of the chief characteristics of spirit, according to Adorno, is its "objectivity." Spirit is said to possess this attribute in at least two senses. First, it is objective insofar as the artist, regardless of any ability to mimic the world's beauty, is never sufficiently in control of the creative process to render spirit precisely as intended. Hence the spirit of a work of art never fully corresponds to the specific subjective designs of the artist. Klee's remark that "the paintings look at us" attests to the fact that a work of art always achieves a life of its own—a discrete existence. Secondly, spirit is objective also to the extent that it is not something transported to the work of art from outside it, that is, from the creative agent. Artists cannot inject spirit into their art work as they can place paint on the surface of the canvas. All they can do is the latter. And it is only by means of their skills in this regard, as expressed, for example, in the compositional arrangement of elements within the work, that its spirit can shine forth. Spirit therefore originates in the art object alone, even though the art work itself is a product of the artist as subject. It is because spirit is objective in this dual sense that Adorno maintains the artist is as much the art object's agent as its creator.

As noted, artists through their work make nature's mute language speak. The criterion for authenticity in a work of art has been said to be its capacity to manifest spirit. Adorno argues further that in this lies its "truth content," as well. A work of art is "true" to the extent that it conveys spirit through its appearance. However, just as the spirit of an art work is never fully expressive of the intentions of its creator, so is its truth content subject to the same constraint. That too is objective. So while a work of art may speak to us through its spirit, its medium of communication hardly leads to unequivocal interpretation. For this reason the truth content of an art work is never ready-made. Although the work of art itself possesses a certain stability by virtue of its 'thing'-like character, this does not mean that its truth is equally fixed. For just as our appreciation of nature's beauty is historically conditioned and hence contingent, so is our reading of an art work's spirit susceptible to multiple interpretations across time and space.

The indeterminacy of art's truth is attributable as well to its over-ridingly enigmatic character. For Adorno, art's power to confound is explainable in terms of the means it necessarily employs to manifest spirit and truth. One of the limiting conditions of art is the fact that it portrays spirit sensually. Its truth, as a result, can never be revealed transparently as pure concept. The truth content of an art work, which shines through and out of appearance, remains inextricably bound to that appearance. The work's spirit, in short, is localized: It always appears somewhere specific. One cannot experience the truth of a work of art unless one stands before it, in some determinate location. For Adorno, works of art are enigmatic precisely because the true and the particular are conjoined in them in this way. Thus in contrast to the truth of modern science or of discursive knowledge, which is "undisguised" (or purely conceptual) and indeterminate (that is, nowhere and everywhere), the truth of art is determinate but "disguised."[12] It is the very tangibility of a work of art which ironically lends an air of obscurity to its truth, which appears to have no fixed origin, being simultaneously both in and beyond the work itself. Its obscurity is only compounded, one might add, if we approach a work of art believing that questions concerning truth and reason can be meaningfully posed only in universalistic terms.

The significance of art in a disenchanted world is two-fold, according to Adorno. On the one hand, art serves to keep alive "the memory of ends-oriented reason" in an age given over to purposive rationality.[13] It can do so because its *ratio* is "qualitative," because it has as its end the reproduction of the experience of being-in-the-world. Artists, in other words, do not confront the world with the intention of mastering it by using it as a means for self-expression or self-aggrandizement. Rather, they stand before it seeking to reconcile themselves in their work to its objective quality—its aura. It is important to note that the desire for reconciliation with the world does not presuppose that artists are at one with it. Artists, no less than scientists, are alienated from their natural environment.

The mimetic impulse that drives the artist is born from the anxiety that accompanies the experience of the ineffability of nature. In the final analysis, then, creative expression is a means of quelling this existential unease. But as we have seen, it realizes this end not by dominating the world, as does science, but by exteriorizing this anxiety through material means. Klee echoes this view in his metaphorical description of the creative process.

> Allow me to make use of a parable, the parable of a tree. Take an artist sufficiently well-oriented in the world and in life to be able to organize phenomena and experiences. This orientation of things in nature . . . I would like to compare to the roots of a tree. From here, the sap mounts towards the artist, trying to pass through . . . him and his eyes: He is thus taking on the function of the trunk. Urged on and *agitated* by this powerful flux, he transmits to the work what he has seen. And the work, like the top of the tree, unfurls into time and space. No one would demand that the tree should form its top in the image of its roots. . . [emphasis added].[14]

The artist, as Klee portrays him, functions as a transmitter of the "orientation of things in nature," or what Adorno would call nature's "beauty." But, by Klee's own admission, the transmitted image is not a straightforward reproduction, for a work of art can never be identified with its initial source of creative inspiration. Moreover, to the extent that he refers to the initial inspiration as producing a sense of "agitation," he seems to concur with Adorno's assessment of the tension that lies at the root of the creative impulse and that only artistic expression can mollify.

Apart from the fact that art keeps alive questions concerning the ends of human existence, it performs the additional important function, as Adorno notes, of retaining the memory of an objectivity that lies beyond conceptual frameworks.[15] The claim Adorno puts forth is one that lies at the core of the disenchantment thesis. We have noted that an era informed by technical rationality takes the empirical world to be mere *res extensa*—homogeneous generic 'matter'—operating in conformity with the universal laws of nature. Thus for all the talk of the 'prosaic' character of our technological age, we are incapable of appreciating the prose of the world—its appearance as concrete substance. Such an appreciation necessarily would entail the development of sensitivities capable of discerning the qualitative in nature. Adorno seems to suggest that art, in both its creation and enjoyment, provides us with the means to develop precisely these sensitivites. In short, it enables us to experience more fully the "real" world. The irony of the fact that art, and not science, allows us to experience the 'other' does not escape Adorno's notice. For art commonly is said to be an "illusion" by virtue of the fact that it is an "after-image" of the world, a "second-order" reflection of something which cannot be.[16] Nonetheless, as Adorno doubtless agrees, it is an illusion that has the power to liberate nature from its silence and to reveal its truth.

There are limits to art's capacities, however. When we look at the power of art within the horizon of our disenchanted contemporary world, we note that its perceived ability to reveal truth is greatly diminished in relation to pre-modern times. Hegel was one of the first to realize that art is "a thing of the past," since it is no longer comprehended as a presentation of the divine in an unproblematic way. Weber came to a similar conclusion when he observed that it is "not accidental that our greatest art is intimate and not monumental. . . ."[17] Adorno follows suit when he asserts that an "age of silence" has befallen art in that it no longer functions positively by giving concrete expression to substantive ideas, as did Greek art in its depiction of the idea of Beauty, for instance.

In keeping with the tenor of his *Negative Dialectics*, Adorno argues that art in modernity operates negatively by reflecting the technological complexion of our world back to itself. But art not only refuses to play the "world game"—the game of domination—it aspires as well to show the world the irrational nature of the game it is playing. Art accomplishes this by providing a foil against which the rationality pervading the disenchanted world can be brought into relief and exposed to scrutiny. Art, then, is said to be the "truth about society" in that it reveals society's technological character and its making a fetish of means. And to the extent that art presents us with "an after-image of man's repression of nature," Adorno holds out hope that art has the power to neutralize the ethic of domination.

At this point in our investigation it is necessary to take stock of where Adorno's esthetic theory has led us. We began by suggesting that Habermas's plan to decolonize the lifeworld failed to address the central concern of the disenchantment thesis, namely, the question concerning domination. In fact, we claimed, the forces of domination would only be still further enhanced should instrumental rationality be supplemented with a more comprehensive communicative rationality. Thus we chose to reconsider the merits of attempting to overcome disenchantment from within the paradigmatic strictures of the so-called philosophy of consciousness.

To this end, we adumbrated Adorno's alternative to mythopoeic and disenchanted modes of understanding. He argued that art, while not opposed to reason *per se*, works against "the rigid juxtaposition of rationality and particularity" that informs the modern scientific world view. In its capacity to conjoin the true (reason) and the particular, art for Adorno forms the phenomenological link that integrates human

understanding with the world of which it is a part. And insofar as disenchantment signifies the dissolution of this bond, Adorno's account of
the esthetic experience appears to meet the challenge we have laid out
for ourselves.

To a great extent it has. Adorno's depiction of a non-repressive
mode of relating self to world is highly persuasive on many counts.
Most important, it presents a compelling argument against the claim,
explicit in Habermas, that the relationship between humans and nature is incapable of being rendered intelligible other than in a purposive rational manner. However, whether an esthetic relationship to
the world represents a rational experience is more problematic. As
stated earlier in this chapter, there are arguments in support of such
a claim; however, they are not likely to prove convincing to those who
uphold the traditional identification of reason and speech.

If there is a major shortcoming with Adorno's esthetic theory, it
lies in its incompleteness. It fails to articulate in sufficiently clear
terms the ontological dimension of the esthetic experience, an aspect
of his thought which I take to be of singular importance to his own
analysis and which is becoming increasingly central to our ongoing investigation. The questions may be posed: What must pertain to account for the artist's capacity to 'read' the "plus" of nature's
appearance? What is the medium of communication and how can it be
spoken of intelligibly? Adorno at best supplies only oblique responses
to questions of this sort, which may explain in part Habermas's dis-
tress over his conclusions. In furtherance of the general approach to
the issue of disenchantment initiated by Adorno, I now refer to Merleau-Ponty and his analysis of the problem of perception.

Merleau-Ponty: From Perception to Ontology

Weber tells us that in a disenchanted world nature is perceived as
devoid of magical qualities, as emptied of spirit or inner life. Set
against the 'inert stuff' of nature are humans, in possession of that
which nature lacks, namely, spirit or mind. It is the incommensurability of the human and natural domains—an ontological discrepancy—that either authorizes the domination of nature by man or
provides a *de facto* justification of its practice.

Disenchantment, however, encompasses more than just a
despiritualized nature. For the human/nature dualism is accompanied
by a corresponding mind/body dualism within humans themselves.
Hence it is apparent that if Adorno is to succeed in shattering the
received framework of disenchantment—that is, if he wishes to
destroy the categorical distinction between myth and enchantment, on

the one hand, and a prosaic world informed by technical rationality, on the other—he must satisfy two demands, at minimum. First, he must give an account of the manner in which the being of humans and nature are implicated, one in the other. Second, he must give an account of the ontological unity of mind and body.

We are now in a position to assess more judiciously the relative strengths and weaknesses of Adorno's esthetic theory. His implicit claim that art enables us to experience more fully what it means to exist within the "objective" world satisfies the first demand in a qualified sense, as noted at the end of the previous section. However, with respect to the second demand, Adorno's analysis of the esthetic experience yields less positive results.

Adorno does not consider, for instance, the relationship, if any, between artists as mediators of nature's "plus of appearance" and their existence as appearing beings themselves. One could ask of Adorno whether the fact that the artist is an appearing being (or "body," among other human and non-human bodies) has any bearing on the artist's capacity to read that which transcends the merely bodily. Perhaps one could ask of Adorno even more fundamental questions concerning the nature of the 'perceptual organ' that apprehends nature's aura. Is it corporeal, spiritual, or some combination of both? What is its relationship to the bodily substance of artists and of their natural environment? It is the absence of answers to questions of this sort, as well as the shortcomings of his response to the first demand, that necessitate a further exploration of the human–nature nexus. As stated, it is to Merleau-Ponty that we redirect our attention in search of replies to queries of this sort.

Merleau-Ponty's extended analysis of what might broadly be called the phenomenology of perception is animated by the same concern that drew Adorno to an investigation of the esthetic experience. It is a concern precipitated by what might be termed the "challenge of disenchantment." Merleau-Ponty sought to meet this challenge in his early writings by addressing the question of perception. The phenomenological exhortation to "return to the things themselves" means for him a "return to that world that precedes knowledge, of which knowledge always speaks," and without the experience of which "the symbols of science would be meaningless."[18] Adorno and Merleau-Ponty share the conviction that science, precisely because it devotes its energies to the manipulation of 'things,' "gives up living in them."[19] In *Phenomenology of Perception*, Merleau-Ponty argues that access to this primal world can be gained only through what he refers to as "perceptual consciousness."[20] In contrast to the transcendental consciousness of the modern philosophical tradition, the consciousness that perceives the world preceding knowledge is for Merleau-Ponty incarnate or "embodied." The use of this latter term is especially appropriate, since it conveys forcefully the extent to which perceiving consciousness is a datum of the empirical world along with the objects it perceives.

Because the seat of consciousness is incarnate, the act of perception requires some kind of bodily alignment of perceiver and perceived. As Merleau-Ponty says: "To perceive is to render oneself present to something through the body."[21] And because the body, indeed like all natural entities, has specific spatiotemporal coordinates within the world, the perceiving body is necessarily directed toward its object from a particular vantage point in space and time. That is to say, perception is an inherently perspectival phenomenon since the perceived object necessarily exists for consciousness alone—by virtue of its being perceived by embodied consciousness. Hence "being" is said to be synonymous with "being for myself." However, the fact that perceiving consciousness has no access to the 'thing in itself' does not mean that the perspectival encounter with an object is a distorting imposition of a 'subjective' point of view. For one can speak meaningfully of perception as distorting in this sense only if there exists an 'objective' point of view against which to contrast it. But clearly, no sentient being is capable of perceiving from everywhere simultaneously, as objective perception would require. As Merleau-Ponty says:

> Perspective does not appear to me to be a subjective deformation of things but, on the contrary, to be one of their properties, perhaps their essential property. It is precisely because of it that the perceived possesses in itself a hidden and inexhaustible richness, that it is a 'thing.'[22]

From this statement we can conclude that variations in perspective account ultimately for what we might call, along with Adorno, "nature's enigmatic appearance." As noted, Adorno attributed nature's "plus of appearance" to the artist's ability to read its non-sensual aura. For Merleau-Ponty, on the other hand, nature says more than what it phenomenally reveals to consciousness to the extent that the perceived object always eludes the absolute (objective) gaze. Because our perception of the empirical world as it presents itself to us can never exhaust its density as a 'thing,' the world always is more than what it perceptually reveals itself to be from any given perspective. Moreover, because the primary constitutive property of perception— its perspectival character—accounts for the "mystery" of nature, this mystery for Merleau-Ponty is no more a problem to be solved than perception itself. So despite the difference in their accounts of nature's "plus," both Adorno and Merleau-Ponty agree on one essential point: the objective of contemporary thought is to recover the mystery of the experiential world which has been neglected in an age given over to the domination of nature through technical means.

By arguing that the perceiving consciousness is embodied, Merleau-Ponty attempts to undermine the epistemological idealism that supports both positivism and world disenchantment. In his early writings, the primacy of perception is related to the so-called "primacy of the world," in that they both underscore the centrality of the pre-reflective experience that unites perceiving consciousness and the object of perception. He argues that there can be no conscious perception of an object unless one first has sensed, however remotely, the givenness of a world of which perceiver and perceived are integral components. Obviously, recognition of this world can never be a product of reflective thought, for, as Merleau-Ponty says, the world "is not what I think, but what I live through."[23] It is the pre-reflective experience of its facticity which assures us of our possession of worldly existence, or which gives us a sense of the *"Weltlichkeit der Welt,"* the worldliness of the world.[24] It confirms the authenticity of the experience of being in the world.

A difficulty remains in Merleau-Ponty's account of the primacy of the world, however. Despite his insistence on the need to regain a sense of the 'worldliness' of the world, the force of this experience is diminished somewhat by the presence of a lingering dualism in his elaboration of perceiving consciousness. It can be argued, in the final analysis, that his *ego percipio* is but a modification of Descartes's *res cogitans*. For although the perceiving ego is "concrete," it is an ego nonetheless, and as such it stands apart from its object—the *cogitatum*. This much is tacitly revealed in the previously quoted statement depicting the world as what "I" live through. The challenge that confronts Merleau-Ponty at this point, and of which he himself becomes increasingly aware, is how to conceive of perception in a way that does not reinstitute a rupture between perception and its object.

With the publication of a middle-period work entitled *Themes from the Lectures*, Merleau-Ponty begins to question some of the assumptions underlying his phenomenological approach to an analysis of perception, and to suggest new directions for investigation. During this transitional stage in his thought he still holds the view that the concrete ego determines the "true" in nature. Yet he counterbalances this assertion by stressing that the discontinuity of perceptual perspectives presupposes a "common dimension," a shared "core of being," within which perception occurs. It is in a chapter entitled "Nature and Logos: The Human Body," that Merleau-Ponty finally reveals a strategy that radically advances the shift from the primacy of perception to that of the "world," to an ontological primacy. He begins by challenging directly the Cartesian dualism of self and object. Merleau-

Ponty now argues that a phenomenological investigation of perception reveals that "life is not a simple object for a consciousness." Abandoning the centerpiece of his previously formulated theory of perception—the *ego percipio*—he argues that it is "the human body . . . which perceives nature."[25] To be sure, insofar as Merleau-Ponty asserts that the body "perceives," there remains in his reformulation a continuity with his previous work. However, as we shall see, the implications of the shift from "perceiving consciousness" to "perceiving body" are rather striking.

The most significant of these consequences is that Merleau-Ponty is no longer confined, as he was when he conceived perception in terms of an embodied consciousness, by the strictures of a person's "two natures." He no longer is faced with the conundrum that attends an understanding of humans as composite beings comprised of an unwieldy union of a thinking and a bodily element. In all such configurations, there remains the problem of explaining how "consciousness"—either disembodied *(ego cogito)* or embodied *(ego percipio)*—relates to the "non-conscious," to the object of thought or perception. Merleau-Ponty makes what at first glance seems to be a rather sophistic move, when, after dispensing with the "two-natures" hypothesis, he adopts instead the view that the perceiving body possesses a "double nature." However, an examination of his "double-nature" thesis soon eliminates any suspicion that a more sublime form of ontological dualism has reasserted itself.

In contrast to his initial claim that perception is embodied within the concrete ego, Merleau-Ponty now takes perception to be a wholly bodily phenomenon. In his posthumously published *The Visible and the Invisible,* he depicts the body as having a double nature, since it is simultaneously a felt object and a sensing object. As he notes, the body "can be seen and it can see itself; it can be touched and it can touch itself. . . ."[26] Hence Merleau-Ponty speaks of the body as a singular entity possessing "two sides" or "two leaves." From one side, the body is "a thing among things," and from the other side that which "sees and touches them."[27] The reflexivity of the body can be expressed, as well, in terms of a coupling of "passivity" and "activity." As a passive or "sensed" being, the body is of the visible; it shares with the world around it the capacity "to be looked at." According to Merleau-Ponty, precisely because the body is a visible thing, a human being, as body, has access to the visible world. As he says: "He who sees cannot possess the visible unless he is possessed by it, unless he is of it, unless . . . he is one of the visibles, capable, by a singlar reversal, of seeing them—he who is one of them."[28] In short, the body is an active or sensing being to the extent that it shares with the visible world a common texture, or "flesh."

The term *flesh* is not to be misconstrued as a mere material substratum connecting body and world. Rather, Merleau-Ponty wishes us to conceive it as an "element of Being" in which body and world "overlap." Reference to a hypothetical experience of this ontological fusion of visibles may help elucidate further the intended meaning of the word. Suppose, for instance, a person were to walk into a red room. Upon entering, the 'communication' between that person's perceiving body and its visible environment would undergo a profound shift, assuming of course that he did not enter the room from a similarly colored exterior. The fact that body and world overlap would result, in this case, in the general elevation of the body's metabolism.

One could ask at this point: What accounts for this 'dialogue' between the two visibles? One may be tempted to respond that it can be explained solely in scientific terms as a physiological reaction of a subject to its environment. While Merleau-Ponty may not be entirely dissatisfied with such a response, it would not in his view address his central concern. For he is not as interested in the actual physiological interrelation of body and world as he is in recovering an awareness of that which sustains such intercourse and without which there could be none. It is precisely the world's flesh—a mode of Being that grounds the visible (i.e., being)—that accounts for the interconnectedness of body and world, according to Merleau-Ponty.

Perception would not be possible unless the body and the visible overlapped within the world as flesh. This intersection, however, is not to be thought of as a simple coinciding or merging of see-er and seen. Perception can not be defined in terms of the superimposition of the body on the world, or vice versa. Rather than employing the static imagery of two concentric circles to depict this overlapping, Merleau-Ponty chooses (although not explicitly) to represent it in the form of a "chiasma." The appeal of this imagery is readily apparent when we realize that a chiasma—a support structure used in architectural construction—takes the shape of an *X*. The very image of reversibility, of projection and introjection, the chiasma is well suited to symbolize Merleau-Ponty's characterization of perception as an inherently dynamic process. Speaking of the see-er and the seen, he describes perception as an event where "each borrows from the other, takes from or encroaches upon the other, intersects with the other, is in chiasm with the other."[29] Perceptual experience is thus in part an excursion into the world. It is, says Merleau-Ponty, a "magical relation" whereby "I lend them [visible entities] my body in order that they inscribe upon it and give me their resemblance. . . ."[30] As we see, however, this active insertion of the body into the visible is possible only because the world is receptive to the body's gaze or touch. Perceptual experience, therefore, relies equally on the encroachment of the body on the visible world and possession of the body by the visible world.

Merleau-Ponty, then, depicts the human–nature relationship as an interpenetration or intertwining of body and world. When viewed in this manner, the visible is seen as a prolongation of the body and the body as a prolongation of the visible. Hence the natural or visible world is to be understood as "the other side of man," and humans the other side of the visible world.[31] In the final analysis, the mutual interpenetration of humans and nature is possible only because they are of the same flesh, a flesh through whose pores the body enters the world and the world enters the body. Understanding the world as flesh leads to the re-establishment of what Merleau-Ponty calls our "perceptual faith," the "openness upon the world" that informs us of our connectedness with the world through our bodies. It rekindles "our living bond with nature" which disenchantment has all but extinguished.[32]

As noted, the neglect of our living bond with nature renders nature transparent to our gaze. A disenchanted world possesses no secrets. In contrast, both Adorno and Merleau-Ponty have tried to illustrate, in their respective ways, that the experience of being-in-the-world is defined precisely as an openness to nature, to its mystery. Before his turn to ontology, as we have seen, Merleau-Ponty accounted for this mystery in terms of the impenetrable density of the object as 'thing.' However, by the time of his writing *The Visible and the Invisible*, he was forced to re-evaluate this matter from within the parameters of the "philosophy of the flesh."

The basic lineaments of Merleau-Ponty's account of the world's mystery remain unchanged after his ontological turn. He continues to argue, for instance, that the enigmatic character of the world is attributable to the perspectival nature of perception, notwithstanding his reinterpretation of what constitutes perception. And despite the fact that he now refers to the world's mystery as the "invisibility of the visible," there remains a continuity in his thought, for the visible is said to be invisible because it "resists becoming totally visible."[33]

However, the changes in his ontological rereading of the world's mystery are considerable. For whereas previously Merleau-Ponty equated mysteriousness with the impenetrable facticity of the object as 'thing,' he now argues that the mystery of the world—its invisibility—is centered around the visible's "nucleus of absence"—its Being.[34] In order to understand what he means by this, it is necessary to reconfirm the fact that because the visible is never totally visible, it eludes, he says, being "all actual under the [gaze]." That is to say, the visible is never wholly 'present' to the perceiving body. Yet it "promises this total actuality" or visibility, because, as Merleau-Ponty states, "it is there."[35] Hence it is the very facticity—the "thereness"—of the visible that eludes total actuality which accounts for the so-called "promise" of total actuality. The promise of the visible's complete presence in the face of the world's perceived incomplete visibility comprises the "absence" within the visible—its Being. And because the visible suggests or portends Being, while never revealing it, the world can be said to be "mysterious."

In the final analysis, then, the world's enigmatic character is inseparable from what Merleau-Ponty refers to as the "paradox" of Being. For both describe a single phenomenon—the invisibility of the visible—from its related yet analytically distinguishable 'sides.' As stated, when viewed from the perspective of the perceiving body, the world's mystery is a function of its intimation of completeness, or Being. On the other hand, when observed from the perspective of Being, the mystery of the world can be traced to the fact that Being discloses itself as an absence—as the "hidden armature"—within the core of the visible. The world is mysterious because it reveals itself only as a pre-figuration of its totality.

The centrality of art, especially painting, to Merleau-Ponty's analysis of perception is well established in his writings. In his article entitled "Eye and Mind," published shortly before he began work on *The Visible and the Invisible*, we find a particularly illuminating account of the artist's affinity to "wild" perception, to a mode of perception attuned to the mystery of the world. In order to expound further on Merleau-Ponty's phenomenological ontology, we now turn to his analysis of art and the esthetic experience of the world.

The appeal of artistic expression for Merleau-Ponty, as for Adorno, is in large measure due to the concreteness of activity in the arts. As Merleau-Ponty puts it, "We cannot imagine how a mind could paint."[36] Of course, it is the body that paints and the body paints what it perceives. But perception itself is problematic. We have noted that, in contradistinction to "wild perception," so-called "profane" vision disregards the fundamental overlapping of body and world. It takes perception to be an operation of thought that sets before the mind "a picture or representation" of the world. The entire thrust of Merleau-Ponty's philosophy of the flesh is to disabuse us of the Cartesian propensity to posit the world as 'out there' beyond the self, and correspondingly to regard vision as a mental representation of this exterior 'reality.' Theoretical considerations aside, common sense alone ought to tell us that we are in the world. This much we know, Merleau-Ponty says, when we realize that "the world is all around me, not in front of me."[37]

"Wild perception" acknowledges that the perceiving body is immersed in the world, is a part of its flesh. Accordingly, the perceiver in no way 'appropriates' the visible. He does not from the outside 'take it in.' Rather, he opens himself to the world in the act of perceiving it. As noted in our discussion of *The Visible and the Invisible*, this reception of the world is chiasmatic in that body and world interpenetrate. By opening oneself to the world, the body not only enters into the world, it is likewise entered into by the world. Hence the eye, for example, is said to be an instrument that both advances into the world in that it "moves itself," and is encroached upon by the world to the extent that it is "moved by some impact" upon it. Due to its reflexive nature, vision cannot be construed merely as the sensory representation of that which lies beyond the organ of sight. For the eye is a component of a perceiving body that is itself a visible entity among other visible entities, a part of the world's flesh.

Seeing and the object of sight therefore must take place within this flesh. This is why Merleau-Ponty asserts that vision is possible only because the object of sight has an "internal equivalent" in the see-er. Those properties of the visible—light, color, depth, etc.—that we see, are before us "because they awaken an echo in our body and because the body welcomes them."[38] This echo within the body which the visible incites can be likened to a kind of bodily reverberation of the perceived within the perceiver. Without this bodily resonance—this "secret visibility," as Merleau-Ponty calls it—there could be no profane or "manifest visibility."

The artist is especially sensitive to the fact that his vision is situated within the world's flesh. His work is not born out of a desire to reproduce nature's beauty as it appears before his seeing mind. On the contrary, it is a response to a kind of visceral excitation invoked by the visible. What leads an artist to paint, says Merleau-Ponty, is that "in the immemorial depth of the visible, something moved, caught fire, and engulfed his body. . . ."[39] Painting, therefore, is an answer to this bodily incitement. We are reminded here of Klee's observation that the artist, like a tree, gathers up and transmits forces "welling up from the depths," forces which, because he is "a fragment of nature in the natural world," are congruent with the orientation of things in nature itself.[40]

As a result it is pointless to argue that nature 'ends' at a particular boundary and that humans and esthetic expression 'begins' beyond that boundary. Both are for Merleau-Ponty moments within a closed circuit or within the seamless web of Being. This is another way of saying that the artist is de-centered vis-à-vis his relationship to the world. Nature speaks through him. Like Adorno, Merleau-Ponty claims that the artist transmits nature's primal voice not by imitating its appearance but by capturing for the senses that which transcends the merely visible. This entails, he says, giving "visible existence to what profane vision believes to be invisible," that is, to Being.[41]

There is a strong sense in which the correlative of invisibility for Adorno—that is, nature's "plus" or "objective quality"—carries with it overtones of what Merleau-Ponty means by "Being." This is most forcefully suggested in Adorno's observation that a work of art "brings back the terror of the primal world" over which stand the objects of appearance.[42] The "terror" that art is capable of invoking can be interpreted as a psychophysiological reaction—what Adorno refers to as a "prehistorical shudder"—to the mute Being of the primal world.

Despite this implied reference, however, nowhere does Adorno clearly identify with Being either the "plus of appearance" or the spirit of art. As alluded to in the previous section, this may be accounted for by the fact that he does not ground his esthetic theory in a fully articulated theory of perception. Yet a theory of perception is central to any discussion of the suprasensible aspect of the visible, for the simple reason that the invisible (i.e., Being or the "plus of appearance") necessarily shines forth from appearance, and appearance is always appearance for a perceiving being. Thus the perceiver by definition is implicated in the appearance of the world both as 'thing' and Being. Merleau-Ponty's advantage over Adorno lies precisely in his explicit analysis of the relationship between the perceiver and the perceived. He shows us that if art is capable of making the invisible visible—or manifesting spirit, as Adorno would say—then this is because artists are able to draw upon their own experience of embeddedness within nature's invisibility or flesh.

As a consequence of their insertion within the flesh of the world, artists do not set out to imitate the visible, to sensually reproduce some aspect of the world as it appears before them. Rather, they "render visible" the world's invisibility—its flesh—as given to them through perception. It is in this sense that Merleau-Ponty refers to the artist's gaze as "voracious," as reaching beyond the "visual givens." For in his work the discrete sensory images are merely *caesurae*, or punctuations, within the texture of Being.[43] This is why he argues, agreeing with Gadamer, that controversies over the merits of figurative versus nonfigurative art ultimately are misguided. For the artist's objective is to convey the "voluminosity of the world," the sheer presence of the world. This can be achieved regardless of the specific form of the painting's content, because no work of art, no matter how "abstract," can escape Being.[44] Perhaps Merleau-Ponty expresses this sentiment best when he says: "I do not look at it [an art work] as I do at a thing; I do not fix it in its place. My gaze wanders in it as in the halos of Being. It is more accurate to say that I see according to it, or with it, than that I *see* it" (emphasis in original).[45] Just how closely Merleau-Ponty's thoughts on art conform to Klee's is evident in Klee's complementary statement: "Formerly we used to represent things visible on earth, things we either liked to look at or would have liked to see. Today we reveal the reality that is behind visible things. . . . There is a striving to emphasize the essential character of the accidental."[46]

Summary and Conclusion

It was stated at the beginning of the chapter that our reconsideration of modernity would call for the realization of two objectives. On the one hand, we would have to evaluate Habermas's response to the disenchantment thesis, and on the other, to rethink disenchantment in light of this evaluation.

With respect to the first task, we eschewed an appraisal of Habermas's reaction to disenchantment that focused on either uncovering possible misinterpretations of Weber's argument or on highlighting internal weaknesses in Habermas's solution to the problem of disenchantment. We avoided such a route, not to suggest that shortcomings of this sort are nonexistent, but simply to lend as strong a reading as possible to Habermas's counter-thesis.

However, in so doing, we discovered that even from this position of relative strength, Habermas's argument remained mired in the technological ethic of domination. As noted, de-technologizing the system—which Habermas regards as necessary to affirm the centrality of communicative action within contemporary society—would require subordinating the system to the controlling demands of the lifeworld. It has been argued that, to the extent Habermas responds to the disenchantment of the world by transposing the function of societal steersman from the system to the lifeworld, his thesis remains bound by the logic of domination and mastery.

The claim put forward here is that the challenge of disenchantment—at the center of which lies the issue of technological control—can be effectively met only by first realizing that the technological ethic reflects a general human orientation toward being *per se*. Hence, Habermas's assertion that societal ills in a disenchanted world arise merely from a failure of politics was found wanting. As a result of Habermas's inability to meet the challenge of disenchantment, it became apparent that the realization of the chapter's second objective (i.e., the rethinking of disenchantment) would require broadening our study to include an examination of the human–nature relationship. The import of Adorno and Merleau-Ponty's esthetic theories to our investigation was shown to lie precisely in the fact that they underscore the fundamental interdependence of the human and natural worlds.

In conclusion, we noted that of the two esthetic theories reviewed, Merleau-Ponty's was the more promising because it better accounted for how we, as perceiving beings, may attune ourselves to what disenchantment has purged from the world, i.e., its mystery. Our remaining task—culminating in the endpoint of our reconsideration of modernity—is to elucidate the repercussions of this orientation for politics.

V

EMBODIED POLITICS

> Because every actor moves among and in relation
> to other acting beings, he is never merely a "doer"
> but always and at the same a sufferer.
>
> Hannah Arendt, *The Human Condition*

Weber informs us that science is "meaningless" because it is neutral with respect to ends. While it expands our power of control over nature and man, it remains silent on the question concerning how we ought to live. Science, he says, "presupposes that what is yielded by scientific work is important in the sense that it is 'worth being known.' " But this presumption cannot be verified by scientific means, and so we left to interpret its value according to "our ultimate position toward life."[1] It is precisely because science leaves aside the question concerning whether or not it ultimately makes sense to master life technically that Weber places so much emphasis on the need to articulate and uphold value orientations. The urgency of this task is heightened if we take into account the fact that he lived in a time when it was becoming abundantly clear that the realm of *technē* had been all but transformed into an end in itself.

This development—the ultimate consequence of the world's disenchantment—was of enormous concern to a number of observers. Before Weber, Nietzsche had prophesied that the modern landscape would be home to the "last men," those creatures who lived a tensionless existence in the here and now and who contented themselves in the vapid consumption of whatever lay before them. Weber himself, we have seen, spoke disparagingly of the advent of technicians—those "specialists without spirit"—and his equivalent of the last men—those "sensualists without heart." Horkheimer and Adorno warned us of the dawning of an age of "barbarism," where the masses are reduced to mere objects of administration.[2] Ellul predicted the "suppression of the subject" in the wake of technology's becoming "the determining factor in society."[3]

Others, whom we have not formally addressed in this study, are equally disconcerted over the repercussions of disenchantment. Alexandre Kojève, for instance, in his commentary on Hegel's *Phenomenology of Spirit*, hypothesizes that the collapse of the tension between the "is" and the "ought" within the liberal technocratic (universal and homogeneous) state would produce a reanimalized man, a being who "would play like young animals, and would indulge in love like adult beasts."[4] George Grant argues that because technology has become our new "religion," we have effectively lost our capacity to comprehend that which transcends the technological.[5] Hans Jonas concurs with this assessment when he says that technology has "turned into an infinite forward thrust of the race, its most significant enterprise, in whose permanent, self-transcending advance to ever greater things the vocation of man tends to be seen. . . ."[6]

Of course, Habermas too is deeply troubled by the determinative power of technology and system imperatives: Left unchecked, he fears the technological ethos would destroy communicative practices. Merleau-Ponty likewise is apprehensive over what might prevail in a world wholly given over to "operational" thinking. He alerts us to the fact that if

> this kind of thinking were to extend its reign to man and history . . . then, since man really becomes the *manipulandum* he takes himself to be, we enter a cultural regimen where there is neither truth nor falsity concerning man and history, in a sleep, or a nightmare, from which there is no awakening.[7]

Each of these individuals responds, in a particular way, to the crisis precipitated by the disenchantment of the world.[8] We have the call for an "overman" (Nietzsche's *übermensch*), for responsible scientific and political leadership in an ethically ambiguous universe (Weber), for openness to that which lies beyond mere human will (Ellul, Grant), for a revival of the kingdom of ends through politics (Habermas), for a reawakening of esthetic sensibilities (Adorno) and the experience of being-in-the-world (Merleau-Ponty).

What I intend to do at this point is explain the sense in which Merleau-Ponty's phenomenological ontology meets the challenge of disenchantment more satisfactorily than the other responses we have examined, especially those of Weber and Habermas. This critical examination will, in turn, provide a foundation for an analysis of a politics beyond disenchantment.

The Problem with 'Politics'

Notwithstanding obvious differences in their conclusions, both Weber and Habermas share the view that the challenge of disenchantment can be met effectively only through political action. Weber, as mentioned, was acutely aware of the modern propensity to subsume ends to means. Repeated reference to the loss of freedom experienced in a bureaucratized world is evidence of Weber's sensitivity to the negative repercussions of the disenchantment process. Yet, beneath gloomy prognostications about life in the iron cage, there remains in his thought an element of hope that offsets his otherwise dire forecast.

We noted that this guarded optimism stems from his conviction that the operations of reasoning and valuing are incommensurable. Because Weber asserted that the two are distinct, he was able to conclude that the increasingly technical nature of thought and action in modernity does not necessarily lead to a comparable restriction of our capacity to formulate values. In other words, the disenchantment process has left unimpaired our ability to articulate ends that are not mere rationalizations of the technological order's own internally generated demands. To be sure, Weber was well aware that the technological order in fact was fast becoming a "system," and that this development could lead only to the further entrenchment of purposive rational modes of action. However, for him this merely served to show the extent to which authentic valuation in modernity had become increasingly marginalized. In no way did he take this to be an indication of its fundamental incapacitation or irrelevance.

Given Weber's portrayal of the contemporary world as disenchanted, stripped of intrinsic value, he turns to politics as a principal means of reintroducing meaning to the world. If the world itself, he seems to say, no longer suggests the ends of human existence, then we must look to ourselves for such answers. The introspection required places the task beyond the reach of the means-ends mentality of the bureaucrat. The shaper of value must by definition be an artist of sorts. Such an individual must be able to both articulate a vision of the political good, and, importantly, command the means needed to realize this vision.

To this end, the supreme societal architect, the political leader, utilizes whatever means available to fashion a world that accords with a valuative vision. In a configuration of this sort there is a clearly defined hierarchical relationship between the realm of ends, or politics, and the realm of means, as technical modes of action. Hence, ideally, the administrative and technological "machines" are to be put to work in the service of the ends of the state as articulated by the political leader.[9] In the final analysis, then, Weber holds out hope against the irreversibility of the disenchantment process by arguing that the technological order and purposive rational forms of social organization are (as they have always been) value-neutral instruments and thus capable of being employed to realize subjectively held ends, the content of which is immune from the influence of the rationalization process itself.

As we have seen, Habermas is critical of Weber's assertion that effective resistance to the rationalization of the world can originate within the individual political actor alone. He argued in contrast that only by foresaking the philosophy of consciousness, which blinded Weber and others from seeing the potential for collective forms of political control, can a truly effective means be found for combatting the imbalance of forces (systemic versus communicative) that threatens society. Yet despite this putative correction, Habermas and Weber concur that the revitalization of "politics"—defined in general terms as the act of value articulation—is a prerequisite to overcoming the problems generated by disenchantment.

Aside from the previously stated concern over the spirit of domination that haunts Habermas's plan for rectifying societal anomie, there remains in his and indeed in all overtly political solutions to disenchantment a certain naiveté with respect to the overwhelming power and seductiveness of the technological ethos. The lifeworld, it can be argued, already is so thoroughly infiltrated by system imperatives that it is difficult to imagine how the process of decoupling these imperatives from communicative practices could be realized. This is especially true if one sympathizes with Grant's observation that technology has become our new religion. For if technology in fact constitutes the unanalyzed ideational horizon of the contemporary world, then it no longer makes sense to describe technology in terms of a discrete ensemble of technical practices that somehow has infiltrated a pre-existing communicative domain and therefore in principle can be filtered out. It becomes increasingly difficult to continue to identify technology as a pathogen invading the body politic after it has been so thoroughly incorporated by the patient.

It would be more accurate to say that we are dealing with a qualitatively new phenomenon, where communicative interactions have become so thoroughly reworked by system imperatives that it becomes pointless to identify them, however remotely, with what they once might have been. This is to argue that there is a difference between an interpretation that regards the advent of instrumental rationality as anathema to the logic of politics, and thus the source of its potential demise, and one that sees the technological ethos as comprising a lens through which our understanding of what constitutes politics is focused. The difference is between a reading that construes the impact of technology as distorting, and one that takes it to be thematizing.[10]

This difference is substantial, for it rests upon fundamentally divergent perceptions as to the nature of technology. Habermas, we have seen, insisted that only by realigning the imbalance of forces within society—that is, by favoring communicative over technical rationality—could the pathology afflicting society be overcome. To uphold such a view, however, presupposes that the technological ethos is delimitable and that its realm of influence can be restricted in the manner he suggests. We have argued here that Habermas's proposed solution is unsatisfactory precisely because it fails to meet the challenge it set for itself. In the final analysis, his reconstituted societal order is no less informed by the technological ethos than the order he attempted to rectify. The evidence is the fact that the move from a pathological to a non-pathological societal order entails nothing more than a reversal of the power relationship between systems and lifeworld, a move that does not alter the relationship's status as one of power.

That the logic of domination persists in Habermas's reconstructed social order illustrates the extent to which the technological ethos has a firm hold even on one of the most penetrating contemporary critiques of disenchantment. Not only does the revival of politics as envisioned by Habermas fail to undermine this ethic, it actually reinforces that ethic. For as we have seen, the ultimate objective of politics is to establish control over the self-generating technical imperatives that heretofore have propelled the disenchanted societal order—control that can be realized only by injecting value into an otherwise value-neutral world. The problem with politics so defined is that it seeks to surmount the ethic of instrumentalism from within the parameters of technical means, that is, while adhering to the major premise of instrumentalism. It is erroneously assumed that the disenchantment problematic can be resolved by mastering those forces that currently control operations within the natural and human environments.

We have presented reasons here for abandoning the political solutions of Weber and Habermas in favor of a more comprehensive approach to the problem. This does not mean, of course, that a critical response to disenchantment would not have a political component. Rather, we argue that such a response would require the establishment of an alternative ethos or world view upon which politics then could be grounded. For this reason I redirected our inquiry toward Adorno and Merleau-Ponty, for in their writings on esthetics and perception we find an attempt to formulate a non-technological mode of relating humans to the world.

The esthetic experience, we have noted, provides both Adorno and Merleau-Ponty with a model for a more muted relationship between self and other than is provided by arrangements based on mere mastery. Artists, more keenly than most people, realize there exists a genuine relationship between themselves and their natural and human environment. The world does not stand before them as an alien "thing," but as an "other" with which they share a certain complicity. Adorno, for one, portrayed artists as those who transcribe nature's aura, and intimated as well that this feat would be inconceivable if they and the world were not somehow attuned to each other.

Merleau-Ponty, as argued here, expressed more satisfactorily than Adorno a way in which we can account for this attunement. He depicted the incarnate subject as an opening within the texture of the world, and "wild perception" as the means by which the subject experiences this primal environment. Most important, Merleau-Ponty claimed that perception thus understood constitutes the ground of all reflective thought and therefore warned that reified conceptual thinking can only lead to disembodiment—to a self-understanding that overrides the concrete experience of being-in-the-world. The technological ethos promotes precisely this forgetfulness of the linkage between reflective thought and the direct perceptual experience of the world from which it arises and to which it ought to return. The hubris of this ethos lies in the mistaken assumption that the visible world, far from promising total actuality, is indeed "all actual under the perceptual gaze." The technological ethos denies the perspectival origin of reasoning in its presumption of the total synthesis of all possible perspectives or horizons. As a consequence, scientific reasoning transcends the experience of the world—which is invariably fragmentary—and constructs in its stead a closed "universe of meaning." The primary aim of Merleau-Ponty's critique of the scientific or technological ethos, then, is to underscore the violence that ethos perpetrates against the lived experience of the world.

Yet we cannot jump from this to the conclusion that science and perception are mutually antagonistic. Each can, under certain conditions, support the other. Merleau-Ponty cites Cézanne's admiration of the scientific principles of design and color as an example of a concrete instance where the two have worked in tandem. Here we see an artist who utilized whatever means were at his disposal in furtherance of his craft. However, Merleau-Ponty is quick to point out that the artist's craftsmanship—and hence the scientific principles that support it as well—ultimately remains subservient to the perceived world. What motivates the painter's movement, he says, can never be simply perspective or geometry or the laws governing color. . . . Motivating all the movements from which a painting gradually emerges there can be only one thing: the landscape in its totality and in its absolute fullness. . . .[11]

Merleau-Ponty in this passage is asserting, in a way comparable to Nietzsche, that what is of ultimate interest is not the nature of the resources used in the performance of some intellectual or esthetic act, but the rationale informing their usage. Whereas Nietzsche's criterion for determining the value of a thought or action hinged on whether or not it was "life-affirming," Merleau-Ponty seems to suggest it be based on the affirmation of perceptual experience. Accordingly, scientific reasoning is censurable only if it fails to enrich such an experience.

Because Merleau-Ponty takes our condition as beings in the world to be constitutive not only of reflective thought and esthetic expression but action as well, it remains to be seen how the "natural stance" plays itself out in the realm of human interrelations, or "politics" broadly defined. Hence this discourse on disenchantment will conclude with an analysis of the implications for politics of a non-technological mode of relating self to world. This will be accomplished in reference to what hereafter will be called "embodied politics."

Embodied Politics

An initial step toward the positive identification of embodied politics is taken when we account for what it is not, or, similarly, when we contrast it against its complement—disembodied politics. The chief characteristic of the latter is the presumed dissociation of the realm of ends from that of means. Political actors who function in a disembodied manner perceive themselves primarily as thinking subjects, or as thinking subjects who act. This is reflected in their understanding of politics as the business of determining the ends of society, the realization of which is then given over to the administrative apparatus and the technical milieu in general. Because politics here is understood primarily as an ends- or value-generating activity, it is, as with any operation cut off from the experience of the lived world, given to the formulation of closed systems of meaning. It is, in short, inclined toward the production of ideologies—universes of meaning that pertain to the proper ordering of human interactions.

If we re-examine Habermas's political prescriptions in the context of such an analysis, we see enfolded within them the tenets of disembodied politics. For one, there exists in his ideal societal order a clearly delineated division of function between the decolonized lifeworld and the ensemble of technical means. The former, as noted, comprises the social order's normative command center, whereas the latter operates as its delivery system. Moreover, one can argue, to anticipate Habermas's defense of the non-ideological character of communicative interaction, that his reconstituted social order's commitment to the ethos of control renders questionable the open-endedness of its politics. To be sure, the political domain is characterized by an interplay of valuative discourses and as such is indeterminate. However, when the social order is viewed comprehensively, it is evident that these discourses issue from a single, unifying ethic—the means-ends ethic.

In positive terms, embodied politics presupposes a reorientation in our understanding of the relationship between humans and world along the lines suggested by Merleau-Ponty's phenomenological ontology. There can be no concrete politics if the participating actors themselves are unaware of their embeddedness in the experiential world. A reinterpretation of what constitutes politics follows from Merleau-Ponty's admonition to "recover the primal world," as is evident when it is realized that for him the "visibles" of the world include all natural objects, human as well as non-human. Thus the alter ego—the other human being—occupies the same relationship to the incarnate subject as do non-human entities. Both are the "other side" of his flesh. This means, in effect, that the self and the other are oriented toward a single world; they are co-perceivers of this world because as they are exposed to the same field of being through their bodies.

Hence Merleau-Ponty can say that the "other" is not "an accident intruding from the outside upon a pure cognitive subject," but "a kind of replica of myself, a wandering double which haunts my surroundings."[12] Of course, the other is a duplication of myself in obviously being not literally myself. The other is merely a co-perceiver, but a co-perceiver with whom I nonetheless can identify to the extent that I realize our embeddedness in a common world.

Merleau-Ponty argues that this realization is possible only because we are able to generalize our own experience of openness toward the world. What is meant by this can be explained by the following example. Suppose that I, as a typical embodied perceiver, were to witness another person wiping his brow under the midday sun. I am able to perceive this individual and his actions only because he has entered my field of vision. However, if, as an embodied subject, my perception of him were not an opening upon the *same* world as his, then he would remain a mere "other" whose actions would have no meaning for me. For it is only because I perceive him while simultaneously experiencing the sun's heating effect upon my own body that I am able to interpret his gestures as a response to a world in which both he and I participate. In short, I would not be able to generalize myself—that is, to interpret his actions as a possible duplicate of mine—unless I first sensed our bodily co-presence within the world.

The co-presence of humans in the world manifests itself in ways other than through mute gesturing, however. Speech, for Merleau-Ponty, is also a kind of gesture and is generally taken to be the most evolved mode of human communication. While certainly not denying the centrality of speech, his reference to it as a gesture—or, more specifically, a "word-gesture"[13]—is an explicit attempt to convey the sense in which speech is a bodily phenomenon along with the non-linguistic gesture. In order to explain this affinity, it is important that we first take into account Merleau-Ponty's definition of speech as "the surplus of our existence over natural being."[14]

If we return momentarily to our previous analysis of esthetics, we see that artistic expression also has been shown to arise from a similar "surplus." Artists are physiologically constituted in such a way that their bodily sensitivity to being-in-the-world "commands" them, so to speak, to express the essence of their existential encounter. Were artists simply at home in the world, were their metabolism in perfect balance with its being, there would be no impulse, no surplus, urging them on to creative expression.

Speech, at least in a primordial or gestural sense, likewise is a way in which the body expresses its "surplus" over and above nature. It is a fundamentally bodily response to the way the incarnate subject is moved by the world. Merleau-Ponty refers to it as that form of emotional or dramaturgical gesticulation through which we come to "sing the world's praises."[15] There could be no speech, then, if humans were not part of the world's flesh, if they were not already sub-linguistically attuned to the world. In short, speech for Merleau-Ponty presupposes silence or a silent dialogue with nature. Speech is the power which literally gives voice to this silent communication.[16]

Having said this, it is obvious that human beings could not communicate to other human beings the meaning of their utterances unless they were to collectively assign specific meanings to particular word-gestures. For this reason gestural speech objectifies into language, into a culturally conditioned set of ready-made verbal significations. As speakers of language, people are able to make use of these sedimented word-gestures in ways that help them express their significative intentions. In describing this process, Merleau-Ponty wants to impress upon us the fact that beneath these sedimentations of speech there continues to exist a speech capable of initiating meaning or significance. This speech embodies a kind of creativity that renders it not a mere tool, but "a manifestation, a revelation of intimate being and of the psychic [ontological?] link which unites us to the world and our fellow men."[17] Merleau-Ponty's intention here is to show us that as practitioners of a language—of a cultural institution that is a repository for objectified significations— we risk overlooking the "miracle" of speech upon which it is founded and therefore the "worldly" origin of speech, as well. The danger of this oversight is akin to that which befalls operational thought. For just as the scientific mode of reasoning tends toward system-building as it becomes increasingly isolated from its perceptual origins, language in its removal from gestural speech exhibits a similar propensity toward becoming self-referential.

This being said, it is axiomatic that we live in a world where speech has become largely institutionalized. This means that speech "always comes into play against a background of speech. . . ."[18] Indeed, if this were not the case, there could be no communication between persons. For, Merleau-Ponty notes, our speech reaches the other, penetrates the other, only insofar as it creates a resonance within the other's pre-established linguistic significations. Thus without a common linguistic world—a ready-at-hand stock of shared significations— our words could never be received by the other as meaningful. Again, the form of the relationship between humans and nature is reproduced in that of interpersonal communication. Whereas the co-participation of the perceiving body and non-human entities in the world's natural flesh enables the two to interpenetrate and communicate chiasmatically, the co-participation of speaking subjects in the world's cultural flesh—that is, in language—enables them to interpenetrate linguistically and communicate meaningfully.

As previously stated, meaningful communication demands more than the mere exchange between individuals of meanings or understandings already in their possession. It requires as well that meaning be brought into existence, that new perspectives be opened up for consideration. Hence truly expressive dialogue must fulfill two seemingly contradictory requirements. First, the speaker must speak the language of the discussant in the sense that the speaker must make use of a stock of significations into which the other is capable of entering. Second, if the speaker is to bring meaning into existence, the speaker must shake the web of significations "in order to tear a new sound from it."[19] Of course, this latter requirement is not in truth incompatible with the former because the expression of a "new sound" necessarily requires only the disruption, not the abandonment, of pre-established significations. In other words, although truly expressive speech demands that an individual voice a significative intention without making reference to a given stock of sedimented signifiers, its expression, if it is to be communicable, always must retain at least an oblique reference to objectified meaning. Expressive speech, then, can contribute to the enrichment of language only by operating through the language which it disrupts.

In shaking the web of language, gestural speech confronts "the background of silence" surrounding it and constituting its ground. Speech elicits from its ground possible meanings that a given language has not yet signified. Hence authentic communication entails a kind of play, a delicate to-and-fro balance, between speech that reaffirms the cultural world of the discussants and speech that unsettles language by opening up fissures within it through which new concretions of meaning appear. This is why Merleau-Ponty says that "speech renews the mediation of the same and the other," for speech both preserves the existing linguistic tradition and simultaneously transcends it in the creation of new meaning.[20] Without this dual capacity, communicative speech would falter. For without the element of repetition, each discussant increasingly would retreat into a private world of meaning, and without the element of innovation, speech would be tedious, since nothing novel could be uttered.

The message underlying Merleau-Ponty's account of communication between embodied subjects can be summarized in the following manner. There is a tendency, not surprisingly in a world given over to technical reasoning, to view communication as an exercise in which participants use pre-established patterns of speech to "get across" the meaning they wish to convey. What is presupposed here is both a certain fixity with respect to the content of meaning and a faith in the capacity of these patterns of speech to capture that content adequately. What is absent from this understanding is what Merleau-Ponty takes to be the fundamental ambiguity of language and of ourselves as speaking beings. Just as natural objects are never "all actual under the perceptual gaze," so does the world elude complete expression through speech. And just as the incompleteness of the visible world is not a problem to be solved but rather is constitutive of the very act of perception, so is the indefinite power of speech not an obstacle to be overcome but a precondition of the possibility of communicating. Speech is inherently ambiguous because it is not, contrary to certain idealist readings, the "cipher of an original text" of meaning. Rather, as noted, it has the power of giving significance, of "singing the world," whose allusiveness is rooted in our "surplus" over and above nature. Thus the notion of "complete speech" is as nonsensical for Merleau-Ponty as the idea of "total visibility."

Since speech is invariably incomplete, linguistic communication itself must likewise exhibit the characteristic of inconclusiveness and hence be grounded in an openness to what is unfamiliar. Expressive speech has the power, against the backdrop of the cultural world, to draw together the participants within a dialogue, to account for our capacity to say the unexpected, to reveal the previously unrevealed, and to project it toward whomever our words are directed. In other words, whereas language assimilates speaking beings within a common "universe" of meaning, expressive speech accounts for the differentiation of meanings. But for Merleau-Ponty even this differentiating capacity of speech ultimately is conditioned by the cultural context of language. That is to say, it has a social origin in that our capacity to shake the web of significations always is modified by our dialogue with others. Simply put, we necessarily speak according "to what the other is saying."[21] Thus our capacity as speaking beings to both preserve and extend the limits of our speech never fully transcends the cultural world of language. Even when we inject new meaning into the world, we do so only by virtue of our participation "in a common effort more ancient than we," an effort which Merleau-Ponty observes, "concerns us, seduces us, trails us along, transforms us into the other and him into us. . . ."[22]

We are now at the point where we can begin to address directly the issue that prompted this overview of speech and language. In Merleau-Ponty's analysis of both esthetics and language there emerges a recurring pattern of features that seem to constitute the essence of being-in-the-world.[23] The first of these is that our perceptual and linguistic interactions with the world are of the kind that simultaneously encroach upon and are encroached by their 'object.' While this hardly denotes the relationship as antagonistic, it does convey the sense in which being-in-the-world is a dialogue between elements of Being, a dialogue sustained through the mutual invasion of these elements. The condition of being-in-the-world, then, is characterized in part by what I will call "the principle of reciprocal incursion." Secondly, we have seen that this feature of being-in-the-world presupposes the existence of a medium that supports it, namely, the world's flesh.[24] This mediating stratum that grounds the principle of reciprocal incursion, and which constitutes the other central characteristic of our embeddedness in the world, henceforth will be referred to as "the principle of ontological inclusiveness."[25]

If we assume that perceiving and speaking beings likewise are embodied when they act, then it follows that embodied politics must manifest the principles of reciprocal incursion and ontological inclusiveness as well. The question then becomes: What kind of politics is a politics informed by these principles? The answer to this question will provide us with a fuller, more positive understanding of embodied politics.

By applying the principle of reciprocal incursion to the realm of human relationships, we find that, for Merleau-Ponty, politics inescapably involves a measure of "violence."[26] That is to say, people's actions intrude upon one another's just as their perceptions encroach upon the visible and their speech invades the alter ego. Reference to politics as the domain of human interaction acknowledges the fact that human action is necessarily interconnected, that one's actions have an impact on—even alter the course of—the actions of others. Violence, then, is for Merleau-Ponty an irreducible feature of embodied politics. Every political act is bound to intrude, favorably or otherwise, on others' spheres of action and alter the nature of their commitment to them.

Because political choice, Merleau-Ponty notes in *Humanism and Terror*, occurs "only against a background of violence," an attempt to eliminate violence from political life would be as futile as the effort to articulate 'complete' speech.[27] Again, as with 'total' visibility or 'complete' speech, political violence is not to be viewed as a problem to be solved but as an unavoidable—indeed, an ontological—precondition of all political action. Thus the presence of violence *per se* within political life is insufficient grounds for reproving it. Merleau-Ponty observes, because we do not have a choice between purity and violence but between "different kinds of violence," an evaluation of political conduct can only operate on the assumption that certain forms of violence are more reprehensible than others.

An appraisal of political violence can proceed from either of two levels of analysis, one formal and the other substantive. When we approach political violence from the formal perspective, we witness Merleau-Ponty's antipathy toward any form of political violence that practices dissimulation. Hence, for instance, he censures traditional liberalism not for being a system of violence, but for not "seeing its own face in violence."[28] Likewise, his disillusionment with Communism arises from his dissatisfaction with its presumption that violence—which for Merleau-Ponty constitutes the very structure of political history—can be superceded in history. Both ideologies, therefore, are grounded in the myth of an age of innocence, the only difference between the two being that one assumes that the age has arrived while the other, that it is imminent.

Given Merleau-Ponty's criticism of the naiveté of both liberalism and Communism on the issue of violence, it is not surprising to find him attracted to Weber's political thought. He is not, however, drawn to the Weber who looked admiringly to those political leaders capable of guiding the social order out of its technical orbit. For according to Merleau-Ponty, even if such a leader were in a position of authority, he would have to contend with other actors in the public realm who are vying for a measure of political influence. As a result, he is partial to that aspect of Weber's thought which, although not in direct conflict with the need for political leaders, tends to stress political pluralism to a much greater degree. Merleau-Ponty is attracted, in short, to

Weber's so-called "new liberalism." Here we have an understanding of politics which acknowledges its violent backdrop and takes its end to be the business of procuring tentative balances between competing interests and relative truth claims.

What Merleau-Ponty admires most about Weber's new liberalism, this "militant . . . suffering, heroic" liberalism, as he calls it, is its self-doubt concerning its own claim to ultimate truth.[29] Just as speech for Merleau-Ponty constitutes truth rather than being constituted by it, political truth is not a given, not a "law of things," but that which forever "perseveres in becoming such a law."[30] Weber's wisdom, therefore, lies in his understanding of politics as an ongoing struggle to articulate and realize a conception of the good in a world that permits of multiple and contending conceptions. This also accounts for Merleau-Ponty's positive reception of Machiavelli's reading of history as "so many disorders, so many oppressions, so many . . . turnings-back," all of which suggested to Machiavelli that it was not predestined to achieve a final harmony.[31]

By acknowledging the ineradicability of political violence, a space is opened up within which it is possible to distinguish between a minimal or acceptable level of violence and one which exceeds it. The determination of this cut-off point requires an evaluation of the issue at hand from the second of Weber's perspectives, that is, from a substantive point of view. This in turn demands that we take into consideration the impact of the principle of ontological inclusiveness on politics and political violence.

Political problems, Merleau-Ponty tells us, arise from the fact that although we are all subjects, we invariably "look upon other persons as objects."[32] To a certain extent this is unavoidable, because action necessarily implies encroachment. However, just as the encroachment of my speech upon another can result in an enhancement of understanding, so too can action generate an enrichment of the political experience. What comprises this enrichment is not problematic, for the principle of ontological inclusiveness informs us that others, whether in their capacity as perceiving, speaking, or acting subjects, are the "other side" of my flesh. Thus our perceptions, speeches, and actions are necessarily directed toward elements (things, persons) of a world whose Being encompasses both poles of the interchange. Flesh perceives, speaks, and acts upon flesh. It follows, then, that embodied politics must aim at eliminating all violence that originates in the treatment of others as non-participants in the world's flesh, as mere *manipulanda*, as Merleau-Ponty might say. Therefore, any form of political life grounded in what could be called a "participatory ethic," is, from a substantive point of view, true to our condition as beings-in-the-world.

What precisely is meant by a "participatory ethic" needs to be addressed at this point. First, it should be noted that embodied action is participatory for the very reason that perception itself can be similarly described. Merleau-Ponty argued that because all subjects are exposed to the same field of being through their perceiving bodies, they are capable of entering into—or participating in—the perceptual experience of the other, thus bridging the epistemological gap separating perceiver and perceived, the latter in this instance being another perceiving being. The relationship between self and other in the realm of action is fundamentally comparable to this. The relationship of self and other, too, is participatory, in the sense that actors are able to enter into the behavioral experience of the other by virtue of their sharing a common world. But in this instance the "world" refers, not to the non-human realm, but to the created sociopolitical environment. Thus the ethic of participation implies the notion of "community," an awareness among actors of their co-presence within a given public space.

The term *community* is used here with some trepidation, for it is generally assumed that the establishment of a sense of belonging depends upon an agreement among actors about the ends of political life. However, community thus understood represents the ideal of disembodied, rather than embodied, politics. From the perspective of embodied politics, establishing a community of ends is not only undesirable but impossible (save with great violence), given the indeterminateness of our power to ascribe meaning, political or otherwise, to the world. True community, therefore, denotes a recognition amongst persons of their being situated in a world of their own making, yet whose meaning can never be unequivocally disclosed. This is to say that "community" suggests a shared context of experience more than a commonality of purpose. To assume that "community" ought to imply the latter is to ask of politics what cannot be satisfied even by an individual, namely, a definitive response to the question: "What am I?" or "What is my nature?" That we remain mysteries to ourselves as persons means, with all the greater force, that we remain a mystery to ourselves as a people or community. By embracing this indeterminateness, embodied political life necessarily becomes something "lived through," as opposed to "lived out" in accordance with determinate yet abstract principles of order. It acknowledges in its actions the insight that persons who act invariably have to deal with—or react to—the consequences of their actions, not all of which are foreseeable, no matter how well thought out in advance. One is reminded here of Hannah Arendt's observation that since "action acts upon beings who are capable of their own actions, reaction, apart from being a response, is always a new action that strikes out on its own and affects others."[33] To "live through" politics, then, is to perform deeds knowing that the political condition is such that no clean division separating 'acting' and 'being acted upon' exists.

Disembodied politics disregards this fundamental insight. It looks upon the business of politics as just another form of making, where the 'object' acted upon is taken to be ontologically distinct from the force acting upon it. The consequences of this oversight are particularly troubling when it is realized that neglect of the reciprocal character of action is often accompanied by a similar response to the limits of political knowledge. Hence the undeniable power of disembodied politics—its capacity to shape and control the human universe—is sustained by a double illusion. On the one hand, it presumes the body politic to be a 'thing' out there that can be molded in such a way as to approximate some posited ideal, as if it were not always already a part of the very process that seeks to reconstitute itself. On the other hand, disembodied politics necessarily operates under the pretence that the order to be realized is indeed "ideal," that it holds within it a simulacrum of truth.

Merleau-Ponty admires Weber's new liberalism precisely because it resists succumbing to either of these illusions. With respect to political 'truth,' Weber remained a steadfast skeptic. Liberalism in his view is characterized by the belief that no matter how fervently one ascribes to a set of political convictions, no claim can be rightfully made to its absolute truth. Contending political visions therefore must co-exist in an uneasy and evolving tension with each other. In Merleau-Ponty words, Weber's liberalism "recognizes the rights of its adversaries, refuses to hate them, relies only upon their own contradictions and upon discussions which oppose these."[34] It rests, in short, upon the principle of political toleration, a principle rooted, not in indifference to political commitments, but in the belief that these commitments are fundamentally irreconcilable and hence are deserving of mutual respect. It is a belief that Merleau-Ponty holds as his own.

Weber articulated as well another great insight into the political condition—the ambiguity of action. His liberalism, accordingly, is heroic not only to the extent that it acknowledges the fragility of 'truth,' but because it takes into account the consequences for politics of the interdependence of acting beings. When Weber commented on this aspect of the political condition as the "ethical irrationality of the world," he was merely observing what he took to be a truism. The realm of action is irrational or absurd because the reverberations set off by a person's deeds more often than not produce unintended results. Every public actor knows from experience that conviction and perspicacity are necessary but insufficient determinants of success in politics, that is, of one's capacity to realize intended objectives. A truly prudent actor responds by measuring the real consequences of the actions against their intended effect, and compensates for the difference by resetting his or her political sights. Weber's call to disengage politics from morality or "the ethic of ultimate ends" is grounded precisely on the fear that unyielding adherence to so-called "right principles" absolves actors of the responsibility for the consequences of their actions, and it is the consequences of actions, as much as actions themselves, which comprise the stuff of politics, in his view. Thus we can conclude by hypothesizing that a central feature of embodied politics is its self-conscious "unprincipledness," based on the acknowledged limitations of rule-bound action.

Merleau-Ponty cites Machiavelli along with Weber as a political thinker most acutely aware of the ambiguity of action. We are told that Machiavelli withdrew politics from moral judgment because he realized that "goodness is sometimes catastrophic and cruelty less cruel than the easy-going mood."[35] The message in both instances is the same: The actors who possess wisdom or *virtu* in political matters realize that they alone are responsible for the world they create. They cannot shirk this responsibility by claiming that their actions are dictated by the will of some inscrutable transcendent force, that they contribute to the further unfolding of the logic of history, or that they manifest the urgings of a personal daimon. Being situated in their own era, they are thoroughly and inextricably embroiled in the politics of the day. And having no completed text of action—no comprehensive political 'master plan'—they must maneuver within the existing political horizon with a sober sense of their own power and its limitations. Notwithstanding Merleau-Ponty's reservations over the specific content of the teachings of Machiavelli and Weber, he commends their underlying "humanism," that is, the seriousness with which they put in the hands of political actors the 'fate' of their community. Herein resides their virtue, in his estimation.

Merleau-Ponty's attraction to political humanism is understandable only when we see it for what it truly is, an attempt to refute the totalizing philosophies of history which explain the development of political affairs in terms of some overarching and extra-human dialectic, ideal or otherwise. What these philosophies of history necessarily presuppose is the transparency of humanity. They are constructs built on the assumption that humankind is an 'object' whose meaning is capable of being fully revealed to the perceptive observer. Merleau-Ponty vociferously rejects any such notion on the grounds that no 'object,' not an single person, let alone the totality of persons, can ever be "all actual under the gaze." The spatiotemporal situatedness of the perceiving and thinking subject rules out in advance the 'total gaze' required by the philosopher of history. In fact, if humans are in any sense predestined, their fate, according to Merleau-Ponty, leads them precisely in the opposite direction. That is to say, humans are ordained to remain a mystery to themselves in that their being is grounded in a world whose Being forever lies beyond their total perceptual or cognitive grasp. The mystery of humankind is inseparable from the mystery of Being.

If humans are destined to remain a question to themselves, as Merleau-Ponty asserts, then there is a density to their political existence which resists a single interpretation and accounts for their capacity to act in unforeseen ways. Each decision to act, Merleau-Ponty tells us, brings unforeseen consequences to which humans respond "by inventions which transform the problem." Therefore there is, in his estimation, "no situation without hope . . . no choice which terminates these deviations . . . and put[s] an end to his history."[36] Thus in the final analysis Merleau-Ponty agrees with Weber's observation that politics must be reclaimed by the "the political man."[37] Merleau-Ponty's critique of totalizing philosophies of history leads him ineluctably to conclude that the decisions of political actors do in fact make a difference, and that the repercussions of their decisions yield results which cannot be accounted for by referring to some logic of history.

There remains in Merleau-Ponty's treatment of embodied politics an outstanding difficulty that needs to be addressed at this point. I will do so by first sketching the backdrop against which this problem appears.

Merleau-Ponty's reflections on *virtu* seem to have been animated by his interest in a particular political phenomenon. Specifically, it has to do with the discrepancy between political rhetoric and action, so evident in both Marxist and liberal regimes, he notes. For Merleau-Ponty the only true measure of the worth of a society is the value it places upon the world of human relations.[38] An analysis of political rhetoric, as experience has taught us, is of little or no use in determining such worth. More often than not it knowingly obfuscates the actual status of such interrelations. One therefore is forced to look to real patterns of political action for answers. This Merleau-Ponty did, and, as we know, he uncovered in the process many instances of real eradicable violence flourishing in both Marxist and liberal regimes. What he appeared less interested in, it seems, was determining whether these patterns of eradicable violence within the two types of regime revealed any shared characteristics, or whether they issued from a common origin.

It has been argued in many circles for some time now, certainly prior to recent political developments in Eastern Europe and the now defunct Soviet Union, that the tension between the world's dominant ideologies as commonly formulated is largely spurious.[39] The critics claim that both liberalism and Communism are simply variants of "collective housekeeping." That is to say, differences in their rhetoric notwithstanding, both political systems seek primarily to supply their citizenry with the comforts of material life and create the conditions necessary to secure them. Hannah Arendt argued as much when she noted that modern politics concerns itself almost entirely with matters that the ancient Greeks considered were of interest within the private sphere alone. By making a public concern of what was once thought to be a private interest, politics today preoccupies itself with tending the economic garden, with cultivating an environment capable of both producing consumer goods and providing the means to their consumption. Because politics increasingly defines its active role in these terms, it effectively has aligned itself with the fate of technology and the domination of nature, for these are the primary means by which "the good life" is realized.

The world's leading ideologies (or should one say ideology?) take as axiomatic the interconnectedness of politics and technology, implicitly if not explicitly. The current demise of Communism therefore cannot be attributed to a unique flaw in its world view, which is largely indistinguishable from that of Western liberalism. Rather, the eclipse of Communism can be ascribed to the fact that over time the economic system most closely associated with it—the so-called "command economy"—has proved to be less efficient in delivery than the mixed economies of the First World. Communism is dying because it finds itself increasingly unable to justify in ideological terms an economic system that has failed to measure up to the only criterion of legitimacy in the technological era, the standard of efficiency.

It could be argued, then, that judging from appearances, the technological ethos holds sway over the politics of modernity and accounts for the value we place on our relations with others. If it is the force that shapes our age—the age of *Gestell*, as Heidegger put it—then one must ask in this context: Whither 'virtu? For if, as Merleau-Ponty tells us, virtuous political action demands in part being fully aware of one's time and its possibilities, and if, as it appears, the possibilities of our time are conditioned by the technological ethos, then it follows that politics cannot easily reclaim for itself an independent existence. Do we therefore resign ourselves to the fact that political virtue today entails no more than the search for and implementation of increasingly efficient delivery systems?

On a different level altogether, we could ask whether or not the temper of our times is at all conducive to the establishment of political community, as embodied politics requires. How reasonable is it to assume that political actors in our age, or in the foreseeable future for that matter, are capable of reversing the tendency to treat human beings as objects when politics' preoccupation with economic concerns—and hence with mastering nature—bespeaks of a continued fascination with the ethic of mastery? Has it not been, after all, a central theme of our discourse in this text that domination within the political sphere is but a manifestation of a more fundamental ethos and that without a reinterpretation of the human–nature nexus the difficulties associated with the political are bound to persist?

There is no simple answer to these questions. But in the absence of a definitive response I wish to make the following critical comments. Merleau-Ponty's observations on politics contain certain strengths and weaknesses. On the positive side, his political humanism acts as a countervailing force to the despair brought on by the recognition of the 'inevitability' of historical processes. Although it may seem to some a rather slim reed on which to lean, Merleau-Ponty's politics remains a politics of hope and as such it provides us with a standard of action which, if not realizable in our society as a whole, continues at least to serve as a model for our personal dealings with others as subjects. Acknowledging its circumscribed utility in this way may appear to be an admission of its impotence; however, one could just as easily interpret this supposed liability as its greatest strength. For as I have argued, the problem with politics traditionally conceived is its assumption that the difficulties attending disenchantment can be satisfactorily resolved by mobilizing forces themselves conditioned by the ethos they seek to overcome. In contrast, I have submitted that a genuinely effective challenge to disenchantment can arise only with the emergence of an ethic that comprehends the complicity of the human and the world, which lies beyond the capacity of mere 'political' agency.

The primary shortcoming of Merleau-Ponty's understanding of politics, on the other hand, is that it fails to integrate sufficiently the realm of action within the overarching context of being-in-the-world. It tends, on the contrary, to present political life exclusively in its own terms, as the discrete phenomenon of being-in-the-political-world. Political problems thus tend to be viewed in isolation from other sorts of difficulties. We have noted that Merleau-Ponty believes problems arise when people treat each other as objects rather than as subjects. Consequently, the solution for him involves incorporating more fully into political life the principle of ontological inclusiveness for the purpose of establishing what I have referred to as "community." What is intimated in this line of reasoning is that the political problem has a directly political solution.

I have maintained, in contrast, that no such solution exists, because the problem is not exclusively political in scope. To be sure, if the objectification of relations between persons were a problem of uniquely social origin, then Merleau-Ponty's reflections on *virtu* or embodied action doubtless would merit very serious consideration. That is why, when looked at on its own terms, his political writings (along with those of Weber) have an undeniable appeal. Thus we can say that the problem with Merleau-Ponty's politics has nothing to do with his politics *qua* politics. Rather, it has to do with the fact already mentioned in this chapter that embodied politics is only a partial solution to a more comprehensive and systemic problem.

The key to the solution of this larger problem I would argue already is contained within the rational core of Merleau-Ponty's phenomenological ontology. Specifically, it lies in the realization that the principle of ontological inclusiveness—of the world as flesh—is truly inclusive and therefore conjoins the political world with worldliness *per se*. Hence the solution hinges upon the realization that our capacity to interact with other human beings is, in addition to all other forms of communication, a general condition of being-in-the-world.

It perhaps would be wise at this point to reflect in a more leisurely manner on the endpoint of our discourse and its relation to the theme of disenchantment. The preceding chapter gave reasons explaining why Merleau-Ponty's phenomenological ontology, in theory at least, enables us to surmount particular difficulties associated with the Weberian and Habermasian responses to disenchantment. The present chapter then explained the way in which the basic principles underlying the experience of being-in-the-world are reflected in Merleau-Ponty's understanding of language and politics. It could be argued that if his insight into the human–nature nexus is a valid antidote to disenchantment, and if his political insights are grounded in a outlook consistent with his more directly theoretical claims, then Merleau-Ponty's politics ought to represent a clear alternative to disembodied politics.

However, as I hope is clear from the preceding discussion, I have asserted that Merleau-Ponty's politics ultimately must be examined from within a context more comprehensive than the merely political. In our case, this means that his politics must be understood in relation to the ethos that informs our age, the technological ethic. Doing this we see, as in reference above to Merleau-Ponty's analysis of *virtu*, that his political response to a disenchanted or rationalized world is inadequate. It is lacking precisely because it tends to isolate the outstanding political problem of our times—the treatment of persons as objects—from its underlying association with the rationalist tradition from which it springs.

I have argued here that if any real progress is to be made toward solving this political problem, it will come about only when questions pertaining to the ethic of domination have been thought through to their core. This discourse on disenchantment has attempted to do just that. We have concluded that because the technological ethos is sustained by a perceived discrepancy between the (mindless) being of nature and the (mindful) being of humans, the ethos is best counteracted by showing the ontological interrelatedness of the two kinds of beings. Thus ontology, according to this reading, is prior to politics—even to what has been referred to here as "embodied politics"—because humans' comportment toward each other as human beings is a special case of their bearing toward the "other" in general. Merleau-Ponty himself seems to have realized this much later in his career, when overtly political concerns commanded less of his attention.

Making such a claim, however, opens up very real possibilities for misinterpretation. For instance, it could be assumed that by asserting the priority of ontology over politics I am saying, in effect, the following: If only we could understand our embeddedness in the world, as outlined by Merleau-Ponty, then we would know how to act within the human world in a non-technological fashion. It might appear from this that the argument ironically ends up giving precedence to the very thing it originally set out to dethrone, disembodied thinking. This critique holds, however, only if it is assumed that being-in-the-world is fundamentally an intellectual experience. But this is precisely what it is not. Granted, one can reflect on it, as Adorno, Merleau-Ponty, Klee, and others have done. But thinking about the experience of worldliness is not to be confused with the experience itself. I have stressed the need to reflect on worldliness only because, in an age where the prevailing ethos is profoundly unworldly, an introduction to the experience requires self-conscious effort on our part. One has to somehow be forced into recognition of it.

This would be in sharp contrast to an age where the dominant ethos is characterized by worldliness. There people would tacitly acknowledge the living interconnection of humans and the world. Within the domain of politics, they would act with the understanding that no one either commands or obeys absolutely.[40] This is not to say that instrumental considerations in the sphere of political action would be ruled out entirely. Rather, it is merely to argue that political actors would remain attentive to the lived experiences of those whose lives they order as they formulate and implement policies. Thus the political upshot of Merleau-Ponty's ontology is quite unspectacular: It is nothing more and nothing less than a call for pragmatism based on an acknowledgement of the limits of 'rational' thought within the realm of action.

An objection could be raised at this point concerning the incompleteness of my analysis of embodied politics. More specifically, it could be argued that I have not spoken about it in sufficiently "concrete" terms, a grave shortcoming given my critique of the overly abstract orientation of its opposite, disembodied politics. It is true that there is a good deal of irony in an argument that stresses the importance of the concrete yet remains highly allusive and theoretical in its analysis of a matter as down to earth as politics. Yet this apparent inconsistency can be accounted for. My primary concern in this study has not been to articulate a reconstructed science of politics for the purpose of challenging the disenchantment thesis. I have avoided entering into this kind of argument because, as already stated, the difficulties we are faced with are more of an ontological than a straightforwardly political nature. As a result, I have indirectly argued that if these kinds of concerns were first addressed and then absorbed into what amounts to a world view, then the kind of politics that would ensue would exhibit the general features of what I have called "embodied politics." My primary concern here, then, has been to take this initial step.

Despite this defense, one still could imagine an argument underscoring the need to sketch a more substantive picture of this admittedly hypothetical political order. However, I have reservations about the appropriateness of even such an undertaking. For if I were to supply the reader with a detailed analysis of these political arrangements, this 'concrete' portrayal of embodied politics would no less continue to abide in the ether of speculation and theory. It would be yet another intellectual exercise in outlining a comprehensive framework for political action far removed from its actual execution. It would, in short, constitute the very kind of activity that lies at the root of disembodied politics.

As my argument stands, the gap between the ideal (embodied) and the real (disembodied) is substantial, and not predisposed to facile reconciliation. I realize that this conclusion is not liable to satisfy the demands of some for a more immediate and tangible response to the challenge of disenchantment. For them, arguments of the sort found in Bruce Wilshire's *The Moral Collapse of the University* will be more reassuring.[41] From a strategic viewpoint, at least, such studies may in fact be invaluable, for they bring to light and hence destabilize preconceptions about practices that have been moulded by the prevailing ethos of disembodiment. It is my hope that critiques of this sort may serve ultimately to reinforce the more general claims I have made here concerning a possible solution to the disenchantment problematic.

EPILOGUE

Mr. Palomar, the eponymic figure in Italo Calvino's novel, finds himself in a courtyard of the Ryoanji of Kyoto, one of Japan's most renowned Buddhist temples. He stands in silence and surveys the sand garden before him. What does he see? He sees a visual representation of an uneasy harmony between the human and non-human natural worlds. He sees the swirling patterns of "mankind-sand" flowing past and around the hard and indifferent substance of "world-boulder."[1] The harmony is tenuous because the human and non-human realms possess opposing logics. The latter exhibits a strangely capricious coherence, whereas the former is characterized by the search for continuity in order and meaning. Yet out of this tension an equilibrium is forged. It is realized to the extent that the cultural realm conforms to the vicissitudes of the natural world by adopting a similar kind of pliancy in its ordering.

Of course, because the object of Mr. Palomar's reflections is not of our time, neither is the substance of his reflection. He is a traveler, after all, a visitor not only from a different land but of another era as well. Still, the symbolism of the Japanese garden is not too removed from our present understanding of the human–nature relationship to make the garden of antiquarian interest only, for we share with the creators of the sand garden the view of the non-human natural world as indifferent to our concerns.

In contrast to what we might call the Japanese accomodation—or the Lucretian, for that matter—we moderns have chosen to resolve the tension between the human and natural orders by humanizing the latter through technological means. In principle, and increasingly in practice, the natural world for us is no longer viewed as 'other,' as an autonomous power capable of limiting the collective technological will. What limitations remain are perceived as mere challenges to mastery, challenges that, as Ellul tells us, we have every confidence of overcoming. But of course this is only half the story. This same ethos, referred to repeatedly here as "the technological ethos," claimed new territory when it trained its sights on the sociopolitical order as 'other.' The human world thus came to be perceived as an object, like any other, capable of being self-consciously remade to accord with an image of good order. The result has been the formation of a technological society, or what Michel Foucault prefers to call a "disciplinary society."

Whenever Weber speaks about our technologized or disenchanted world, one gets the distinct impression that his interest in it is guided by a practical concern, namely, how to live in the world as it is given in such a way that makes it worth living. There is in all of this no hint of nostalgia, no sense that he harbored any illusions about escaping modernity's iron cage by fleeing through the back door of metaphysics. In short, for Weber there is no turning back, no "journey home." The world in his view cannot be saved from its inherent meaninglessness through the self-defeating act of willing its meaningfulness. It cannot, in short, be self-consciously re-enchanted. Weber doubtless is right on this score. There is no journey home.

Or is there? The answer ultimately depends on one's understanding of a key term. On the one hand, if by "home" one means the initial point of departure, then there can be no turning back for the reason given above. However, if the word is interpreted more liberally as "habitat" or "dwelling place," then a return of sorts is possible. For the journey home in this instance would denote the act of entering the dwelling place—the earth or world—that constitutes the seat of human experience.

With Merleau-Ponty as guide, I have tried to show how this return might be conceived of. As noted in the Introduction, the journey home does not lead us back to the point from which we originally embarked. Rather, it brings us to a point outside the binary opposition "enchantment–disenchantment." It leads us to the world, to the place that sustains this dualism yet has never been truly entered into by either of its dialectical aspects. Viewed from this vantage point, both enchanted and disenchanted ages share one important characteristic—they are in flight from the world. In the former instance the world is discounted to the extent that it is perceived as a mere epiphenomenon of the supernatural, whereas in a disenchanted epoch the world's remove from the human realm triggers a response that leads to its humanization through technology.

With the aid of Merleau-Ponty I have indirectly asserted that the impulse to retreat from our embeddedness in the world, especially as it reveals itself in the disenchanted age, originates from a particular ontological disposition—from what might be referred to as "disenchantment with the world." As with an erstwhile friend with whom we have grown disillusioned, we have come to resent the perceived otherness of the natural and social worlds that resist our total command. We seek revenge by redoubling our commitment to the project of mastery, which, in turn, only serves to aggravate our sense of alienation.

By taking "disenchantment" to signify not simply the rationalization process, as did Weber, but the ontological condition that facilitates this process, we are closer to understanding the significance of Merleau-Ponty's contribution to this study. For precisely through neglect of our faith in the perceived world we have come to view the world, both natural and human, as mere extended matter and therefore a 'thing' to be worked over by the controlling mind. When read through the lens of Merleau-Ponty's phenomenological ontology, disenchantment reveals itself as a revolt against our status as beings-in-the-world.

As I have illustrated, those attempts to think through disenchantment which ignore our complicity with the world meet with an insurmountable difficulty. Interpreting the problematic as the flight of meaning from the world, they respond in kind by attempting to reinsert "value" into it. For Weber this is accomplished when leaders within the political community come to terms with the goals of their actions and assume personal responsibility for the consequences of these actions. Habermas, on the other hand, wishes to reinstate the vitality of communicative action as a means of articulating the ends of the societal order.

The problem with these 'political' solutions, it is argued, is that they effectively exacerbate the very phenomenon—i.e., disenchantment, or the alienation of humans from the world—they seek to discourage. While the reinsertion of value into the world might appear to be a viable cure for an age given over to instrumentalism, it ends up actually reinforcing that instrumental character by generating 'images' of order that purposive rational modes of action then set out to realize. That these images are to further truly human interests (as opposed to those supportive of technological control for its own sake) does not alter the fact that solutions of this sort are conditioned by their perception of politics as a form of "making" or *poiesis*. That is to say, they presuppose a fundamental distinction between the political actor as artist—as the bestower of meaning—and the meaningless raw materials employed in the furtherance of those ends.

Regardless of whether the articulation of ends is conceived of as originating within an individual (Weber) or a community of individuals (Habermas), there persists in these configurations a subject/object dualism that mirrors the epistemological rupture between the thinking ego and the object of thought, the rupture that precipitated the world's disenchantment. Given the fact that Weber and Habermas take politics to be an essentially productive enterprise, they refuse to situate the crisis of modernity in the realm of means— of purposive rational action—for at least this aspect of the productive process is fully operational. Rather, in their own separate ways, Weber and Habermas argue that the crisis arises from abdication of our responsibility to direct the realm of purposive action toward ends that satisfy truly human needs and wants, however they may be defined. They claim the modern project can be vindicated, then, only by regaining for ourselves the function of artificer.

Merleau-Ponty, in contrast, argues that the crisis of modernity lies not in our failing as 'artists' but in our adherence to an understanding of art as *poiesis*. To conceive of art as the production or concretizing of a concept is to assume the priority of mind (the image-maker) over body (the instrument of its materialization). In upholding this view, we remain locked within a horizon that gives pride of place to the ego and sustains disenchantment. Merleau-Ponty, as we know, counters this conception of art by asserting that art is the surplus expression— the overflow—of the artist's embodied relationship with the world. The esthetic temperment therefore is characterized by an acute sense of worldliness or being-in-the-world. But it is important to note that the capacity to experience the world is not privy to the artist alone, for, as embodied beings, all people, in principle at least, are open to the world in which they are situated. Indeed, every human gesture, as manifested in art, speech, action, or simply one's bodily comportment, reveals and expresses its connection to the world. Without belittling the term, we could say that all expressive human beings are artists whether they realize it or not. Of course, the point Merleau-Ponty wants to get across is that should we fail to acknowledge our human condition—our incarnate participation in the world—our gestures will register this failing. We will speak and act as if we were the sole authors of our utterances and deeds, having lost sight of the worldly context that supports authentic communication and action.

The challenge that disenchantment sets before us, then, cannot be met simply by injecting meaning into an otherwise meaningless world, as Weber and Habermas would have us believe. Rather, we must see to it that the meaning we retrieve from the world, and according to which we order our speech and actions, does not break with the ground that sustains it. It is only when a breach of this kind occurs that the question of meaning becomes a problem in the first place. For only then do we lose sight of the fact that the generation of meaning is not wholly arbitrary—that it is not what the thinking ego merely wills—but is conditioned by the worldly context within which we find ourselves.

Nowhere are the consequences of such forgetfulness more in evidence than in Weber's understanding of science. To recall, science for him is literally meaningless because it is neutral with respect to ends. It cannot, in short, supply an answer to questions of the sort: To what end ought our manipulation of the world be directed? Given its incapacity to do so, Weber concludes that science is merely an instrumental power in need of purposive guidance. What he overlooks in all of this is that the very phrasing of the question reflects a particular hidden 'value' orientation, i.e., a disenchanted attitude. For he assumes the power that allows us to manipulate the natural order does not itself issue from a particular way of conceiving the 'value' of this order. Thus he ignores the value-laden character of science and asserts its mere instrumentality on the grounds that it functions as if it were an instrument.

Of course, science does in fact function like an instrument if one presumes that what is—the being of the world—is incapable of possessing value. When the tangible world of things is believed to be valueless, no one acting within it would think of looking to this world to provide the 'ends' of that involvement. Weber clearly is committed to such a view. The same can be said for Habermas. What both overlook in the process is what such an orientation reveals about their and our unexamined relationship to the world. What it illustrates, I have argued, is our rejection of the world's communicative embrace. The technological 'world' we have created for ourselves is a tangible and forceful reminder of the fact that the world no longer commands our respect and hence has ceased to hold value. It reveals the extent to which humans have cut themselves off from the things that can speak for themselves.

The unspoken side of the disenchantment thesis, then, is its ontological underpinnings. That is the part glossed over by Weber and others in debates on the question of meaning in a disenchanted world. By focusing on this hidden dimension, as I have done here, with the help of Merleau-Ponty, a path opens up that allows us to extricate ourselves from the difficulties attending disenchantment without capitulating to its ethos. The first step along this path is taken when we realize that neither the disenchanted nor the traditional philosophic world views are capable of generating a definitive answer to questions concerning the ends of existence. As we know, the traditional philosophies took refuge from the surfeit of meaning by claiming that meaning originates from a source above the world. However, we also know that, in so doing, philosophy was unable to achieve its intended goal of stilling the flux of meaning. The proliferation of 'transcendent truths' continued apace. Entry into a post-metaphysical or disenchanted age did little to curb this tendency. In fact, as we are aware, it only served to intensify it by redirecting the locus of meaning outside the world, that is, within the isolated and unworldly *ego cogito*.

It has been argued here that an alternative to both these responses would be to locate meaning in the world. Hence resolving the disenchantment problematic would require realizing that meaning is neither simply subjective nor merely objective. It is not subjective because value is in the world as much as it is within the realm of the human. I have stressed the importance of Merleau-Ponty's analysis of speech in this discourse precisely because it presents us with an account of meaning that locates meaning in that which conjoins the human and the non-human, in the flesh of the world. On the other hand, for all this meaning is also not simply objective, because the world's flesh is open to multiple readings. There are innumerable ways to sing the world's praises, as Merleau-Ponty might say.

The political corollary to all this is that 'values' generated within the public sphere similarly issue from the unacknowledged "in-between" that binds acting selves. Accordingly, political actors neither have access within the world to the objective meaning of their world nor are at sea in their private imaginings as to its significance. The web of interactions that constitute the flesh of the public realm is the source of all political meaning, yet it is sufficiently multilayered to ensure that no single reading can adequately capture its complexity.

The solution to the challenge of disenchantment I have adumbrated in these pages is admittedly idealist. It is far removed from the real world of politics and technology. The question that invariably and understandably arises in such circumstances pertains to the value of an exercise that is of negligible practical consequence. I would respond first by noting that the grip the technological ethic has on our disenchanted world is so firm that it is becoming increasingly difficult to even imagine an authentic response to it, let alone realize such a response. Habermas's failing in this regard illustrates the point quite well. So there is a pressing need to articulate the contours of the problem and suggest at least a viable theoretical remedy.

The first objective, the primary concern of this study, is achieved when we realize that disenchantment cannot properly be ascribed to the retreat of meaning from the world *per se*, but to the disappearance of the world from modern consciousness. Almost none of the main actors in our discourse have responded to the disenchantment problematic in this manner because each, in his own way, assumes that what is missing in a rationalized world is authentic value. Hence, as we have seen, Weber looks to the political actor to lead us out of the technological wasteland, Lukács, to the collective consciousness of the proletariat, Blumenberg, to science itself, Ellul, to Christian ethics, Habermas, to the untapped communicative potential of the democratic masses, and so on.

The common failing of these responses is the assumption that because authentic value cannot be retrieved from a rationalized and disenchanted world, we are forced to look for it elsewhere—either in one of the few remaining enclaves within the world that resists its dominant ethos, or beyond the world altogether.

Outlining an alternative to this flawed strategy has required that we pursue a very different route. Rather than responding to the challenge of disenchantment by seeking refuge from our technological environment and its attendant "will to mastery," we critically examined this environment and found it to rest on a indefensible premise, i.e., our status as controlling, disembodied egos. By showing the extent to which such a premise betrays our living connection with the world we inhabit, we underscored the need to sustain and nurture the bond that unites us with the world, and with each other as inhabitants of the world.

Nurturing this bond, it has been argued, requires the development of an esthetic sensibility. Without it—without attuning ourselves to the "experience" of being-in-the-world—our subsequent reflections, not to mention the actions that flow from these reflections, will invariably turn back upon the world, seeking their revenge.

Notes

Preface

1. Apart from Alexandre Kojève's own commentary on the universal and homogeneous state in *Introduction to the Reading of Hegel*, tr. James H. Nichols, Jr. (Ithaca, NY: Cornell University Press, 1980), see also Barry Cooper, *The End of History: An Essay on Modern Hegelianism* (Toronto: University of Toronto Press, 1984); Tom Darby, *The Feast: Meditations on Politics and Time* (Toronto: University of Toronto Press, 1982); and Francis Fukuyama, *The End of History and the Last Man* (New York: Free Press, 1992).

2. Others whose writings have been influenced by Heidegger's depiction of modern technology in terms of a "will to planetary order," but who have not been included in this study, are Jacques Derrida and Michel Foucault. At the other end of the philosophical spectrum, the conservative reaction to disenchantment as articulated by Leo Strauss and Eric Voegelin remains unexplored as well.

Introduction

1. Max Horkheimer and Theodor Adorno, *Dialectic of Enlightenment*, tr. John Cumming (New York: Herder and Herder, 1972), p. 57.

Chapter One. The Setting

1. Aristotle, *Nicomachean Ethics*, tr. Martin Ostwald (New York: Library of Liberal Arts, 1962) see Book 6, 1140a–1141b 20. It should be noted at this point that my main concern is to elucidate the classical distinction between the theoretical sciences, on the one hand, and the productive sciences, on the other. Of course, there exists the practical sciences as well, the highest of which Aristotle held to be *politikē epistēmē*, or political science.

2. Aristotle, Book 6, 1140a 10. Aristotle phrases it in the following manner: "All art is concerned with the realm of coming-to-be, i.e., with contriving and studying how something which is capable of being and not being may come into existence. . . ."

3. René Descartes, "Discourse on the Method of Rightly Conducting the Reason and Seeking Truth in the Field of Science," in *Descartes: Philosophical Essays*, tr. Laurence J. Lafleur (New York: Library of the Liberal Arts, 1985), part 6, p. 45.

4. Descartes, pp. 45–46.

5. Quoted in Hiram Caton, *The Origin of Subjectivity: An Essay on Descartes* (New Haven, CT: Yale University Press, 1973), pp. 45–46.

6. René Descartes, "Rules for the Direction of the Mind," in *Descartes: Philosophical Essays*, Rule III, p. 154. Descartes notes that unreliable knowledge in past ages was not due to deficiencies in "common sense" or "reason," which he claims to be "mankind's most equitably divided endowment," but to an inability to use it well (part 1, p. 3). His codification of the "rules" of the mind is meant to rectify this shortcoming.

7. Descartes, "Discourse on the Method," part 2, p. 15.

8. René Descartes, "The Meditations Concerning First Philosophy," in *Descartes: Philosophical Essays*, Second Meditation, pp. 86–91.

9. Richard Rorty, *Philosophy and the Mirror of Nature* (Princeton, NJ: Princeton University Press, 1979). See his ch. 1 for an insightful analysis of the vital role played by Descartes and Bacon in the turn toward epistemology.

10. Francis Bacon, *The New Organon*, ed. Fulton H. Anderson (New York: Library of Liberal Arts, 1960), p. xxvi.

11. Immanuel Kant, "An Answer to the Question: 'What is Enlightenment'?" in *Kant's Political Writings*, ed. Hans Reiss (Cambridge: Cambridge University Press, 1970), p. 54. Kant explains his statement by arguing that: " 'Immaturity' is the inability to use one's own understanding without the guidance of another. The motto of enlightenment is therefore: *Sapere aude!* Have the courage to use your *own* understanding!" (emphasis in original).

12. Immanuel Kant, "Inquiry into the Distinctness of the Principles of Natural Theology and Morals," Fourth Observation. The quotation is in Ernst Cassirer, *Kant's Life and Thought*, tr. James Haden (New Haven, CT: Yale University Press, 1981), p. 233.

13. Auguste Comte, *The Essential Comte*, tr. Margaret Clarke, ed. Stanislav Andreski (New York: Barnes and Noble, 1974), p. 25.

14. Comte, pp. 23, 39.

15. Morris Berman, in *The Reenchantment of the World* (Ithaca, NY: Cornell University Press, 1981), argues persuasively in favor of the view that Newton, largely for political and economic reasons, found it prudent to remove the hermetic elements from his published scientific writings. See his ch. 4 for a more complete analysis.

16. Comte, pp. 27, 215.

17. Wilhelm Dilthey, *Gesammelte Schriften*, vol. 5, (Stuttgart: Teubner, 1961), pp. 12–13. (Author's translation)

18. Dilthey, vol. 5, p. 27. See also Ilse Bulhof's *Wilhelm Dilthey: A Hermeneutic Approach to the Study of History and Culture* (The Hague: Martinus Nijhoff, 1980), p. 25. (Author's translation)

19. Dilthey, vol. 5, p. 89. See Bulhof, pp. 25–29.

20. Quoted in Bulhof, p. 37.

21. Bulhof, pp. 41–56.

22. Bulhof, pp. 19–21.

23. Friedrich Nietzsche, "Birth of Tragedy," in *Basic Writings of Nietzsche*, tr. Walter Kaufmann (New York: Modern Library, 1968), sect. 1, p. 18.

24. Nietzsche, sect. 10, p. 74.

25. Friedrich Nietzsche, *Beyond Good and Evil*, tr. R.J. Hollingdale (London: Penguin, 1972), part 1, sect. 14, p. 26.

26. Friedrich Nietzsche, *Daybreak: Thoughts on the Prejudices of Morality*, tr. R.J. Hollingdale (Cambridge: Cambridge University Press, 1982), no. 450, pp. 189–190. The passage from which this observation is taken reads: "Does it not thrill all your senses—this sound of sweet allurement with which science has proclaimed its glad tidings, in a hundred phrases and in the hundred-and-first and fairest: 'Let delusion vanish!'?"

27. See Ofelia Schutte, *Beyond Nihilism: Nietzsche Without Masks* (Chicago: University of Chicago Press, 1984), pp. 48–56.

28. Thomas Hobbes, *Leviathan*, ed. Michael Oakeshott (New York: Collier, 1962), p. 19.

Chapter Two. The Disenchantment Thesis

1. Max Weber, *Roscher and Knies: The Logical Problems of Historical Economics* (New York: Free Press, 1975), p. 48.

2. Max Weber, " 'Objectivity' in Social Science," in *The Methododology of the Social Sciences*, ed. Edward A. Shils and Henry A. Finch (Glencoe, IL: Free Press, 1949), p. 81.

3. Friedrich Nietzsche, "On the Genealogy of Morals," in *On the Genealogy of Morals and Ecce Homo*, ed. Walter Kaufmann (New York: Vintage, 1969), Third Essay, sect. 12, p. 119.

4. Max Weber, "Science as a Vocation," in *From Max Weber: Essays in Sociology*, ed. Hans H. Gerth and C. Wright Mills (New York: Oxford University Press, 1946), p. 139.

5. F.M. Cornford, *From Religion to Philosophy: A Study in the Origins of Western Speculation* (New York: Harper and Row, 1957), p. 92.

6. Weber, "Science as a Vocation," p. 139.

7. Cornford, p. 158.

8. Lucretius, *The Nature of Things*, tr. Frank O. Copley (New York: Norton, 1977), p. 4.

9. Lucretius, p. 34.

10. Weber, "Science as a Vocation," p. 138.

11. Max Weber, *The Protestant Ethic and the Spirit of Capitalism*, tr. Talcott Parsons (New York: Scribner's, 1958), p. 113.

12. For an excellent analysis of Weber's multiformed notion of rationality, see Rogers Brubaker, *The Limits of Rationality* (London: George Allen & Unwin, 1984), especially chs. 1–3.

13. Max Weber, *Gesammelte Aufsätze zur Wissenschaftslehre* (Tübingen: Mohr, 1922), p. 408. See also Weber's "The Meaning of 'Ethical Neutrality'," in *The Methodology of the Social Sciences*. There Weber makes the distinction between a subjectively "rational" action and a "rationally 'correct' action, i.e., one which uses the objectively correct means in accord with scientific knowledge" (p. 34). Rogers Brubaker discusses this distinction, as well, in his *The Limits of Rationality*, pp. 53–60.

14. Weber, "Science as a Vocation," p. 147. See also Stephen K. White, *The Recent Work of Jürgen Habermas* (Cambridge: Cambridge University Press, 1987), p. 74.

15. This is a rereading of the line: "Many of the old gods ascend from their graves; they are disenchanted and hence take the form of impersonal forces," from Weber's "Science as a Vocation," p. 149.

16. Max Weber, "Religious Rejections of the World and Their Directions," in *From Max Weber: Essays in Sociology*, pp. 331–333.

17. Weber, *Protestant Ethic*, p. 182.

18. Weber, "Science as a Vocation," p. 144. Elsewhere he states that "the question of the appropriateness of the means for achieving a given end [i.e., a value] is undoubtedly accessible to scientific analysis" (" 'Objectivity' in Social Science," p. 52). That is all that is amenable to scientific scrutiny, however, according to Weber. Science therefore is a non-valuative instrument, a purely technical means, for the attainment of some desired end.

19. Weber, " 'Objectivity' in Social Science," p. 57.

20. Weber's thoughts on politics in a disenchanted world will be discussed in more detail in Chapters 3 and 5.

21. Weber, "Science as a Vocation," p. 139.

22. Michael Lowy, *Georg Lukács: From Romanticism to Bolshevism*, tr. Patrick Camiller (London: NLB, 1978), p. 109.

23. Georg Lukács, *History and Class Consciousness: Studies in Marxist Dialectics,* tr. Rodney Livingstone (Cambridge, MA: MIT Press, 1971), p. 88.

24. Lukács, pp. 84–86.

25. Gillian Rose, *Melancholy Science: An Introduction to the Thought of Theodor W. Adorno* (London: Macmillan, 1978), p. 3.

26. Max Horkheimer, *Eclipse of Reason* (New York: Oxford University Press, 1947), p. 176.

27. Horkheimer, p. 176.

28. Max Horkheimer and Theodor Adorno, "Excursus I: Odysseus or Myth and Enlightenment," in *Dialectic of Enlightenment*, tr. John Cumming (New York: Herder and Herder, 1972), pp. 43–80.

29. Horkheimer and Adorno, p. 55.

30. Horkheimer and Adorno, p. 6.

31. Horkheimer and Adorno, pp. 7–9.

32. Horkheimer and Adorno, p. 16.

33. Horkheimer and Adorno, p. 57.

34. Horkheimer and Adorno, pp. 18–27.

35. Horkheimer and Adorno, p. 25.

36. Horkheimer, *Eclipse of Reason*, p. 175.

37. Theodor Adorno, *Negative Dialectics*, tr. E.B. Ashton (New York: Seabury Press, 1974), p. 183.

38. Theodor Adorno, *Aesthetic Theory*, tr. Christian Lenhardt (New York: Routledge & Kegan Paul, 1984), p. 64.

39. Emile Durkheim, *The Rules of Sociological Method*, ed. George E.G. Catlin (New York: Free Press, 1964), p. 103. Durkheim's statement reads: "Society is not a mere sum of individuals. Rather, the system formed by their association represents a specific reality which has its own characteristics."

Hannah Arendt, for one, is critical of the functionalist stress in systems analysis. As she sees it, the "specific reality" of modernity suppresses "individual life" by redefining and reducing the end of life (for individuals) to laboring. For *homo laborans*, the end of existence is simply "the survival of the animal species man," she notes in *The Human Condition* (Chicago: University of Chicago Press, 1958), p. 321.

Richard J. Bernstein comments on Arendt's insights into the triumph of *homo laborans* in modernity in his *Philosophical Profiles: Essays in a Pragmatic Mode* (Philadelphia: University of Pennsylvania Press, 1986), ch. 9, "Rethinking the Social and the Political," pp. 238–259.

40. Some of the more illuminating texts on cybernetic theory include: R.W. Ashby, *An Introduction to Cybernetics* (London: Chapman and Hall, 1956); Edgar Morin, "Complexity," *The International Journal of Social Sciences*, vol. 26, no. 4 (1976), pp. 555–581; J. von Neumann, *Theory of Self-Reproducing Automata* (Urbana: University of Illinois Press, 1966); Norbert Wiener, *The Human Use of Human Beings* (New York: Avon, 1950) and *Cybernetics: Or Control and Communication in the Animal and the Machine* (Cambridge, MA: MIT Press, 1960). See also Tom Darby, ed., *Sojourns in the New World: Reflections on Technology* (Ottawa: Carleton University Press, 1986).

41. Jacques Ellul, *Perspectives on Our Age: Jacques Ellul Speaks on His Life and Work*, tr. Joachim Neugroschel, ed. William H. Vanderburg (Toronto: Canadian Broadcasting Corporation, 1981), p. 50.

42. Ellul, p. 34.

43. Jacques Ellul, *The Technological Society*, tr. John Wilkinson (New York: Vintage, 1964), p. 74.

44. Ellul, *Technological Society*, pp. 142–144.

45. Ellul, *Technological Society*, p. 136.

46. The following synopsis of Niklas Luhmann's social theory has been garnered primarily from his *The Differentiation of Society*, tr. Steven Holmes and Charles Larmore (New York: Columbia University Press, 1982). Secondary sources include Peter Beyer's introduction to Luhmann's *Religious Dogmatics and the Evolution of Societies*, tr. Peter Beyer (New York: Edwin Mellen, 1984), and Jonathan H. Turner, *The Structure of Sociological Theory* (Chicago: Dorsey, 1986, 4th ed.), pp. 102–125.

47. Jacques Ellul, *Perspectives on Our Age,* pp. 104–111.

Chapter Three. Modernity Vindicated

1. All references are to Thomas McCarthy's two-volume English translation of *The Theory of Communicative Action*, tr. Thomas McCarthy (Boston: Beacon Press, 1981).

2. Karl Löwith, *Meaning in History* (Chicago: University of Chicago Press, 1949), p. 192.

3. Eric Voegelin, *The New Science of Politics* (Chicago: University of Chicago Press, 1952), p. 121.

4. Hans Blumenberg, *The Legitimacy of the Modern Age* (Cambridge, MA: MIT Press, 1983), pp. 8–9.

5. Blumenberg, p. 116.

6. Blumenberg, p. 33.

7. Blumenberg, p. 46.

8. Blumenberg, pp. 137, 142.

9. Blumenberg, pp. 141–142.

10. Blumenberg, pp. 142, 177–178.

11. Max Weber, "Parliament and Government," in *Economy and Society*, ed. Guenther Roth and Claus Wittich (New York: Bedminster Press, 1968), p. 1438. For secondary commentary on this important issue, see Guenther Roth and Wolfgang Schluchter, *Max Weber's Vision of History: Ethics and Methods* (Berkeley and Los Angeles: University of California Press, 1979). The most pertinent chapters are "The Paradox of Rationalization: On the Relation of Ethics and World" and "Value-Neutrality and the Ethic of Responsibility."

12. George Grant speaks most eloquently about the dire consequences for the politics of freedom, and the protection by law of the rights of the individual, of a society ordered in accordance with the precepts of cybernetic control—the most salient being the principle of efficiency. He regards contractarian liberalism as an ally of the technological drive, as a co-contributor to the erosion of Western civilization's heretofore most cherished social and political virtues. The clearest presentation of Grant's position is contained in his *English-Speaking Justice* (Notre Dame, IN: University of Notre Dame Press, 1986). An excellent secondary source on Grant is to be found in Joan E. O'Donovan's *George Grant and the Twilight of Justice* (Toronto: University of Toronto Press, 1984).

13. Jürgen Habermas, *Toward a Rational Society: Student Protest, Science, and Politics*, tr. Jeremy J. Shapiro (Boston: Beacon Press, 1970), pp. 56–61. Habermas argues that as a result of these unplanned consequences precipitated by the advancement of technological forces, the human species has "challenged itself to learn not merely to affect its social destiny, but to control it." Hence, he concludes, the "challenge of technology cannot be met with technology alone," for, as a good Weberian, Habermas realizes that the control of objective processes in no way is concomitant with a knowledge of their value. See pp. 60–61.

14. Habermas, p. 57; see also Habermas, *Theory and Practice*, tr. John Viertel (Boston: Beacon Press, 1973), p. 155.

15. Jürgen Habermas, *Knowledge and Human Interests*, tr. Jeremy J. Shapiro (Boston: Beacon Press, 1971), p. 292.

16. Habermas, *Theory and Practice*, p. 44.

17. Habermas, *Theory and Practice*, p. 264.

18. Thomas McCarthy, *The Critical Theory of Jürgen Habermas* (Cambridge, MA: MIT Press, 1978), pp. 62–65.

19. Habermas, *Toward a Rational Society*, p. 61.

20. Habermas, *Theory and Practice*, p. 281.

21. Habermas, *Knowledge and Human Interests*, p. 292.

22. Habermas, *The Theory of Communicative Action*, vol. I, tr. Thomas McCarthy (Boston: Beacon press, 1984), pp. 6–7.

23. Habermas, *Theory of Communicative Action*, vol. I, pp. 173–274.

24. Habermas, *Theory of Communicative Action*, vol. I, p. 354.

25. Habermas, *Theory of Communicative Action*, vol. I, p. 372. Habermas is ill at ease with Lukács's claim that the proletariat remains fundamentally immune to reification. As he notes:

Lukács merely assures us that "while the process by which the worker is reified and becomes a commodity . . . dehumanizes him and atrophies his "soul," it remains true that precisely his *human nature* is not changed into a commodity" (emphasis added) (vol. I, p. 368).

26. Habermas, *Theory of Communicative Action*, vol. I, p. 364.

27. Habermas, *Theory of Communicative Action*, vol. I, p. 363.

28. Habermas, *Theory of Communicative Action*, vol. I, pp. 368–372.

29. Habermas, *Theory of Communicative Action*, vol. I, p. 379.

30. Habermas, *Theory of Communicative Action*, vol. I, p. 376.

31. Habermas, *Theory of Communicative Action*, vol. I, p. 378.

32. Habermas, *Theory of Communicative Action*, vol. I, p. 382.

33. Habermas, *Theory of Communicative Action*, vol. I, p. 384.

34. Habermas, *Theory of Communicative Action*, vol. I, p. 383. In short, Habermas maintains that mimesis cannot be spoken about. There can be no rational account, no *logos*, of the mimetic capacity. This shortcoming is said to automatically disqualify art from serious consideration as a legitimate and useful concept in critical theorizing.

35. Habermas, *Theory of Communicative Action*, vol. I, p. 385.

36. As Habermas puts it:

The program of early critical theory foundered not on this or that contingent circumstance, but from the exhaustion of the paradigm of the philosophy of consciousness. I shall argue that a change of paradigm to the theory of communication makes it possible to return to the under-standing that was *interrupted* with the critique of instrumental reason . . . (emphasis in original) (Habermas, *Theory of Communicative Action*, vol. I, p. 386).

37. Habermas, *Theory of Communicative Action*, vol. I, p. 391.

38. Habermas, *Theory of Communicative Action*, vol. II, tr. Thomas McCarthy (Boston; Beacon Press, 1987), pp. 301, 307.

39. Habermas, *Theory of Communicative Action*, vol. II, p. 303.

40. Habermas, *Theory of Communicative Action*, vol. I, p. 15.

41. Habermas, *Theory of Communicative Action*, vol. I, p. 388.

42. Habermas, *Theory of Communicative Action*, vol. I, p. 398.

43. Habermas, *Theory of Communicative Action*, vol. II, p. 323.

44. Habermas, *Theory of Communicative Action*, vol. II, p. 325.

45. Habermas, *Theory of Communicative Action*, vol. II, p. 153.

46. Habermas, *Theory of Communicative Action*, vol. II, p. 318.

47. Habermas, *Theory of Communicative Action*, vol. II, p. 186.

48. Habermas, *Theory of Communicative Action*, vol. II, p. 357.

49. In general terms, the task of "universal pragmatics" is to reconstruct the universal and rational conditions that account for consensual interaction (understanding), or, what amounts to the same thing, to unearth the "validity claims" that facilitate such an understanding. Habermas expounds on his theory of universal pragmatics in the following texts: *Communication and the Evolution of Society*, tr. Thomas McCarthy (Boston: Beacon Press, 1979), pp. 1–68; "On Systematically Distorted Communication," *Inquiry*, vol. 13 (1970), pp. 205–218; "Towards a Theory of Communicative Competence," *Inquiry*, vol. 13 (1970), pp. 360–375; "Some Distortions in Universal Pragmatics," *Theory and Society*, vol. 3 (1976), pp. 155–167. Insightful secondary sources on the matter include: Fred R. Dallmayr, *Language and Politics* (Notre Dame, IN: University of Notre Dame Press, 1984), pp. 123–136; Thomas McCarthy, "A Theory of Communicative Competence," *Philosophy of the Social Sciences*, vol. 3 (1973), pp. 135–156; Albrecht Wellmer, "Communications and Emancipation: Reflections on the Linguistic Turn in Critical Theory," in John O'Neill, *On Critical Theory* (New York: Seabury Press, 1976), pp. 231–263.

Chapter Four. Modernity Reconsidered

1. Jürgen Habermas, *The Theory of Communicative Action*, vol. I, "Reason and the Rationalization of Society," tr. Thomas McCarthy (Boston: Beacon Press, 1984), p. 398.

2. Habermas, p. 390.

3. This claim appears in volume II of Habermas's *The Theory of Communicative Action* (1987), pp. 275–276, but is extracted from Thomas McCarthy's introduction to the first volume of the two-volume English translation of the work (p. xxxi).

4. Plato, "Phadreus," in *The Collected Dialogues of Plato*, ed. Edith Hamilton and Huntington Cairns (Princeton, NJ: Princeton University Press, 1961), 230d, p. 479.

5. John Caputo, *Radical Hermeneutics: Repetition, Deconstruction, and the Hermeneutic Project* (Bloomington: Indiana University Press, 1987), pp. 223–224.

6. Paul Klee, *The Diaries of Paul Klee: 1898–1918*, ed. Felix Klee (Berkeley and Los Angeles: University of California Press, 1964), p. 194.

7. Theodor Adorno, *Aesthetic Theory*, tr. Christian Lenhardt (New York: Routledge & Kegan Paul, 1984), p. 116.

8. Adorno, p. 109.

9. Adorno, p. 105.

10. One is reminded here of Gadamer's observation:

Like a crystal, it [a work of art] has its own timeless necessity: folds of being itself, eroded lines, runes in which time itself comes to a standstill. Abstract? Concrete? Objective? Non-objective? It is a pledge of order.

See Hans-Georg Gadamer, "The Speechless Image," in *The Relevance of the Beautiful and Other Essays*, tr. Nicholas Walker (Cambridge: Cambridge University Press, 1986), p. 91.

11. Adorno, p. 129.

12. Adorno, p. 183.

13. Adorno, p. 453.

14. This quotation is taken from a lecture Klee gave in 1924 during an exhibition of his work in Jena. It is quoted in Constance Naubert-Riser's text, *Klee*, tr. John Greaves (London: Bracken, 1988), pp. 31–32.

15. Adorno, p. 453.

16. Adorno, p. 160.

17. Max Weber, "Science as a Vocation," in *From Max Weber: Essays in Sociology*, ed. Hans H. Gerth and C. Wright Mills (New York: Oxford University Press, 1946), p. 155.

18. Maurice Merleau-Ponty, *Phenomenology of Perception*, tr. Colin Smith (London: Routledge & Kegan Paul, 1962), pp. viii, ix.

19. Maurice Merleau-Ponty, "Eye and Mind," in *The Essential Writings of Merleau-Ponty*, ed. Alden Fisher (New York: Harcourt, Brace and World, 1969), p. 252.

20. Merleau-Ponty, *Phenomenology of Perception*, p. 395. See also the chapter entitled, "The Cogito," pp. 369–409.

21. Maurice Merleau-Ponty, *The Primacy of Perception*, ed. James M. Edie (Evanston, IL: Northwestern University Press, 1964), p. 42.

22. Maurice Merleau-Ponty, *The Structure of Behavior* (Boston: Beacon Press, 1963), p. 201.

23. Merleau-Ponty, *Phenomenology of Perception*, pp. xvi–xvii.

24. Merleau-Ponty, *Phenomenology of Perception*, p. xvii.

25. Maurice Merleau-Ponty, "Nature and Logos: The Human Body," in *Themes from the Lectures*, tr. John O'Neill (Evanston, IL: Northwestern University Press, 1970), p. 128.

26. Maurice Merleau-Ponty, "Working Notes," *The Visible and the Invisible*, ed. Claude Lefort (Evanston, IL: Northwestern University Press, 1968), p. 129.

27. Merleau-Ponty, *Visible and Invisible*, p. 137. Merleau-Ponty comments further:

> We have to reject the age-old assumptions that put the body in the world and the see-er in the body, or, conversely, the world and the body in the see-er as in a box. Where are we to put the limit between the body and the world, since the world is flesh? . . . The world seen is not "in" my body, and my body is not "in" the visible world ultimately: As flesh applied to a flesh, the world neither surrounds it nor is surrounded by it. A participation in and kinship with the visible, the vision neither envelops it nor is enveloped by it definitively. The superficial pellicle [membrane] of the visible is only for my vision and for my body. *But the depth beneath this surface contains my body and hence my vision.* My body as a visible thing is contained within the full spectacle. But my seeing body subtends [extends under] this visible body, and all the visibles with it. There is a reciprocal insertion and intertwining of one in the other (emphasis added) (p. 138).

28. Merleau-Ponty, *Visible and Invisible*, pp. 134, 135.

29. Merleau-Ponty, *Visible and Invisible*, p. 261.

30. Merleau-Ponty, *Visible and Invisible*, p. 146. As Merleau-Ponty explains elsewhere in the text:

My body is made of the same flesh as the world (it is a perceived), and [because] this flesh of my body is shared by the world, the world reflects it, encroaches upon it and it encroaches upon the world. . . . They are in a relation of transgression or of overlapping. . . (p. 248).

31. Merleau-Ponty, *Visible and Invisible*, p. 274.

32. Merleau-Ponty, *Visible and Invisible*, p. 28.

33. Merleau-Ponty, *Visible and Invisible*, pp. 136, 149.

34. Merleau-Ponty, *Visible and Invisible*, p. 229. Merleau-Ponty says of Being that: "It is the invisible of this world . . . which inhabits this world, sustains it, and renders it visible, its own and interior possibility. . ." (p. 151).

35. Merleau-Ponty, *Visible and Invisible*, p. 191.

36. Merleau-Ponty, "Eye and Mind," p. 255.

37. Merleau-Ponty, "Eye and Mind," p. 273.

38. Merleau-Ponty, "Eye and Mind," p. 257.

39. Merleau-Ponty, "Eye and Mind," p. 283.

40. Naubert-Riser, *Klee*, p. 32.

41. Merleau-Ponty, "Eye and Mind," p. 259.

42. Adorno, p. 118.

43. Merleau-Ponty, "Eye and Mind," pp. 259, 260.

44. Merleau-Ponty, "Eye and Mind," p. 259.

45. Merleau-Ponty, "Eye and Mind," p. 258.

46. This quotation is taken from an essay entitled "Creative Credo," published in 1920 in the symposium *Schopferische Konfession*. It is quoted in Will Grohmann's *Klee* (New York: Harry N. Abrams, 1985), p. 16.

Chapter Five. Embodied Politics

1. Max Weber, "Science as a Vocation," in *From Max Weber: Essays in Sociology*, ed. Hans H. Gerth and C. Wright Mills (New York: Oxford University Press, 1946), p. 143.

2. Max Horkheimer and Theodor Adorno, *Dialectic of Enlightenment*, tr. John Cumming (New York: Continuum, 1988), p. 38.

3. Jacques Ellul, *Perspectives on Our Age: Jacques Ellul Speaks on His Life and Work*, tr. Joachim Neugroschel, ed. William Vanderburg, (Toronto: Canadian Broadcasting Corporation, 1981), pp. 49, 69.

4. Alexandre Kojève, "Note to the Second Edition," *Introduction to the Reading of Hegel*, tr. James H. Nichols, Jr. (Ithaca, NY: Cornell University Press, 1980), p. 159.

5. George Grant, *Lament for a Nation: The Defeat of Canadian Nationalism* (Toronto: McClelland and Stewart, 1965), pp. ix, 55, 56, 58.

6. Hans Jonas, *The Imperative of Responsibility: In Search of an Ethics for the Technological Age* (Chicago: University of Chicago Press, 1984), p. 9.

7. Maurice Merleau-Ponty, "Eye and Mind," in *The Essential Writings of Merleau-Ponty*, ed. Alden Fisher (New York: Harcourt, Brace & World, 1969), pp. 253, 254.

8. Alexandre Kojève is excluded from the list because he claims, in essence, that there can be no challenging response. He accepts the view, as Bloom notes in his introduction to Kojève's text, that the liberal state affirms in principle the dignity of all humans, and that all there is left to do is realize our humanity throughout the world.

9. As Max Weber says, the bureaucrat or "genuine official" is not engaged in politics but in impartial "administration." He is a follower insofar as he executes "the order of the superior authorities." His ultimate superior is the political leader who, unlike him, takes a stand and "fights" for a cause. The true political leader, then, exercises authority because his dictates are not conditioned by a pre-existing set of rational rules but are a product of a passionate commitment to a vision of the political good. See especially "Politics as a Vocation," in *From Max Weber*, pp. 78–96.

10. Martin Heidegger is the most influential exponent of the thesis claiming technology to be a thematizing phenomenon. See *The Question Concerning Technology and Other Essays*, tr. William Lovitt (New York: Harper and Row, 1977).

11. Maurice Merleau-Ponty, "Cézanne's Doubt," in *Sense and Non-Sense*, tr. Hubert Dreyfus and Patricia Dreyfus (Evanston, IL: Northwestern University Press, 1964), p. 17.

12. Maurice Merleau-Ponty, "Dialogue and the Perception of the Other," in *The Prose of the World*, tr. John O'Neill (Evanston, IL: Northwestern University Press, 1973), pp. 139, 134.

13. Maurice Merleau-Ponty, "The Body as Expression and Speech," in *Phenomenology of Perception*, tr. Colin Smith (New York: Routledge & Kegan Paul, 1962), p. 194.

14. Merleau-Ponty, "The Body as Expression," p. 197.

15. Merleau-Ponty, "The Body as Expression," p. 187.

16. If Merleau-Ponty is correct, if speech arises from a silent communication with the world, then reason too has its origin in the unsaid, the unspoken. But if this in turn is true, then it no longer makes sense to

differentiate reason *qua* speech from so-called extra-linguistic modes of reasoning, as Habermas and others insist, for all modes of reasoning spring from the same silent ground.

17. Merleau-Ponty, "The Body as Expression," p. 196.

18. Maurice Merleau-Ponty, "Indirect Language and the Voices of Silence," in *Signs*, tr. Richard McCleary (Evanston, IL: Northwestern University Press, 1964), p. 42.

19. Merleau-Ponty, "Indirect Language," p. 46.

20. Merleau-Ponty, "Dialogue and the Perception of the Other," in *The Prose of the World*, ed. Claude Lefort (Evanston, IL: Northwestern University Press, 1973), p. 142.

21. Merleau-Ponty, "Dialogue," p. 145.

22. Merleau-Ponty, "Dialogue," p. 144.

23. The approach I have taken in my analysis of embodied politics is indebted to Monika Langer's article, "Merleau-Ponty: The Ontological Limitations of Politics," in *Domination*, ed. Alkis Kontos (Toronto: University of Toronto Press, 1975), pp. 102–113.

24. I mean by "flesh" both the Being of the world and what I previously have defined as the world's cultural flesh, namely, language.

25. In stating that this principle is ontologically grounded, it would be misleading to assume the principle of reciprocal incursion is not as well, since it is a characteristic of being-in-the-world.

26. The applicability of Merleau-Ponty's ontology to overcoming domination through politics could be questioned by noting that he whose theoretical claims I have used to resolve the problems of disenchantment, was, in his overtly political writings, an apologist for Stalinist terror (see *Humanism and Terror: An Essay on the Communist Problem*, tr. John O'Neill (Boston: Beacon Press, 1969)). While it is true that Merleau-Ponty at one point did not reject force to achieve his desired political end—(a world free of political and economic domination)—it is equally true that he soon became disillusioned with the ideological rigidity and the repressive policies of Communist parties in Europe and the Soviet Union. He was, in short, no ideological sycophant. This is clearly evidenced in his eventual repudiation of Communist doctrine and his alignment with Weber's "new liberalism." The point to be made here is that Merleau-Ponty's politics underwent an evolutionary change, just as did his more straightforwardly theoretical insights.

As my interest in Merleau-Ponty's theoretical writings focuses primarily on his later work on the "philosophy of the flesh," so too am I mainly concerned with his analysis of a new liberalism, which I think better reflects the content of what I refer to as "embodied politics" than his earlier political orientation. Beyond this, I want to make it clear that I do not believe my presentation of embodied politics stands or falls with the particulars of Merleau-Ponty's political views, early or late. I refer to his politics only to suggest the general contours of a politics beyond disenchantment.

27. Maurice Merleau-Ponty, "From the Proletarian to the Commissar," in *Humanism and Terror*, p. 109.

28. Merleau-Ponty, "Bukharin and the Ambiguity of History, in *Humanism and Terror*, p. 35, fn. 11.

29. Maurice Merleau-Ponty, "The Crisis of Understanding," in *Adventures of the Dialectic*, tr. Joseph Bien (Evanston, IL: Northwestern University Press, 1973), p. 26.

30. Merleau-Ponty, "Crisis of Understanding," p. 9.

31. Merleau-Ponty, "A Note on Machiavelli," in *Signs*, p. 218.

32. Merleau-Ponty, "From Proletarian to Commissar," p. 110.

33. Hannah Arendt, *The Human Condition* (Chicago: University of Chicago Press, 1958), p. 190.

34. Merleau-Ponty, "Crisis of Understanding," p. 26.

35. Merleau-Ponty, "Note on Machiavelli," p. 216.

36. Merleau-Ponty, "Crisis of Understanding," p. 23.

37. Merleau-Ponty, "Crisis of Understanding," p. 28.

38. Merleau-Ponty, "Author's Preface," in *Humanism and Terror*, p. xiv.

39. This critique is hardly exhaustive. See arguments presented in Alexandre Kojève, *Introduction to the Reading of Hegel*, tr. James H. Nichols Jr., ed. Allan Bloom (Ithaca, NY: Cornell University Press, 1969); Tom Darby, *The Feast: Meditations on Politics and Time* (Toronto: University of Toronto Press, 1982); Francis Fukuyama's article, "The End of History?" in the Summer 1989 issue of the Washington quarterly, *National Interest*, along with critical commentary in both the Summer and Fall issues of that periodical; and Francis Fukuyama, *The End of History and the Last Man* (New York: Free Press, 1992).

40. Bernard P. Dauenhauer, "Merleau-Ponty's Political Thought: Its Nature and Challenge," in *Phenomenology in a Pluralistic Context*, ed. William L. McBride and Calvin O. Schrag (Albany: State University of New York Press, 1983), p. 18.

41. Wilshire attributes what he perceives to be the crisis of "professionalism" in the modern university to a Cartesian-inspired fear of "mimetic engulfment," the term used to denote the intertwining of self and other. Thus university professors, through numerous "purification rituals," distance themselves from the uninitiated—their students, faculty members in disciplines unrelated to their own, etc. See Bruce Wilshire, *The Moral Collapse of the*

University: Professionalism, Purity, and Alienation (Albany: State University of New York Press, 1990).

Epilogue

1. Italo Calvino, *Mr. Palomar,* tr. William Weaver (New York: Harcourt Brace Jovanovich, 1983), pp. 91–94.

Bibliography

Primary Sources

Adorno, Theodor W. *Aesthetic Theory.* Translated by Christian Lenhardt. Gretel Adorno and Rolf Tiedemann, eds. New York: Routledge & Kegan Paul, 1984.

———. *Negative Dialectics.* Translated by E.B. Ashton. New York: The Seabury Press, 1974.

Adorno, Theodor, and **Horkheimer, Max.** *Dialectic of Enlightenment.* New York: Continuum, 1988.

Arato, Andrew, and **Gebhardt, Eike,** eds. *The Essential Frankfurt School Reader.* New York: Routledge & Kegan Paul, 1978.

Aristotle. *Nicomachean Ethics.* Translated by Martin Ostwald. New York: The Library of Liberal Arts, 1962.

Bacon, Francis. *The New Organon.* Fulton H. Anderson, ed. New York: The Library of Liberal Arts, 1960.

Blumenberg, Hans. *The Legitimacy of the Modern Age.* Cambridge, MA: The MIT Press, 1983.

Comte, Auguste. *Auguste Comte: The Foundation of Sociology.* Kenneth Thompson, ed. New York: John Wiley & Sons, 1975.

———. *The Essential Comte.* Translated by Margaret Clarke. Stanislav Andreski, ed. New York: Barnes and Noble, 1974.

———. *A General View of Positivism.* Translated by J.H. Bridges. New York: Robert Speller and Sons, 1957.

Descartes, René. *Philosophical Essays.* Translated by Laurence J. Lafleur. New York: The Library of Liberal Arts, 1985.

Dilthey, Wilhelm. *Gesammelte Schriften.* Stuttgart: B.G. Teubner Verlagsgesellschaft, 1961.

Durkheim, Emile. *The Rules of Sociological Method.* George E.G. Catlin, ed. New York: The Free Press, 1964.

Ellul, Jacques. *Perspectives on Our Age: Jacques Ellul Speaks on His Life and Work.* Translated by Joachim Neugroschel. William H. Vanderburg, ed. Toronto: Canadian Broadcasting Corporation, 1981.

———. *The Technological Society.* Translated by John Wilkinson. New York: Vintage Books, 1964.

Habermas, Jürgen. *Communication and the Evolution of Society.* Translated by Thomas McCarthy. Boston: Beacon Press, 1979.

———. *Knowledge and Human Interests.* Translated by Jeremy J. Shapiro. Boston: Beacon Press, 1971.

———. *Legitimation Crisis.* Translated by Thomas McCarthy. Boston: Beacon Press, 1975.

———. "On Systematically Distorted Communication." *Inquiry*, vol. 13 (1970), pp. 205–218.

———. *The Philosophical Discourse of Modernity.* Translated by Frederick Lawrence. Cambridge: Polity Press, 1987.

———. "Some Distortions in Universal Pragmatics." *Theory and Society*, vol. 3 (1976), pp. 155–167.

———. *Theory and Practice.* Translated by John Viertel. Boston: Beacon Press, 1973.

———. *The Theory of Communicative Action.* 2 vols. Translated by Thomas McCarthy. Boston: Beacon Press, 1984, 1987.

———. *Toward a Rational Society: Student Protest, Science, and Politics.* Translated by Jeremy J. Shapiro. Boston: Beacon Press, 1970.

———. "Towards a Theory of Communicative Competence." *Inquiry*, vol. 13 (1970), pp. 360–375.

Horkheimer, Max. *Eclipse of Reason*. Oxford: Oxford University Press, 1947.

Horkheimer, Max, and Adorno, Theodor. *Dialectic of Enlightenment*. Translated by John Cumming. New York: Continuum, 1988.

Kant, Immanuel. *Critique of Pure Reason*. Translated by Norman Kemp Smith. New York: The Humanities Press, 1950.

Klcc, Paul. *The Diaries of Paul Klee: 1898–1918*. Felix Klee, ed. Berkeley and Los Angeles: University of California Press, 1964.

Luhmann, Niklas. *The Differentiation of Society*. Translated by Steven Holmes and Charles Larmore. New York: Columbia University Press, 1982.

———. *Religious Dogmatics and the Evolution of Societies*. Translated by Peter Beyer. New York: The Edwin Mellen Press, 1984.

———. *A Sociological Theory of Law*. Translated by Martin Albrow. London; Routledge & Kegan Paul, 1985.

———. *Trust and Power*. 2 vols. Translated by Howard Davis, John Raffan, and Kathryn Rooney. Tom Burns and Gianfranco Poggi, eds. Toronto: Wiley & Sons, 1979.

Lukács, Georg. *History and Class Consciousness: Studies in Marxist Dialectics*. Translated by Rodney Livingstone. Cambridge, MA: The MIT Press, 1971.

Merleau-Ponty, Maurice. *Adventures of the Dialectic*. Translated by Joseph Bien. Evanston, IL: Northwestern University Press, 1973.

———. "Eye and Mind." In *The Essential Writings of Merleau-Ponty*. Alden Fisher, ed. New York: Harcourt, Brace and World, 1969.

———. *Humanism and Terror: An Essay on the Communist Problem*. Translated by John O'Neill. Boston: Beacon Press, 1969.

———. *Phenomenology of Perception*. Translated by Colin Smith. London: Routledge & Kegan Paul, 1962.

———. *The Primacy of Perception.* Translated by William Cobb, Arleen Dallery, Carleton Dallery, James Edie, John Flodstrom, Nancy Metzel, and John Wild. James M. Edie, ed. Evanston, IL: Northwestern University Press, 1964.

———. *The Prose of the World.* Translated by John O'Neill. Evanston, IL: Northwestern University Press, 1973.

———. *Sense and Non-Sense.* Translated by Hubert Dreyfus and Patricia Dreyfus. Evanston, IL: Northwestern University Press, 1964.

———. *Signs.* Translated by Richard McCleary. Evanston, IL: Northwestern University Press, 1964.

———. *The Structure of Behavior.* Translated by Alden Fisher. Boston: Beacon Press, 1963.

———. *Themes from the Lectures at the Collège de France: 1952–1960.* Translated by John O'Neill. Evanston, IL: Northwestern University Press, 1970.

———. *The Visible and the Invisible.* Translated by Alphonso Lingis. Claude Lefort, ed. Evanston, IL: Northwestern University Press, 1968.

Nietzsche, Friedrich. *Basic Writings of Nietzsche.* Translated by Walter Kaufmann. New York: The Modern Library, 1968.

———. *Beyond Good and Evil.* Translated by R.J. Hollingdale. London: Penguin Books, 1972.

———. *Daybreak: Thoughts on the Prejudices of Morality.* Translated by R.J. Hollingdale. Cambridge: Cambridge University Press, 1982.

———. *On the Genealogy of Morals* and *Ecce Homo.* Translated and edited by Walter Kaufmann. New York: Vintage, 1969.

———. *Thus Spoke Zarathustra.* Translated by R.J. Hollingdale. London: Penguin Books, 1961.

Rickert, Heinrich. *Science and History: A Critique of Positivist Epistemology.* Arthur Goddard, ed. Princeton, NJ: D. Van Nostrand, 1962.

Weber, Max. *Economy and Society: An Outline of Interpretive Sociology.* 3 vols. Guenther Roth and Claus Wittich, eds. New York: Bedminster Press, 1968.

—————. *From Max Weber: Essays in Sociology.* Translated and edited by Hans H. Gerth and C. Wright Mills. New York: Oxford University Press, 1946.

—————. *Gesammelte Aufsätze zur Religionssoziologie.* 3 vols. Tübingen: J.B.C. Mohr, 1920–1921.

—————. *Gesammelte Aufsätze zur Wissenschaftslehre.* Tübingen: J.B.C. Mohr, 1922.

—————. *The Methodology of the Social Sciences.* Edward A. Shils and Henry A. Finch, eds. Glencoe, IL: The Free Press, 1949.

—————. *The Protestant Ethic and the Spirit of Capitalism.* Translated by Talcott Parsons. New York: Charles Scribner's Sons, 1958.

—————. *Roscher and Knies: The Logical Problems of Historical Economics.* Translated by Guy Oakes. New York: The Free Press, 1975.

Secondary Sources

Alford, C. Fred. *Science and the Revenge of Nature: Marcuse and Habermas.* Tampa: University Presses of Florida, 1985.

Arendt, Hannah. *The Human Condition.* Chicago: The University of Chicago Press, 1958.

Ashby, R.W. *An Introduction to Cybernetics.* London: Chapman and Hall, 1956.

Barfield, Owen. *Saving the Appearances: A Study in Idolatry.* New York: Harcourt, Brace & World, 1965.

Bendix, Reinhart, and Roth, Guenther. *Scholarship and Partnership: Essays on Max Weber.* Berkeley and Los Angeles: University of California Press, 1971.

Berman, Morris. *The Reenchantment of the World.* Ithaca, NY: Cornell University Press, 1981.

Bernstein, Richard J. *Beyond Objectivism and Relativism: Science, Hermeneutics and Praxis.* Philadelphia: University of Pennsylvania Press, 1985.

————, ed. *Habermas and Modernity.* Cambridge, MA: The MIT Press, 1985.

————. *Philosophical Profiles: Essays in a Pragmatic Mode.* Philadelphia: University of Pennsylvania Press, 1986.

————. *The Restructuring of Social and Political Theory.* Philadelphia: University of Pennsylvania Press, 1976.

Bloom, Allan. *The Closing of the American Mind: How Higher Education has Failed Democracy and Impoverished the Souls of Today's Students.* New York: Simon and Schuster, 1987.

Bottomore, Tom. *The Frankfurt School.* London: Tavistock Publications, 1984.

Breines, Paul, ed. *Critical Interruptions: New Left Perspectives on Herbert Marcuse.* New York: Herder, 1970.

Brubaker, Rogers. *The Limits of Rationality: An Essay on the Social and Moral Thought of Max Weber.* London: George Allen & Unwin, 1984.

Bulhof, Ilse. *Wilhelm Dilthey: A Hermeneutic Approach to the Study of History and Culture.* The Hague: Martinus Nijhoff, 1980.

Butterfield, Herbert. *The Origins of Modern Science: 1300–1800.* London: Bell & Hyman, 1949.

Calvino, Italo. *Mr. Palomar.* Translated by William Weaver. New York: Harcourt Brace Jovanovich, 1985.

Caputo, John D. *Radical Hermeneutics: Repetition, Deconstruction, and the Hermeneutic Project.* Bloomington: Indiana University Press, 1987.

Cassirer, Ernst. *Kant's Life and Thought.* Translated by James Haden. New Haven, CT: Yale University Press, 1981.

Caton, Hiram. *The Origin of Subjectivity: An Essay on Descartes.* New Haven, CT: Yale University Press, 1973.

Cooper, Barry. *The End of History: An Essay on Modern Hegelianism.* Toronto: University of Toronto Press, 1984.

———. *Merleau-Ponty and Marxism: From Terror to Reform.* Toronto: University of Toronto Press, 1979.

Cornford, F.M. *From Religion to Philosophy: A Study in the Origins of Western Philosophy.* New York: Harper and Row, 1957.

Dallmayr, Fred. *Beyond Dogma and Despair: Toward a Critical Phenomenology of Politics.* Notre Dame, IN: University of Notre Dame Press, 1981.

———. *Language and Politics: What Does Language Matter to Political Philosophy?* Notre Dame, IN: University of Notre Dame Press, 1984.

———. *Twilight of Subjectivity: Contributions to a Post-Individualistic Theory.* Notre Dame, IN: University Press, 1981.

Dallmayr, Fred, and **McCarthy, Thomas,** eds. *Understanding and Social Inquiry.* Notre Dame, IN: University of Notre Dame Press, 1977.

Darby, Tom. *The Feast: Meditations on Politics and Time.* Toronto: University of Toronto Press, 1982.

———, ed. *Sojourns in the New World: Reflections on Technology.* Ottawa: Carleton University Press, 1986.

Descombes, Vincent. *Modern French Philosophy.* Translated by L. Scott-Fox and J.M. Harding. Cambridge: Cambridge University Press, 1980.

Dufrenne, Mikel. *In the Presence of the Sensuous: Essays in Aesthetics.* Mark S. Roberts and Dennis Gallagher, eds. Atlantic Highlands, NJ: Humanities Press International, 1987.

Eco, Umberto. *Art and Beauty in the Middle Ages.* Translated by Hugh Bredin. New Haven, CT: Yale University Press, 1986.

Eden, Robert. *Political Leadership and Nihilism.* Tampa: University Presses of Florida, 1983.

Feenberg, Andrew. *Lukács, Marx, and the Sources of Critical Theory.* Totowa, NJ: Rowman and Littlefield, 1981.

Fisher, Alden, ed. *The Essential Writings of Merleau-Ponty.* New York: Harcourt, Brace and World, 1969.

Forbes, R.J. *The Conquest of Nature: Technology and Its Consequences.* New York: Praeger, 1968.

Franklin, Ursula. *The Real World of Technology.* Toronto: CBC Enterprises, 1990.

Fukuyama, Francis. "The End of History?," *National Interest,* no. 16 (Summer 1989), pp. 3–18.

———. *The End of History and the Last Man.* New York: Free Press, 1992.

Gadamer, Hans-Georg. *The Relevance of the Beautiful and Other Essays.* Translated by Nicholas Walker. Robert Bernasconi, ed. Cambridge: Cambridge University Press, 1986.

Gay, Peter. *The Enlightenment: An Interpretation.* 2 vols. New York: Knopf, 1966, 1969.

Giddens, Anthony. *Profiles and Critiques in Social Theory.* Berkeley and Los Angeles: University of California Press, 1982.

———. *Studies in Social and Political Theory.* New York: Basic Books, 1970.

Grant, George. *English-Speaking Justice.* Notre Dame, IN: University of Notre Dame Press, 1986.

————. *Lament for a Nation: The Defeat of Canadian Nationalism.* Toronto: McClelland and Stewart, 1965.

————. *Technology and Empire: Perspectives on North America.* Toronto: House of Anansi, 1969.

Grohmann, Will. *Klee.* Translated by Norbert Guterman. New York: Harry N. Abrams, 1985.

Hamilton, Richard. "Imperial Humanism: Habermas's Interest Theory of Knowledge." In *Sojourns in the New World: Reflections on Technology.* Tom Darby, ed. Ottawa: Carleton University Press, 1986.

Heidegger, Martin. *Nietzsche.* 4 vols. Translated by Frank A. Capuzzi. David F. Krell, ed. San Francisco: Harper & Row, 1982.

————. *The Question Concerning Technology and Other Essays.* Translated by William Lovitt. New York: Harper & Row, 1977.

Heisenberg, Werner. *The Physicist's Conception of Nature.* Translated by A.J. Pomerans. London: Hutchinson, 1958.

Heller, Agnes, ed. *Lukács Revalued.* New York: Harper & Row, 1972.

Hobbes, Thomas. *Leviathan.* Michael Oakeshott, ed. New York: Collier, 1962.

Hodges, H.A. *Wilhelm Dilthey: An Introduction.* London: Kegan Paul, 1944.

Ihde, Don. *Consequences of Phenomenology.* Albany: State University of New York Press, 1986.

————. *Existential Technics.* Albany: State University of New York Press, 1983.

————. *Instrumental Realism.* Bloomington, IN: Indiana University Press, 1991.

————. *Sense and Significance.* Pittsburgh: Duquesne University Press, 1973.

————. *Technics and Praxis.* Dordecht, Holland: D. Reidel, 1979.

Idhe, Don, and **Silverman, Hugh J.**, eds. *Descriptions*. Albany: State University of New York Press, 1985.

Jay, Martin. *The Dialectical Imagination: A History of the Frankfurt School and the Institute of Social Research, 1923–1950.* Boston: Little, Brown and Company, 1973.

Johnson, Galen, and **Smith, Michael**, eds. *Ontology and Alterity in Merleau-Ponty*. Evanston, IL: Northwestern University Press, 1990.

Jonas, Hans. *The Imperative of Responsibility: In Search of an Ethics for the Technological Age.* Chicago: The University of Chicago Press, 1984.

Kelly, Michael, ed. *Hermeneutics and Critical Theory in Ethics and Politics.* Cambridge, MA: The MIT Press, 1990.

Kluback, William, and **Weinbaum, Martin**, eds. *Dilthey's Philosophy of Existence.* London: Vision Press, 1957.

Kojève, Alexandre. *Introduction to the Reading of Hegel.* Translated by James H. Nichols, Jr. Allan Bloom, ed. Ithaca, NY: Cornell University Press, 1980.

Kontos, Alkis, ed. *Domination.* Toronto: University of Toronto Press, 1975.

Koyré, Alexandre. *From the Closed World to the Infinite Universe.* Baltimore: Johns Hopkins University Press, 1957.

———. *Newtonian Studies.* London: Chapman and Hall, 1965.

Langer, Monika. "Merleau-Ponty: The Ontological Limitations of Politics." In *Domination,* Alkis Kontos, ed. Toronto: University of Toronto Press, 1975.

Leiss, William. *The Domination of Nature.* Boston: Beacon Press, 1972.

———. "Utopia and Technology: Reflections on the Conquest of Nature." *International Social Science Journal,* vol. 22 (1970), pp. 576–588.

Lowy, Michael. *Georg Lukács: From Romanticism to Bolshevism.* Translated by Patrick Camiller. London: NLB, 1978.

Madigan, Patrick. *The Modern Project to Rigor: Descartes to Nietzsche.* Washington, DC: University Press of America, 1986.

McBride, William L., and Schrag, Calvin O., eds. *Phenomenology in a Pluralistic Context.* Albany: State University of New York Press, 1983.

McCarthy, Thomas. *The Critical Theory of Jürgen Habermas.* Cambridge, MA: The MIT Press, 1978.

————. "A Theory of Communicative Competence." *Philosophy of the Social Sciences*, vol. 3 (1973), pp. 231–263.

Morin, Edgar. "Complexity." *The International Journal of Social Sciences*, vol. 26, no. 4 (1976).

Naubert-Riser, Constance. *Klee.* Translated by John Greaves. London: Bracken, 1988.

O'Donovan, Joan E. *George Grant and the Twilight of Justice.* Toronto: University of Toronto Press, 1984.

O'Neill, John. *The Communicative Body: Studies in Communicative Philosophy, Politics, and Sociology.* Evanston, IL: Northwestern University Press, 1989.

————, ed. *On Critical Theory.* New York: The Seabury Press, 1976.

Plato, "Phaedrus." In *The Collected Dialogues of Plato.* Translated by Edith Hamilton and Huntington Cairns. Princeton, NJ: Princeton University Press, 1961.

Rabinow, Paul, and Sullivan, William M. *Interpretive Social Science: A Reader.* Berkeley and Los Angeles: University of California Press, 1979.

Rasmussen, David M. *Reading Habermas.* Cambridge, MA: Basil Blackwell, 1990.

Redner, Harry. *The Ends of Philosophy: An Essay on the Sociology of Philosophy and Rationality.* Totowa, NJ: Rowman & Allenheld, 1986.

Reiss, Hans, ed. *Kant's Political Writings.* Cambridge: Cambridge University Press, 1970.

Rorty, Richard. *Philosophy and the Mirror of Nature.* Princeton: Princeton University Press, 1979.

Rose, Gillian. *Melancholy Science: An Introduction to the Thought of Theodor W. Adorno.* London: Macmillan, 1978.

Roth, Guenther, and **Schluchter, Wolfgang.** *Max Weber's Vision of History.* Berkeley and Los Angeles: University of California Press, 1979.

Schlucter, Wolfgang. *The Rise of Western Rationalism.* Berkeley and Los Angeles: University of California Press, 1950.

Schnadelbach, Herbert. *Philosophy in Germany, 1831–1933.* Translated by Eric Matthews. Cambridge: Cambridge University Press, 1984.

Schutte, Ofelia. *Beyond Nihilism: Nietzsche Without Masks.* Chicago: The University of Chicago Press, 1984.

Shapiro, Jeremy. "One-Dimensionality: The Universal Semiotic of Technological Experience." In *Critical Interruptions*, P. Breines, ed. New York: Herder and Herder, 1970.

Silverman, Hugh, and **Ihde, Don**, eds. *Hermeneutics and Deconstruction.* Albany: State University of New York Press, 1985.

Simpson, George, ed. *Auguste Comte: Sire of Sociology.* New York: Thomas Crowell, 1969.

Strauss, Leo. *Natural Right and History.* Chicago: The University of Chicago Press, 1950.

Turner, Jonathan H. *The Structure of Sociological Theory.* Chicago: Dorsey, 1986.

Ulmer, Gregory L. "The Object of Post-Criticism." In *The Anti-Aesthetic: Essays on Postmodern Culture*. Hal Foster, ed. Port Townsend, WA: Bay Press, 1983.

Voegelin, Eric. *The New Science of Politics*. Chicago: The University of Chicago Press, 1952.

von Newmann, John. *Theory of Self-Reproducing Automata*. Urbana: University of Illinois Press, 1966.

Wellmer, Albrecht. "Communication and Emancipation: Reflections on the Linguistic Turn in Critical Theory." *On Critical Theory*. John O'Neill, ed. New York: Seabury Press, 1976.

————. *Critical Theory of Society*. Translated by John Cumming. New York: Herder and Herder, 1971.

White, Stephen K. *Political Theory and Postmodernism*. Cambridge: Cambridge University Press, 1991.

————. *The Recent Work of Jürgen Habermas*. Cambridge: Cambridge University Press, 1987.

Whiteside, Kerry H. *Merleau-Ponty and the Foundation of an Existential Politics*. Princeton, NJ: Princeton University Press, 1988.

Wiener, Norbert. *Cybernetics: Or Control and Communication in the Animal and the Machine*. Cambridge, MA: MIT Press, 1960.

————. *The Human Use of Human Beings*. New York: Avon Books, 1950.

Wilcox, John T. *Truth and Value in Nietzsche*. Ann Arbor: The University of Michigan Press, 1974.

Wilshire, Bruce. *The Moral Collapse of the University: Professionalism, Purity, and Alienation*. Albany: State University of New York Press, 1990.

Wilson, H.T. "The Sociology of Apocalypse: Jacques Ellul's Reformation of Reformation Thought." *The Human Context*, vol. 7, no. 3 (Autumn 1975), pp. 474–494.

Winner, Langdon. *Autonomous Technology.* Cambridge, MA: The MIT Press, 1972.

Woodhouse, Edward. "Re-Visioning the Future of the Third World: An Ecological Perspective on Development." *World Politics,* vol. 25 (July 1973) pp. 1–33.

Name Index

Adorno, Theodor, 2, 3, 4, 46-53, 54, 56, 57, 62, 67, 73, 82, 83, 84, 85, 86, 87, 88, 93, 96, 101, 102, 103, 104-110, 111, 112, 116, 117, 118, 119, 120, 121, 125-126, 142
Arendt, Hannah, 121, 135, 139, 157n39
Aristotle, 10-11, 15, 22, 72, 74, 153n1, 153n2
Ashby, R.W., 158n40

Bacon, Francis, 14
Benjamin, Walter, 52
Berman, Morris, 154n15
Bernstein, Richard, 158n39
Blumenberg, Hans, 3, 5, 55-58, 68-72, 76, 88, 150
Brubaker, Rogers, 156n12

Caputo, John, 103
Cézanne, Paul, 126
Comte, Auguste, 16-17
Cooper, Barry, 153n1
Cornford, F.M., 29-30

Dallmayr, Fred, 161n49
Darby, Tom, 153n1, 158n40, 167n39
Democritus, 31
Derrida, Jacques, 153n2
Descartes, René, 1, 5, 9, 11-13, 14, 22, 33, 35, 154n6
Dilthey, Wilhelm, 17, 18-19, 23, 26, 76
Durkheim, Emile, 54, 157n39

Ellul, Jacques, 3, 5, 55-58, 61, 62, 63, 98, 121, 145, 150

Foucault, Michel, 145, 153n2
Fukuyama, Francis, 153n1, 167n39

Gadamer, Hans-Georg, 119, 162n10
Grant, George, 122, 124, 159n12
Greene, Graham, 9

Habermas, Jürgen, xi, 3-4, 67-68, 73-93, 94, 95, 96-102, 103, 110, 120, 122, 124-125, 127-128, 147, 148, 149, 150, 159n13, 160n34, 161n36, 161n49
Hegel, G.W.F., ix, 82, 83, 109
Heidegger, Martin, xi, 55, 85, 103, 139, 153n2, 165n10
Hobbes, Thomas, 22
Homer, 48, 49
Horace, 95
Horkheimer, Max, 2, 3, 5, 46-52, 53, 54, 56, 57, 62, 67, 73, 82, 83, 84, 85, 86, 88, 93, 101, 104, 121

Jonas, Hans, 122

Kant, Immanuel, 14-16, 18, 19, 23, 76, 77, 154n11
Klee, Paul, 104, 106, 108, 118, 119, 142
Kojève, Alexandre, ix-x, 67, 122, 153n1, 165n8, 167n39

Langer, Monika, 166n23
Leucippus, 31
Löwith, Karl, 68
Lucretius, 25, 32-33, 35
Luhmann, Niklas, 5, 58-62, 63, 91
Lukács, Georg, 2, 5, 43-46, 54, 67, 81, 82, 83, 93, 150

Subject Index

Action theory, 79-80, 86-87

Alchemy, 17, 154n15

Animism, 9, 47

Art, Adorno on, 52-54; as antidote to disenchantment, 108; Gadamer on, 162n10, Klee on, 104, 106, 108; limits of, 109; Merleau-Ponty on, 117-120; as *poiesis*, 147-148. *See also* Esthetic theory

Being: defined, 164n34; and mystery of the world, 116

Being-in-the-world: defined, 113; revolt against, 147

Chiasma, 115

Cogito, 1, 2, 12-13, 15, 16, 45, 51-53, 85, 95, 113, 114, 149, 151

Collective housekeeping, 138-139

Commodity fetishism, 45

Communicative action, 89, 97

Communicative rationality, 68, 97

Communism, 133; collapse of, 138-139; and Merleau-Ponty, 166n26

Community, 135-136

Co-perception, 128

Crisis of culture, 43, 45

Cybernetics, 3, 55, 158n40 159n12. *See also* Systems theory

Demagification, 29-30. *See also* Disenchantment of nature

Disenchantment of nature, 22, 25, 28-34, 49, 110. *See also* Intellectualization, process of

Disenchantment of the world, 34, 37, 38; defined, 28; Ellul on, 56; paradoxical core of, 38-39, 40. *See also* Societal rationalization

Disenchantment thesis, 42

Disembodied politics, 127, 136

Efficiency, principle of, 139; Ellul on, 56

Ego cogito. See *Cogito*

Egological bias, 13

Egological revolution, 16

Embodied politics, 132-133, 134-136, 138-140, defined, 127-128

Empiricism, 14

End of history, ix

Enlightened action, 73-74, 77-78, 87

Enlightenment, the, 14, 49-50, 69

Entropy, 54-55

Epistemology: Descartes on, 12-13; Kant on, 15; turn toward, 25; Weber on, 26-27

Esthetic theory: Adorno on, 52-54, 104-111, 111; Habermas's critique of, 85; Merleau-Ponty on, 117-119, 129; *See also* Art

Ethical irrationalism, 38, 78, 136

Extended substance. See *Res extensa*

Flesh, philosophy of the, 114-116

Formal rationality, 36, 156n13. *See also* Instrumental rationality

Frankfurt School, 46

Green Movement, 99

185